The Life and Times
of Ron Brown

THE LIFE AND TIMES OF RON BROWN

A Memoir by His Daughter

Tracey L. Brown

WILLIAM MORROW AND COMPANY, INC.

NEW YORK

Copyright © 1998 by Tracey L. Brown

All rights reserved. No part of this book may be reproduced or utilized in any form or by any means, electronic or mechanical, including photocopying, recording, or by any information storage or retrieval system, without permission in writing from the Publisher. Inquiries should be addressed to Permissions Department, William Morrow and Company, Inc., 1350 Avenue of the Americas, New York, N.Y. 10019.

It is the policy of William Morrow and Company, Inc., and its imprints and affiliates, recognizing the importance of preserving what has been written, to print the books we publish on acid-free paper, and we exert our best efforts to that end.

Library of Congress Cataloging-in-Publication Data

Brown, Tracey L.
The life and times of Ron Brown : a memoir by his daughter /
Tracey L. Brown. — 1st ed.
p. cm.
ISBN 0-688-15320-8
1. Brown, Ronald Harmon, 1941–1996. 2. Cabinet officers—United
States—Biography. I. Title.
E840.8.B77B76   1998
380.1'092—dc21
[B]   97-32016
                                                            CIP

Printed in the United States of America

First Edition

1 2 3 4 5 6 7 8 9 10

BOOK DESIGN BY BERNARD KLEIN

www.williammorrow.com

This book is dedicated to the heroes who lost their lives on
St. John's Mountain in Dubrovnik, Croatia.

Ronald H. Brown
Gerald Aldrich
Niksa Antonini
Dragica L. Bebek
Duane Christian
Barry L. Conrad
Paul Cushman III
Adam N. Darling
Ashley J. Davis
Gail E. Dobert
Robert E. Donovan
Claudio Elia
Robert Farrington, Jr.
David Ford
Carol L. Hamilton
Kathryn E. Hoffman
Lee F. Jackson
Stephen C. Kaminski
Kathryn E. Kellogg
Shelly A. Kelly
James M. Lewek
Frank Maier
Charles F. Meissner
William E. Morton
Walter J. Murphy
Nathaniel C. Nash
Lawrence M. Payne
Leonard J. Pieroni
Timothy W. Schafer
John Scoville
I. Donald Terner
Stuart Tholan
Cheryl A. Turnage
Naomi P. Warbasse
Robert A. Whittaker

Acknowledgments

Since I began writing about my father's life, countless people have asked me what new or surprising things I have learned about him. Frankly, I have been most surprised at the number of lives he touched. Not just people who knew him but folks young and old who never met him but respected and admired what he accomplished and what he stood for. I thank all of you for recognizing my father as the real American hero that he was.

My family deserves the ultimate thanks for being supportive and sharing their private memories of Dad. Especially my mother, Alma Arrington Brown, for letting me move in and take over the house with my research paraphernalia. And for being strong enough to comfort me and strong enough to let me comfort her. To Michael, you are the best big brother anyone could wish for: brilliant, funny, and always in my corner. To my paternal grandmother, Gloria Brown Carter, for being helpful during one of the most difficult times of her life, and to my maternal grandmother, Dorothy Madison Arrington, for love, understanding, and a little secretarial work. To my sister-in-law, Tami Brown, and my nephews, Morgan and Ryan Brown. To my uncle, Chip Brown, for taking time out during the stress of medical school. To my father's godparents, Fred Wilkinson and Marie Rhone, and our cousin, Bobby Jones. To my great-aunts Charlotte Stewart, Elizabeth Keys, Rebecca Freeman, Gwendolyn Pettis, and Nancy Smith for putting up with my interrogation at a family cookout.

Thanks to all of you who took time out for interviews, some as many as three times. Your candor in sharing memories of my father was invaluable: Betty Adams, Marilyn and Chuck Alston, Yasir Arafat, Larry Bailey, Gary Barron, Marion Barry, Jane Bobbitt, Tommy Boggs, Lisa Handley Bonner, Yolanda Caraway, Maria Cardona, Ken Chenault, Vinnie Cohen, Maudine Cooper, Courtland Cox, Lynn Cutler, Jim Desler, David Dinkins, Terry Donovan, Hazel Dukes, Loretta Dunn, Dalia Elalfi-Traynham, Lauri Fitz-Pegado, Karla Fitzgerald, Betty Ford, Barbara Fredericks, John Galbraith, Charlyn Goins, Rick Greenfield, Wilma Greenfield, Pamela Harriman, Billy Harris, Dorothy Height, Alexis Herman, Ernie and Ardath Hill, Eleanor Holmes Norton, John and Betty Hornbostel, Larry Irving, Jesse Jackson, Charlene Drew Jarvis, Bob Johnson, Lajuan Johnson, Vernon Jordan, Mickey Kantor, Edward Kennedy, Shelia Davis Lawrence, Elliott Laws, Melanie Long, Bob McAlpine, Tim May, Tommy and Maurin Meehan, Wren Mosee Lester, Melissa Moss, John Nailor, Larry Parks, Billy Perry, Billy Pickens, David Pitman, Malcolm Puryear, Charles Rangel, Joe Reeder, Morris Reid, Clyde Robinson, Jonathan Sallet, Barbara Schmitz, Dana Shelley, Jill Shuker, Rob Stein, Mark Steitz, Bob Taylor, Ginny Terzano, Christine Varney, Carl Wagner, Paul Webber IV, Reid Weingarten, Tommy Williams, and Jim Zogby. And to the entire Department of Commerce for your love and support of my family.

I am grateful to President Clinton for his interview and for writing a moving introduction to this book, to Hillary Rodham Clinton for introducing me to a great agent, and to that agent, Bob Barnett, who guided me through an unfamiliar process.

Thanks to Claire Wachtel, my editor at William Morrow, who believed in the importance of this book from the beginning; to literary agent Elizabeth Kaplan for her contribution; to my very helpful research assistant, Tamara Masters Wilds; and to researcher Esther Ratner.

My gratitude to my understanding friends and extended family—Marcelino Ford-Livene, Kent and Carmen Amos, Larkin and Cynthia Arnold, Alison Baker, George Curry, Michael Graves, Cindy Harper-Covington, Charles Hall, Kimberly Hill, Kendall James, Candice Mitchell, Rosa Moreno, Michelle Nunn, Henry Oliver, Chance Patterson, Maria Tildon, and Nikki Webber; to my friends at the Los Angeles District Attorney's Office for not forgetting about me, even though it took me so long to return phone calls—Bobby Grace, Tal Kahana, Henry Kerner, Stephanie Mire, Jacqui Romano; and to my favorite public defenders—Mojgan Aghai and Tamela Cash-Curry.

Finally, to the best collaborator in the business, Sheila Isenberg, who made my words and thoughts come alive and guided me through a very difficult and soul-searching project. I am eternally grateful for your magnificent work and friendship.

Contents

Introduction by
President Bill Clinton

HISTORY remembers great men as collections of great deeds. More than a year after the tragedy that took his life, history remembers Ron Brown as the chairman who returned his party to the White House, as the secretary who revolutionized the Commerce Department, and as the leader who worked to bring all Americans into the new global economy.

For those of us who knew him, though, Ron Brown was more than a mere collection of achievements. He was an incredible life force. Intelligent and successful, caring and determined, Ron was one of the most impressive men I have ever known. He was my friend.

His energy was contagious. As long as I live, I will remember the day Ron Brown forgot I was President and beat me at basketball. We were visiting a sporting goods store in Los Angeles, and in the back of the store we found a basketball court and a group of boys and girls who couldn't wait to show us their jump shots. So we divided up sides—Ron took a few kids, and I took a few kids—and suddenly it didn't matter that Ron was a Cabinet member, or that I was the President. "The President was in my face from twenty feet out," Ron would say afterward. "But when I shot—nothing but net."

His enthusiasm brought out the best in people, and it brought people together. I first met him in 1988, when he was working on Jesse Jackson's campaign. At the end of that year, when Ron announced that he wanted to chair the Democratic National Committee, I knew he was the leader who could rejuvenate the party. And as he broadened the party's foundation, harmonizing the differences between its members, Ron went beyond my expectations.

He announced in 1992 that the world's oldest political party would regain the White House. We had lost the last three presidential elections, and many Americans felt that our party was outdated. But if he felt any doubt, Ron never showed it. His confidence inspired an enormous amount of confidence in those around him.

And after I won the party's nomination, he inspired a greater confidence in me. I could not have become President without Ron Brown.

When I became President, the job of commerce secretary seemed tailor-made for Ron. At that time, the Department of Commerce was a moribund agency with only a negligible role in our nation's everyday life. Yet Ron recognized, as I did, that the department had the potential to transform the American economy. I knew that he was up to the challenge. "This is a big, new world out there," I told him, "and you ought to be secretary of commerce. You could change the future of America, and make a real difference for millions of people around the world."

Ron Brown entered my administration like a force of nature, becoming one of the best commerce secretaries in our nation's history. He re-created the Commerce Department, based on a simple creed that he required his staff to memorize: "The mission of the Department of Commerce is to ensure economic opportunity for every American."

As the first African-American commerce secretary, and a man who never forgot where he came from, Ron focused especially on those Americans who had traditionally been left behind. He treated African-Americans as people with economic potential, rather than economic need, and he challenged minority businesses to join the new global economy. The son of a Harlem hotel manager, Ron had lived the American Dream. He felt it was his duty to give others the same chance, and he worked tirelessly for their opportunity.

Ron also believed that the American Dream was not limited to Americans. Cultivating prosperity abroad as at home, he lifted aspirations around the world. On his final mission overseas, he traveled to Bosnia with hopes that the vigor of the American economy could restore peace to the Balkans.

Filled with excitement about his mission, Ron visited me at the White House shortly before he left. He was proud of the men and women who would accompany him. They were business executives, Commerce employees, journalists, and military personnel—thirty-three courageous Americans who demonstrated the power and the responsibility of the individual to address the concerns of humanity. Like Ron, they were patriots and they were role models who gave up their lives to solve a problem nearly five thousand miles from home.

I will never forget the morning I called Alma Brown to tell her that her husband's plane was missing in the Balkans. "I want you to hear it from me first," I told her. It was one of the saddest moments in my life.

A few hours later, when our worst fears had become our new reality, Hillary and I joined friends and family at the Brown home. He had only been gone for a short while, but we already felt the emptiness of Ron's absence.

Ron Brown walked, ran, and flew through life, with an extraordinary vivacity that touched everyone who knew him. As a daughter's testament to her father, this book captures the deeds that make Ron the stuff of history, the character that makes him worthy of our continuing admiration, and the spirit that won him the love of millions around the world. In our greatest tribute to this legacy, let us follow Tracey Brown's lead, and live by Ron's example.

But those who wait upon the Lord
Shall renew their strength;
They shall mount up with wings as eagles;
They shall run, and not be weary;
They shall walk, and not faint.

—Isaiah 40:31

I laugh every time I remember my twenty-seventh birthday. It was No-vember 8, 1994, and I was in a courtroom, about to make my opening statement as prosecutor on an assault and battery case. The presiding judge had just ordered the jury to be seated when the bailiff whispered to me that I had a telephone call. Hoping the call was not a cancellation by an important witness, I walked over and picked up the phone on the bailiff's desk. In my most professional voice, I said, "This is Tracey Brown." Then I heard Dad, in that baby-talk voice he sometimes used with me: "Twenty-six years ago today, I was in the waiting room at Brookdale Hospital in Brooklyn, New York, when Dr. Josephine En-glish comes in grinning from ear to ear. Of course, we had a female obstetrician, since Mom and I have always been feminists."

I interrupted. "Hurry up, Daddy, the jury is in the box."

But he continued at his normal pace, retelling the story of my birth as he did on my birthday every year: "Dr. English says, 'It's a girl!' and I say, 'It's a girl!' I'm so happy and I run in to see you. Wrapped in a tiny blanket in Mom's arms is this pale baby. You were so white that you were translucent, so I say to Mom, 'That's not my baby. She's too white.' "

The judge was staring at me. "Miss Brown?" he queried, reminding me that the court was waiting.

"If I can have a moment, Your Honor," I responded. Then into the receiver, I whispered, "Daddy, the judge is getting mad."

But Dad was in the midst of our annual birthday ritual and refused to be hurried: "Then I picked you up and looked at your beautiful face and your little mouth and your almond eyes and I knew you were my baby girl. Happy birthday, baby. I love you so much."

"I love you too, Daddy," I whispered, "but I have to go."

"Are you gonna kick some booty in court?"

"Yes, Daddy, but I really have to go."

"Say, 'I'm gonna kick butt.' "

"No, Dad. Have a great day. Gotta go."

"Say it," he teased.

"*I'm gonna kick butt,*" *I whispered, trying not to laugh.*

"*Say it louder.*"

"*Dad, I don't want you to have to fly out here and bail my butt out of jail for being held in contempt of court.*"

"*Okay, okay. Good luck with your trial. Happy birthday, Boli.*" *Boli, short for Tracinda Bolinda, his nickname for me.*

"*Bye, Daddy. I'll call you all tonight. I love you.*"

"*I love you more.*" *We hung up. Then, warmed by his love, with a smile on my face, I turned to the jury. "Good morning, ladies and gentlemen. My name is Tracey Brown and I represent the people of the state of California.*"

~ ONE ~

Losing Dad

I<small>T</small> was my fourth year as a deputy district attorney in Los Angeles. As I battled fierce traffic that Wednesday morning from my apartment in Hollywood to my office in the Criminal Courts Building, I thought about the case I would be trying that day before the famed Judge Lance Ito. Because I was making a court appearance, I was dressed in a suit and heels and was even wearing lipstick, a cosmetic I applied only for jury trials—and visits with my father. Whenever Dad, visiting L.A. on business, took me out to dinner, I'd wear lipstick just to hear him say, "It makes you even more beautiful than you already are!"

That morning, I slid behind my desk a few minutes before eight and had just opened my case file when Bobby Grace, a coworker and friend, appeared in the doorway, looking tense. He asked if I had listened to the news on the way to work. Before I could answer him, another colleague, Jacqui Romano, appeared, also looking nervous.

Thinking something was up on the office grapevine, I laughed and asked, "Why are you both looking so crazy?"

Bobby took a deep breath. "Tracey, your father's plane is missing."

I jumped up and dialed my mother at home in Washington. As soon as she heard me say, "Mom," she started crying. Sobbing, she told me that the President had called and said Dad's plane was off radar and it didn't look good. I couldn't take it in and kept repeating, "What are you saying? What are you saying?" Then I began to cry. I had one thought: to get home as soon as possible. I told Mom I was on my way, hung up, and tried to clear my mind enough to figure out how to get to Washington. Hysterics were setting in as my boss, District Attorney Gil Garcetti, walked in and hugged me. Then he, Bobby, and Jacqui guided me toward the elevator; coworkers patted me on the back as I walked by. In the elevator, I was hyperventilating and sobbing while the other passengers were staring at my swollen, wet face. As Bobby and Jacqui drove me to my apartment to pack, we listened to National Public Radio's conflicting reports about whether the plane had been lost over water or mountains. I couldn't stand to listen. I turned it off.

My parents' friends, Irma Hopkins and Larkin and Cynthia Arnold, were at my apartment when we arrived. First they helped me pack, and talked to me trying to calm me down. Then with the help of Dad's friend Noel Irwin Hentschel they arranged my plane ticket: U.S. Airways Flight 38, leaving LAX at 12:35 P.M. and due at Baltimore-Washington International Airport at 8:22. Then Chip, Dad's half brother and a student at UCLA Medical School, arrived and I grabbed him and crushed my face in his jacket and sobbed. Before we left for the airport, I ran into the bedroom and grabbed the photo I kept on my night table, of me and Dad hugging, big grins on our faces. Holding the picture, I went down on my knees and prayed. I needed God's help. I'd never been especially religious or prayerful, but at this moment I was desperate for something, anything, to relieve my terror. I promised God I would do good for the rest of my life, if He would just let my father be all right.

Irma and Cynthia drove us to Chip's apartment and, while he packed and we waited two hours for flight time, we watched CNN. I wanted to know but I also didn't want to know; it was an impossible situation. Sit in the room, television off, hoping my father was alive. Or turn it on, maybe find out he wasn't.

The newscast was heartbreaking. There was Daddy, all preppy looking, on the tarmac, about to board the fated plane. He looked so beautiful in his barn jacket, black corduroy pants and turtleneck, and plaid flannel shirt, finished off with L. L. Bean duck shoes. CNN showed Dad chatting with American troops stationed in Tuzla, grinning and sharing McDonald's hamburgers with them. Could my father really be gone? It was truly unbelievable.

One Week Earlier, Washington

I think Dad had a premonition about his trip to Croatia. Even though he was excited about this trade mission and the economic opportunities for American business in the war-torn eastern European country, some of his behavior at home before he left, and also in Paris directly before he flew to Croatia, was out of character.

If all went well on the Croatia mission, U.S. companies would negotiate business deals to gain a share of the five billion dollars in aid being fed into the region by international financial institutions and foreign governments; at the same time, these companies would be helping the citizenry recover from a devastating civil war. The foreign-aid money was intended to stimulate the economy of the former Yugoslavia and, as Dad saw it, Boeing and other American companies could profit while helping to rebuild the country. Dad really believed in this mission and viewed it as an opportunity to do good while helping American business. "Peace and stability [will] only be ensured [here] through economic development," he told reporters at an April 2 press conference in France. "The purpose of this trip is to help U.S. companies get in on the ground floor of the competition for up to five billion dollars in upcoming procurement contracts. . . . [My] objective is to enable U.S. companies to establish contacts and participate in the process of converting needs to actual project designs."

Some of the business executives who went to Croatia with Dad were Stuart Tholan, senior vice president of Bechtel Enterprises; Don Terner, president of Bridge Housing Corporation; Leonard J. Pieroni, chairman and CEO of Parsons Corporation, a Pasadena-based engineering firm; and Paul Cushman III, head of Riggs National Bank's international banking operations.

This trade mission allowed my father to combine his economic goals for the United States with his liberal-humanitarian orientation. "Baby, this is big. This mission is big," he told Mom the day before he left for Croatia. But Mom didn't pay too much attention to what he was saying because she'd been ill with the flu for two weeks. She'd been so sick, she was unable to go to work, eat, drink, or share Dad's excitement. And this is one of the reasons we believe he had some sort of premonition: Even though Mom couldn't do a thing but lie in bed, Dad renewed a conversation they had three months earlier, right after Christmas. He wanted to refinance the house because mortgage rates were very low. And he wanted to do it then and there. "We need to do it before I go to the Balkans," he told Mom.

A month earlier, in March, Dad had led a trade mission to Colombia, Panama, and Nicaragua. Mom had been nervous about that trip because of press reports of violence by Colombian drug lords and Nicaraguan rebels. She didn't stop worrying about Dad until he was safely back home. In contrast, when he told her about the trip to the Balkans, she was relaxed. After all, the United States had a considerable presence there, including troops, and she felt an American delegation would be safe.

But when he urged her to come to the bank with him to apply for a new, lower mortgage rate, she couldn't understand his intensity. "Ronnie, I don't feel like doing it," said a bedraggled Mom. "Let's wait until you get back."

"No, we're going to do it. We really need to do it." Dad was insistent.

Mom put him off for days. Then Friday morning, the day before he was to leave for France and Croatia, he walked into their bedroom, where she lay in bed, still quite ill, and told her he had done all the paperwork and made an appointment at the bank. He would come home to pick her up, whisk her to the bank to sign papers, then whisk her back home. Even though she told him she absolutely could not get out of bed, he would not relent.

"Honey," he said, "we have to do it. I want to do this house business before I go." When Mom told me this story later, I was amazed that she finally agreed to go with him; she said he just kept on about interest rates going up, as if they might rise instantly and meteorically.

He came home from work at about four in the afternoon and helped my mother get out of bed and dress. He remarked about her clothes hanging on her; she had lost weight, having eaten no solid food for more than a week, and looked, as she put it, like "pitiful Paula." They drove to the bank, my mother clutching her tissues and cough drops, signed the papers, and went right back home so Mom could crawl into bed.

That evening, Dad packed for the Croatian trip because he would be busy part of the next day, Saturday, playing golf with my brother, Michael, before he caught his plane to Paris: United Airlines Flight 914, leaving at 6:20 in the evening. Mom lay in bed, coughing and hacking, while Dad asked her what she thought the weather would be like, what she thought he should take. She looked in *USA Today* and told him the weather in Paris the next day would be a high of forty-six, a low of thirty-three, and cloudy. Dad was to spend two days in meetings in France before heading to Croatia. Then he climbed into bed and watched a boxing match on television.

Mom always says, "He never got my cold." As if it mattered.

Saturday morning, he played golf at the Robert Trent Jones course in Lake Manassas, Virginia, with my brother, Michael, and two of his friends, Jeffrey Scruggs and Rick Greenfield. Rick told me that Dad was in great form that day and played the best golf he had ever played. As always, after he had been with his Sonny Junior—his nickname for Michael—and after a good game, he was in a great mood as he returned to the house to shower and change before leaving for Europe. Henry Oliver, his longtime driver, was waiting outside to take him to the airport.

When Dad was about to leave, he hugged Mom. "Bye, honey. I'll see you Friday."

Mom said, "Love," which is our family's special way of saying good-bye to each other. Then they kissed.

Right before Dad walked out of the house for the last time, he yelled up the stairs, "I'll call you tonight when I get to Paris. And don't forget to tell Michael to get your medicine."

Mom mumbled, "Okay," and added her usual instructions: "Lock the door and turn the alarm on." Then she went back to sleep. And he was gone.

"I didn't even walk him downstairs," Mom says when she relives that last evening.

March 31 and April 1, Lille and Paris

When Dad arrived in Paris, in keeping with our family's practice of close and constant contact, he called Mom to say hello and to see if Michael had picked up her medicine. He hadn't, so Dad then called my brother and gave him hell and made him promise to pick up the prescription for Mom on Sunday morning.

Dad went first to Lille, a city 136 miles north of Paris, near the Belgian border, to head up the U.S. delegation to the G-7 Conference on Employment. This was a conference of economic and foreign ministers from the world's seven leading industrial countries—the United States, Britain, France, Canada, Germany, Japan, and Italy. There, Dad told the delegates that, under his leadership, America's zealous pursuit of increasing trade with foreign countries included a guarantee that this growth would benefit *all* Americans.

Said Dad, "We can't pursue growth without being concerned about whether it is shared by all Americans. We can't pursue policies that risk slowing our growth or handicapping our private sector in a rapidly changing global economy. . . . We must and will pursue both of these goals."

Afterward, former secretary of labor Robert Reich, who was at Lille, said my father emphasized that a country's standard of living depended on "the skills and education of its workforce."

Dad wasn't leading trade missions only to benefit corporations and their executives; his intention was to enhance the economic well-being of the American people.

When the conference in Lille ended, Dad traveled by train back to Paris for a reception at the American embassy hosted by Pamela Harriman, the matriarch of American Democratic politics and, at the time, our ambassador to France. (Pamela Harriman died February 5, 1997.) With time to spare before the reception, my father told Mrs. Harriman that, even though he'd visited Paris often, he had never explored the city because he was always busy with meetings and conferences. "He said he never had a chance before when he was in Paris, to really see Paris," she said. The ambassador suggested they take a long walk through a few of the arrondissements, or neighborhoods, but warned him that she was quite a seasoned walker. Dad, surprised when the elegant ambassador changed into sneakers, laughingly complained that he might not be able to keep up with her in his suit and dress shoes. He did loosen his tie, which, for him, meant going casual.

They toured the Tuileries and the Louvre, then walked along the Seine to Notre Dame. During their walk, Dad told Pamela his vision of the new global role America would play in the world and, of course, boasted about his children, adding that in a few days I was bringing my "new, serious" boyfriend home to Washington for Easter weekend. Dad was relaxed and at ease that day, enjoying his chance to take a leisurely walk without having to rush to a meeting.

Dad mentioned to Mrs. Harriman that he intended to visit a small chapel named for Saint Catherine Laboure so that he could get some religious medals for me, Mom, and Michael. Their walk finally ended when Dad—who usually never admitted defeat—said he was tired out by trying to match her stride and wanted to return to the embassy. Accompanied by a couple of staff people, Dad then drove to the chapel, where he spent so much time that he was late getting back to the reception at the embassy that was being given in his honor.

That night, Dad called Mom, exuberant about his walk with Ambassador Harriman, adding, "I am so tired. She walked me to death." When he told Mom about the chapel, she listened and didn't say much, still sick and not focusing on what he was saying. Dad was not a particularly religious man, rarely went to church, and that he took the time to go to a chapel to "pick up some things for us" was most unusual.

After the plane crash, we found the medals as well as the text of a prayer inside Dad's briefing book. His leather folder, burned inside and scorched outside, was retrieved from the wreckage. The medals are oval-shaped gold medallions with a raised image of the Virgin Mary and these words: *O Marie, conçue sans peché, priez pour nous qui avons recours a vous.* (O Mary, conceived without stain, pray for us who resort to you.) The medals are dated 1830, the year in which Saint Catherine Laboure was visited by Mary, who instructed her to raise an altar and create medals for the faithful. And taped in the front inside pocket of my father's folder was a prayer:

> Oh, St. Joseph, whose protection is so great, so prompt, so strong, before the throne of God, I place in you all my interest and desire. Oh, St. Joseph, do assist me by your powerful intercession and obtain for me from the Divine Son all spiritual blessings through Jesus Christ our Lord so that having engaged here below your heavenly power, I may offer my thanksgiving and homage to the loving father. Oh, St. Joseph, I never weary contemplating you and Jesus asleep in your arms. I dare not approach. While he reposes in your heart, press him in my name, kiss his fine head and ask him to return the kiss when I draw my dying breath. St. Joseph, patron of my departed soul, pray for me.

Why did Dad have religious medals and a prayer? Did he have a premonition? Could that be why he had been so insistent on refinancing the mortgage before he left? If he had fears or worries about the trip, I wished he had shared them with his family. We could have reassured him, reminded him how much we loved him, how we needed him to come home to us. But Dad never said a word.

I can't even visualize Dad, praying for a kiss from the baby Jesus as plane meets mountain and he draws his dying breath.

April 2, Zagreb

Tuesday night, April 2, after the reception at the embassy, Dad left for Croatia. In addition to facilitating negotiations between American and Croatian businesses, the trade mission was to include talks with Croatian prime minister Zlatko Matesa, a meeting with Croatian president Franjo Tudjman, and the signing of economic agreements between the United States and Croatia. The meeting between Dad and President Tudjman, originally scheduled for Zagreb, was changed to Dubrovnik, a well-preserved medieval fortress city; Matesa had chosen to relocate the meeting to publicize the city's ability to attract tourists and also because some of the executives on the trade mission were in the business of building hotels. It would be a tragic change.

That night, my father's small military plane left at nine o'clock from Villacoublay airport and landed two hours later in Zagreb, Croatia. It was raining when Dad was met by Peter Galbraith, the U.S. ambassador to Croatia; Morris Reid, my father's advance person and close aide; and Tom Mitnick from the American embassy. They were accompanied by Prime Minister Matesa and Croatian ambassador to the United States Miomir Zuzul. As Dad got into his car on the airport tarmac, Morris climbed in to brief him on the identities of the various dignitaries and to remind him that Matesa was someone he had met before. Dad was always briefed in advance on names, faces, and relationships by Morris and aides so that he could properly address everyone he encountered.

Dad greeted his welcoming committee in the airport's VIP lounge, then he, Morris, and Ambassador Galbraith were driven to the Zagreb Sheraton in the ambassador's armored Chevrolet Caprice. During the twenty-five-minute ride, the ambassador brought my father up to date on the Croatian situation and discussed items he might want to focus on during the next day's planned meeting in Dubrovnik. Croatia, having emerged from the war, still had one territory, Eastern Slavonia, under United Nations administration, according to a U.S.-negotiated agreement. The Croatians wanted Eastern Slavonia returned to them by July 15, 1996, but the U.N. mandate had been extended to January 1997. Dad would have to handle the Eastern Slavonia issue, should it come up, diplomatically.

The ambassador also discussed with my father four other subjects to be raised with the Croatians: First, execution of the Eastern Slavonia agreement; second, respect for the rights of Croatian Serbs, including allowing those who had been driven out of their country to return home; third, his support for the Federation in Bosnia-Herzegovina and the Muslim Karat Federation; and fourth, the Boeing deal, of prime importance to Dad on this trade mission. It was my father's intention to disrupt an arrangement between the Croatian government and Airbus Industrie, a European plane-manufacturing consortium. His goal was to convince the Croatians to place their eighteen-plane, one-billion-dollar order with Boeing, an American company.

When they arrived at the Sheraton at midnight, Dad slept in a suite that was often used by U.S. dignitaries; in recent weeks, his bed had been slept in by then–secretary of state Warren Christopher and, later, U.S. Ambassador to the United Nations Madeleine Albright. Since it was late and Dad was due to leave at dawn for Tuzla to breakfast with American troops, Ambassador Galbraith asked Dad if he minded if he didn't see him off. The American embassy had been quite busy with visitors and late arrivals and early departures, and he was tired. Dad, always gracious, said, "That's fine. It's much too early. I'll be okay."

In his hotel room, Dad placed his usual call to Mom and told her that he was looking forward to the day's events: breakfast and lunch with GIs. They chatted for a while, Dad sounding almost nostalgic for his old army days. Before they hung up, he told her he'd call her the next day, from Dubrovnik.

April 3, Zagreb

At five-thirty in the morning, Dad and Morris left the Sheraton and headed for the airport. Dad waited while McDonald's hamburgers, buns, and cooking equipment, as well as sports videos—including the NCAA basketball tournament finals, a game close to my father's heart—were loaded into the plane for Dad to take to the troops in Tuzla. Morris and my father continued a conversation they had begun earlier that morning on the way to the airport. Rather than accompany him to Tuzla, Dad wanted Morris to stay in Zagreb to take care of a problem that had arisen with Enron, a Texas-based natural gas company that was negotiating an agreement with the government of Croatia. Morris disagreed, arguing that he had a responsibility to remain with Dad, since that was his job as advance person. Of course, Dad prevailed and Morris remained behind, planning to meet Dad in Dubrovnik later.

By six o'clock, the plane was airborne for the forty-minute flight to Tuzla. After a brief army ceremony at Eagle Base Camp, my father left by helicopter for Guardian Base, where he had breakfast with the troops, then went on a tour of the Tuzla power plant. At 10:40, he helicoptered to Camp Alicia for a tour and a discussion and press conference with the mayors of Tuzla, Orasje, and Zvornik. Lunch was McDonald's hamburgers with the troops at Camp Alicia. With both groups of GIs, in the morning and at lunch, Dad was a big hit; he communicated well with enlisted men and their enthusiasm warmed him. "Being a former army man myself, I know what being away from home is like," Dad told them.

After lunch, he returned to Eagle Camp for a 2:30 P.M. flight to Dubrovnik. Dad and his delegation were on an Air Force version of a Boeing 737, the very plane that a month earlier had carried the First Lady to Germany, Bosnia, Turkey, and Greece. The plane, which had a perfect safety record and had last been inspected nine months earlier, was used by Defense Secretary William Perry to fly from Zagreb to Tuzla, Sarajevo, Albania, and Egypt before turning around to pick up Dad's group.

1 P.M., Cilipi Airport, Dubrovnik

Morris Reid, who had stayed behind in Zagreb, took care of the Enron problem, then flew to Dubrovnik to prepare for Dad's arrival. Ambassador Galbraith and Prime Minister Matesa also went to Dubrovnik. Their flight left Zagreb at about 1:30 P.M. and experienced turbulence from wind and rain as it approached Dubrovnik. The ambassador and his fellow passengers cracked jokes to relieve the tension. It occurred to him to recommend that the pilot head to another airport; he thought about my father's plane, also, and hoped it would head to the airport in nearby Split. By the time the ambassador had those thoughts, their plane was already circling and preparing to land. When his plane landed at about 2:30 P.M., Ambassador Galbraith heard another coming in behind and thought it was Dad's plane. It wasn't, of course, and turned out to be a Swiss charter carrying the Enron people. Galbraith and the officials with him went into the airport to await my father's arrival.

2:52 P.M., Cilipi Airport

Morris stood on the tarmac, expecting my father's plane momentarily, since it was already twenty minutes late. The last recorded communication between Dad's plane and the tower, at 2:50, was a normal conversation, not a distress call.

Time passed. A minute or two. An eternity.

Two thousand feet up, and eight miles from its destination, my father's plane lost contact with the tower. The pilots, miscalculating wildly, were off course, flying up a valley parallel to the one they should have taken. Then, at 2:52 P.M., as they headed toward what they thought was a runway, they turned left and found, not a safe place to land, but a looming mountain—and death.

∼

All of the Bosnian coast had been hit with intermittent wind and rain. Although flying conditions were unstable, five planes did land at the airport at Cilipi that day. The airport, on the Adriatic coast twelve miles south of Dubrovnik, was considered a difficult place to land. Its technology was outmoded: It relied on a forty-year-old system of beacons to guide planes onto runways.

The pilots of Dad's plane, U.S. Air Force Captains Ashley

Davis and Tim Schafer, veterans both, apparently flew an approach in which they had to rely on instruments until they could establish visual contact with the runway and decide if it was safe to land. Such approaches are easily affected by bad weather.

But this crash was not caused by bad weather. An investigation by the Air Force has found that it was caused by three factors: failure of command, pilot error, and an improperly designed approach. Had any of these three factors not been in place, the crash would not have happened. Two generals, five colonels, six lieutenant colonels, and three majors received reprimands for allowing my father's plane to land at an airport with the most rudimentary landing equipment. Some of their names were made public; others were not. None was court-martialed for dereliction of duty.

3 P.M., Cilipi Airport

Down on the tarmac, Morris heard that the plane had disappeared from radar. "I didn't panic. War-torn country and all that. I thought I would give it some time," Morris said. Considering all the planes my father had flown on, and all the planes Morris had flown on with my dad since he began working for him in 1992, the idea of an accident simply didn't enter his mind.

3:10 P.M., Cilipi Airport
9:10 A.M., Washington

The tower announced to Morris and the others waiting that it had lost contact with the plane but implied that it was no big deal and not an unusual occurrence in that type of storm. Everyone assumed the weather had either delayed the plane or caused the pilot to decide to divert to another airport.

Ten minutes later, after Prime Minister Matesa announced that the plane had disappeared from the radar screen and there was no radio contact at all, the idea of a plane crash became a reality. Ambassador Galbraith reentered the Croatian prime minister's plane to call the U.S. State Department. Secretary of State Warren Christopher was in California but Undersecretary Peter Tarnoff, the most senior State Department official in Washington at the time, was reached. Galbraith told Tarnoff that the plane was feared lost. Then he hung up and helped organize a search-and-rescue operation, a multinational effort that included Croatian military forces and police, as well as NATO forces.

10:30 A.M., Washington

The State Department mobilized, scrambling to gather information, confused by conflicting reports. Tarnoff called Secretary Christopher and Anthony Lake, the President's national security adviser. At 10:30, Lake called the White House press office and staffers Ginny Terzano and another woman went with their boss, White House Press Secretary Mike McCurry, into the top-secret situation room in the basement of the West Wing. Then Lake walked into the Oval Office and informed the President.

11 A.M., Unicorn Lane, Northwest Washington, D.C.

It was Wednesday morning and there had been no phone call from Dad. My mother thought it strange because Dad always called, no matter how busy he was; but Mom put her thoughts aside, assuming he'd call later. She was still sick but tried to talk herself into getting up out of bed. She expected my father home in two days, on Good Friday, and I was due from L.A. the same day, with my boyfriend, Marcelino Ford-Livene. The house was in chaos, there was no food in the kitchen, and Mom knew she had to get organized before we all arrived home for the holiday. Family plans for the weekend included Friday night soul-food takeout from Faces, a restaurant on Georgia Avenue—Dad's favorite fried chicken, fried catfish, collard greens, and sweet potatoes; a round of golf Saturday for Dad, Marcelino, and Michael; and Saturday night dinner at home with Mom cooking her deservedly famous "Chicken à la Alma." Easter Sunday dinner we always had next door with good friends Kent and Carmen Amos.

Figuring that going to work would get her jump-started and out of her malaise, Mom called Monica West, her assistant at Chevy Chase Bank, where she is senior vice president, and told her she'd be coming into work that afternoon.

Mom showered and began to dress, but very slowly because she still had the flu and felt as if she were moving underwater. She couldn't seem to get going. And she didn't turn on C-SPAN, which in our house is on all the time. Mom is addicted to its political coverage. She always shakes her head when she recalls that that was the only morning in her life that she didn't put the television on. When the phone rang shortly before 11 A.M., she was standing in front of the bathroom mirror trying to fix her hair.

She walked into the bedroom and picked up the receiver but there was no one there. Two minutes later, the phone rang again, and again she heard a silence when she picked up. When it rang a third time, she answered in a slightly annoyed tone and heard a voice saying, "Alma, Alma, is that you? This is Bill Clinton."

She said, "Oh, hi, Mr. President! How are you doing?"

"I guess you haven't heard anything," the President said.

Mom didn't know what he was talking about. He said, "I wanted you to hear it from me first. Ron's plane is missing in Croatia."

She sat down on Dad's side of the bed.

"Ron's plane is missing," he repeated. He told her that the plane had been on track to the airport in Dubrovnik until it went off radar. Mom still didn't really understand, so the President finally said, "Alma, it doesn't look good." When she heard those words, she felt as if a giant fist had hit her in the chest. She asked if the plane had been shot down and the President said, "We have no evidence that it's been shot down. But it's missing. And it doesn't look good."

After promising to call her back as soon as he heard anything more definite, he hung up. Mom remained sitting on the side of the bed but turned on CNN and saw an image of the plane with Dad's name flashing across the bottom of the screen. She saw a line of little dots representing the course the plane had been on and followed them as they went off course and collided with a mountain. At that point, there was a graphic depicting a plane crash.

The phone rang again and it was Bill Taylor, Dad's counsel at the Commerce Department. He asked my mother where Michael was and when she said Michael was at Howard University Law School giving a speech, Bill said he would find him. Then my mother called her assistant, Monica, and started to say "Ronnie's plane" but couldn't finish and started crying. Monica said she would be right over. My mother sat on the bed, crying, while all three phone lines in the house began to ring.

Monica arrived and began answering the phones and the door because people started coming. When the President called back, Monica handed the phone to Mom. "Alma. We're going over to the church across the street to say a prayer then Hillary and I will be right over." Within minutes, Michael arrived at the house, and I called from L.A.

Maybe the hardest part was dealing with Nan, Dad's mother, who lived in New York City. She called, sobbing, "Is it true? Is it true?" Nan asked if she should come to Washington, then added that she would never get on a plane again. My mother was numb herself, but she had to deal with Nan. Mom told Nan not to come yet. Since Nan had just recently been discharged from the hospital, Mom felt she should stay in the calm environment of her apartment. Fortunately, my grandmother had Marie Rhone, Dad's godmother, with her, as well as her good friend Bea Gordon.

～

Meanwhile, I was on the longest plane ride of my life. My thoughts were wild, disjointed, almost psychotic. I was certain that Dad could survive a crash over water; he was such a strong swimmer, he would make it to the shore of the Adriatic Sea. I pictured him gasping for breath as he swam, towing along with him someone he'd rescued, a nonswimmer who'd been with him on the plane. I saw him, cold and wet, on the icy shore, waiting for help. Abruptly, that image faded and I mumbled a prayer, clutching our photo, repeating his name over and over. My thoughts jumped again and I saw us both flying through the air, lost—me here, Dad on the other side of the world. Then, I found myself peering intently out the plane window: If he were really dead and on his way to heaven, he might float by and blow me a kiss. I switched gears again, berating myself for leaving my passport in L.A. Surely I would need it when we flew to Europe to bring Dad home from a Croatian hospital.

I had no rational thoughts. I just knew he was alive, but hurt. We'd bring him home, help him recuperate, and everything would be the way it was.

Then, a heavy curtain would fall, crushing my fragile hope and I knew for certain that he was dead: I would never hug him again and our family's life was over.

I relived the last time we were together, three weeks earlier, when Dad came to L.A. on business. That Friday night, we'd had dinner at Chinois in Santa Monica. As usual, we walked into the restaurant hand in hand and held hands at the table. Our family is unusually affectionate, Dad most of all. Once, in San Francisco, Michael and Dad were on the street saying good-bye and, as they always did, kissed on the lips. A passing man clapped and whistled, most likely thinking he was seeing two fellow gay guys in action. At Chinois, Dad and I held hands in between bites of our delicious Szechuan lobster and I told him my most recent life plan; he listened intently, laughing and offering advice.

Whenever I recall that night, it seems that he did have a premonition because he was mushier than usual. I think that he was presenting me with a farewell benediction of love and approval that I would remember always.

Wolfing down the lobster—nothing stopped Dad from loving his food—he said that he understood I wasn't in a rush to move back east and that if I was happy, he was happy. This was so different from his usual suggestion that I return to Washington or New York: "You need to bring your booty home." That night, he said he was proud of me, pleased that I loved trying felony cases in the D.A.'s office, and glad that I was so in love with Marcelino. (My parents have always been closely involved

in my life. A month earlier, when my father was in San Francisco, he took Marcelino to dinner without telling me. "I wanted
to meet this boy that you're always talking about," he said.
When I found out, I wanted to run up to San Francisco, but
they did fine without me and in the end Dad enjoyed Marcelino's company and approved of our relationship.)

When dinner was over, we did one of our routines: Dad reminded me that I was "the most brilliant and beautiful daughter in the world" and I responded that he had "made me that
way." We hugged and kissed, and went our separate ways. I
would never see him again.

As I thought of that night during the interminable plane ride,
I smiled and cried. Then, disbelief and horror flooded my
mind. If the plane had crashed, what about Bill, Carol, and
Kathryn? Bill Morton, a deputy undersecretary at the Commerce Department, my father's aide for years and a good friend
of mine, was close to my whole family. Carol Hamilton, my
father's press secretary, was on the phone with Mom constantly,
they were that close. And Kathryn Hoffman, Dad's special assistant, was a woman I admired for her poise and assurance.
Bill, Carol, Kathryn, all young and bright and full of life. Were
they dead? In a whirl of despair and confusion and hope, I sat
on that plane, each moment bringing me close to the answers
I would find in Washington. Life without my father? Not possible, I thought.

～

Three thousand miles away, my brother, who had also followed
Dad's example and become a lawyer, was speaking before an
audience of first-year law students at Howard University. He
was just finishing his talk on mentoring and the importance of
involving young people in the political process, and was looking
forward to the question-and-answer period to follow. Michael
had inherited my father's ease in front of an audience. No one
could outshine Dad at Q&A, although Michael was a close second. But before the first question could be asked, a man came
up to the podium and handed Michael a note: "You have an
emergency. Please call your office." Without a second's hesita-
tion, Michael exited and went backstage, toward an office with

a phone. He noticed that people were looking at him strangely, just as Bobby and Jacqui had looked at me that morning. Michael instantly assumed that whatever was wrong had to do with Dad; he never thought of Morgan and Ryan, his two-year-old twin boys. He knew it was Dad. He called his office and his secretary, Yvette Coleman, told him there was a problem with Dad's plane. Then he called Mom, who told him to come home right away. In the car, Michael turned on WTOP, D.C.'s all-news station, and heard that Dad's plane was missing but it was unclear how and why. Michael drove and listened, but part of his mind retreated defensively; he wasn't ready to feel.

When he pulled up to the house and saw dozens of reporters camped out, reality intruded and Michael emerged from his dazed state. If indeed something had happened to our father, Michael was prepared to help Mom, to do whatever she needed him to do.

2 P.M., *Unicorn Lane*
8 P.M., *Cilipi Airport*

By afternoon, the house was jammed with Commerce staff, friends, and relatives, and dozens of press people were outside, behind a barricade. Mom was in her bedroom with Michael and Tami, Michael's wife, and I was on a plane flying east, feeling as if my life were over. The President and Hillary arrived at the house in midafternoon and Mom, Michael, and Tami went into the library with them. The President had spent the morning in his office, after canceling his regular appointments, so he could be updated on the status of the search-and-rescue operation across the ocean in Bosnia. Mom and the President and First Lady talked for a long time. When the President told Mom he was going to the Commerce Department to talk to the employees, he asked, "What do you want me to tell them?" At that point, he and Mom felt certain that the plane, and Dad, were gone.

"I want you to tell them that Ron was proud of them, fought for them and believed in them. And tell them that you're going to do that now," Mom said. She chose those words so that all thirty-six thousand individuals who worked at Commerce would not begin worrying about the possibility of the Department being dismantled, something my father had fought during his years as secretary. She also asked the President to read them Dad's favorite passage from Scripture: the verse in Isaiah in which the faithful "soar on wings like eagles."

At the Commerce Department, five hundred employees jammed the building's auditorium to hear President Clinton pay tribute to Dad. Said the President, "I was always amazed at the way he was continually reaching out and trying to bridge the differences between people, always trying to get the best out of people, always believing that we could do more than we have done."

On the other side of the world, in Dubrovnik, Ambassador Galbraith, Morris, and the Croatian and American officials returned to the airport police station to set up an open line to the State Department. At that point, the group also included some Commerce Department personnel and about thirty Croatians, including government officials, security, and police.

The search-and-rescue mission was under way. Dark sheets of drenching rain made the search difficult. Inside the airport police station, the men talked about what they thought had happened. When Morris heard the people around him talking plane crash, he was in shock. For what seemed like endless hours, the group waited while search-and-rescue crews, believing the plane had gone down over the ocean, used helicopters and boats to search the Adriatic near the shoreline at Dubrovnik for signs of wreckage.

After a while, most of the group drove to the mayor's office in the old town of Dubrovnik, to wait for news. At 6:45 P.M., a Croatian villager named Ivo Durkovic called the local police and said that afternoon he had heard a plane flying very low, then had heard an explosion. He assumed it was a grenade. The fog had finally lifted from the area and he was now able to see plane wreckage on a mountain, St. John's Peak, located a mile and a half east of Cavtat. Cavtat is a tiny hamlet with gray stone houses situated on a peninsula jutting into the Adriatic. Rescue teams now began to search for survivors and wreckage on the mountain, with the first team members rappelling down the steep slope, attached by ropes to helicopters over-head.

Back in Washington, my family waited for me. When Chip and I arrived at Baltimore-Washington Airport, an old friend, Mike Graves, drove us home with a police escort. On the way, he said that they'd found the wreckage, that one woman had survived initially, but had died on the way to the hospital. My hopes soared. One survivor meant the possibility of others. Dad was such a fighter, I thought. Surely he would be found alive. When Mike warned us that the press was outside the house, I wondered, naively, why they would invade our privacy at a time like this. He also said that President and Mrs. Clinton, along with various Cabinet members, government and political offi-cials, old friends, and even strangers had been at the house.

My brother had been anxiously waiting in the foyer for me and when Chip and I got to the front of the house, Michael came out to meet us and I actually collapsed in his arms. As he led me up the three flights of stairs to my parents' bedroom, I saw faceless, nameless hordes of people everywhere, on the stairs, in the rooms. I only wanted to get to my mother. In her room, stretched out on her bed, looking small and alone, was Mom. I ran into her arms and she rocked me back and forth as we cried together. Tami and Mere, my mother's mother, Carmen and Kent Amos, our next door neighbors, and a few other people were in there but quickly left when Kent said, "Everybody out of the room."

I was not far from hysteria, screaming, "My Daddy isn't dead. I don't believe it. They'll find him." Mom and Michael hugged me and tried to calm me, saying over and over, "It's okay, Tra, it's okay." In truth, at that moment, I felt that nothing would ever again be okay for me. It hurt so much that I defended myself by developing a delusion that I would hold on to for a long time after the crash: I was certain that, despite the news reports, my father was really alive, wandering, hurt and alone, in the mountains of Croatia.

Of course, CNN was on and as we watched, the horror grew. Between updates on the plane and rescue efforts, the station showed photos and interviews from my father's career as if the eulogy had begun, as if a determination had been made, and my father was officially no longer here. Over and over the head-line was repeated: "Commerce Secretary Ron Brown and thirty-four others presumed dead." When I saw a film clip of Dad laughing and shooting the breeze with GIs in Tuzla that very morning, the pain seemed unendurable.

∼

In Croatia, Morris, the ambassador, and some Commerce peo-ple drove to the site, a long ride in pitch-blackness, on winding dirt roads, some of which were almost completely washed out. At the end of their ride, they came to the foot of St. John's Peak and saw a crowd of police and military personnel. The plane was there, in pieces, on the mountain. Some of the group tried to climb the mountain, but found it impossible and retreated to the mayor's office, then to their hotel. Ambassador Galbraith halted an hour's walk from where the central pieces of wreck-age, and the victims, lay. There were no roads, visibility was almost nonexistent, and Galbraith was told by the rescue team that he would only hinder their operation. He agreed to return in the morning.

Morris Reid refused to leave and stood in the rain, watching. Rescue teams worked until after midnight in rain and fog and located one survivor and nine bodies; none of them was Dad. All through the night, a team of rescuers continued to climb the rough terrain, searching for survivors. Morris argued with the searchers until they agreed to allow him up the mountain. Morris climbed more than two miles uphill, over rocks and dirt, to see what he needed to see with his own eyes: pieces of wreck-age and bodies scattered over a four-hundred-square-meter area.

He saw my father. He saw his friends and coworkers at Com-merce. He then went down the mountain to call us.

2 A.M., Unicorn Lane

Finally, the house cleared out and Michael, Tami, Mom, and I got into my parents' bed and curled up together. Eventually Tami moved to the floor because it was so crowded. I lay between Michael and Mom staring at the ceiling. There was still no confirmation as to whether Dad was dead or alive. I thought of him lying all alone in the rain on that mountain in Croatia. I wanted to be there with him, holding him, fixing his wounds, shielding him from the rain.

The phone rang at 2 A.M. and it was Morris. Michael listened for a few minutes, then said, "Okay, okay. Thanks a lot, Morris. I'll talk to you tomorrow." Michael hung up and turned to us. Morris had been at the crash site, had seen Dad, and removed his watch and chain for us. We began to sob and hold each other.

9 A.M., April 4, Washington

President Clinton called in the morning. "Alma, there are no survivors. They have identified Ron's body." He told Mom that Brigadier General Michael Canavan, special operations commander at the site, had seen Dad. Mom told me and Michael. I felt numb. The President ordered all American flags to be flown at half-mast through April 10 in memory of those who had died in the crash; then, along with some of his staff and some Cabinet members, he attended a memorial service at St. John's Episcopal Church, which is near the White House, to pray for the victims. In addition to my father, the crash had taken the lives of thirty-four others—Commerce employees, business executives, a *New York Times* reporter, crew members, and two Croatians. My family stayed in our house; I continued to feel numb.

11 A.M., Unicorn Lane

Later that morning, the house started filling up again, even more than on the previous day, and our close friend Alexis Herman came in and took over; Alexis, now the U.S. secretary of labor, had been Dad's chief of staff at the Democratic National Committee. Our dining room was made into an office, with staff and computers and phones for tracking telegrams, letters, and flowers, and for arranging food deliveries. Alexis and Kent Amos took care of the funeral arrangements. Friends Nikki and Fay Webber, Diane Cohen, Lisa Handley Bonner, Carmen Amos, and Monica West oversaw flowers and food, letters and phone calls. We remained in the library, unable to do anything but cry. Alexis and Kent would come into the room from time to time to tell us what was going on.

In the meantime, State and Defense worked to determine what had happened to the plane and how to definitively identify the bodies. A press conference was called by the Defense Department and General Howell M. Estes III, Director of Operations on the Joint Chiefs of Staff, told reporters what was known so far:

Thirty-five people had died in the crash. The sole initial survivor, a woman crew member, had died en route to a hospital. Brigadier General Mike Canavan and about thirty members of the rescue team under his command had worked through the night and into the early part of the day, April 4. They reported that the plane, which did not have a black box, had broken into pieces. His team struggled on the muddy incline of St. John's Peak to determine if there were any survivors and to find the bodies of the victims. He described the scene: bobbing flashlights, muted shouts of the rescue team, blasts of thunder and heavy rain, dirt roads turned to mud. Canavan reported that all thirty-three Americans on board had been located. None had been officially identified yet.

I wonder: Where is my father?

The Croatians had set up a temporary morgue at the airport for the victims they are taking off the mountain. Other than the calls from Morris and from the President, we have heard nothing official about Dad. Maybe he survived.

Night, April 4, Unicorn Lane

Thursday night, the President called. "What are you doing?"

"Nothing," Mom replied. "Just sitting around with a few thousand people." At about 10:30 P.M., he came over. By this time, most of our friends had left, with the exception of Kent and Carmen and their children, Debbie and Wesley, Alexis, Howlie Davis, Monica West, and Vernon Jordan. We all sat in the living room with the President and talked. He said he needed to talk about my father and the times they had shared. He told stories about some of my father's funny habits and we actually laughed. When the President finally left, it was about two in the morning.

We still knew little about what had happened. We had no solid information on why and how the plane had crashed. Other than what Morris Reid told us in that brief telephone call, or what the President had told Mom about Canavan's report, we knew nothing specific about how my father had died. It seemed as if Dad had suddenly been swallowed up by the universe. He had disappeared in an instant, without a chance for us to say good-bye.

April 5

By Friday, even I found it hard to believe that Dad had survived. We still didn't know very much about what had happened. We were told that all of the Americans who had been on the plane would arrive at Dover Air Force Base the next day, Saturday. Things had to be done and, all around, people began to do them. But not me. I was in bad shape, hysterical and numb by turns. I lay on the couch alternating between free-floating anxiety and terror. Then I would get into my delusional state and imagine that the next ring of the phone would be Dad. "Tra," he would say when I picked up, "why haven't you all come to get me?"

Kent went with Michael to pick out the casket while my mother and I stayed in the house. I honestly don't know how Michael did what he did, how he held it together. Kent and Carmen moved all the meetings next door, to their house, which helped a lot. Morris remained in Croatia. He insisted that as Dad's advance person, it was his responsibility to accompany him back to Washington.

The President wanted us to ride to Dover on Air Force One with him Saturday when Dad was brought back from Croatia.

He and Hillary would be with us and we could invite a few close friends to accompany us. My mother thought about who to take but I remember not caring at all, not even wanting to hear about it. Besides us—Mom, me, Michael, Tami, and Chip—we took Kent Amos; Dad's longtime secretary, Barbara Schmitz; his driver, Henry Oliver; Michael's best friend, Rick Greenfield; Tommy Boggs, Dad's former law partner and close friend; and his good friend Vinnie Cohen. They were all folks Dad had been very close to and would have wanted there. Mom thought that the trip would be too difficult for Nan and, after we had all been to Dover, we knew how right she had been.

In Dubrovnik, helicopters used winches to lift the crash victims aboard and transport them to a temporary morgue at the airport. We were told that the Americans would not be identified until they returned to the United States. I didn't want to think about what this meant.

We began to hear rumblings of the many factors that had led to the crash, about an officer who was removed from his post after he complained publicly that the Air Force was allowing flights to land in poorly equipped airports such as Cilipi. We also heard that Dad's plane was old, lacked adequate equipment, and was due for an upgrade in 1997. The news was filled with theories and reports and the beginnings of an investigation.

But, in the end, none of it mattered. I had lost Dad.

One sunny May afternoon, a month after Dad's accident, Mom and I were in the kitchen when the doorbell rang. I answered the door and was shocked to see a courier standing there with Dad's luggage, luggage we assumed had gone down with the plane but instead had remained in Zagreb, awaiting his return from what was supposed to be a day trip to Dubrovnik.

I carried his beautiful brown leather garment bag and suitcase, Christmas gifts from Mom, upstairs to the foyer off the kitchen. When Mom saw what it was she pulled me to her and we cried. Seeing his bags made me feel as if he were going to walk in the door any moment. Since he traveled so much, it was a familiar event to have couriers deliver Dad's misplaced or delayed luggage to the house. I ran to the window and looked up and down the street, expecting to see my father. Thank God, I thought, now the nightmare will end.

But he didn't open the door. He didn't climb the steps, come into the kitchen, walk to the refrigerator, and ask, "Honey, what's to eat?" The courier truck pulled away and the street was quiet.

Upstairs we opened his garment bag and touched his suits, even pressing them to our faces to get his smell one last time. When we unzipped his suitcase, we both burst out laughing as four bottles of contact lens solution tumbled out. Dad was always misplacing, forgetting, or losing his saline, so he would buy extras in airport and hotel shops; by the end of a trip, he'd come home with more bottles than he needed.

His portable CD player and some CDs were in a side compartment of his suitcase, so I put on his headphones, turned on the player, and heard the sweet sounds of a jazz group, Fourplay, perhaps the last music he'd listened to. I passed it to Mom so she could listen. Looking through the other discs, I saw some by jazz guitarist Earl Klugh, saxophonist Kenny G, the hip-hop group TLC, and the soundtrack of Waiting to Exhale.

Having seen numerous stellar performances at the Apollo Theater during his years in Harlem, my father was an avid music fan, and musicians had a special place in his heart. He often told me he missed

not having any musical talent. He had never learned to play an in-
strument and his singing was as bad as mine. While he loved best the
sound of a saxophone and preferred the mellowness and soul of R&B
and jazz to my favorite, bass-heavy hip-hop, he appreciated all music.

I took the CD player and discs up to my room, sat on the floor, and
for several hours listened to Dad's music on his CDs. They've never
sounded so good.

Child of Harlem

My Grandmother, Gloria Osborne

M y father's maternal great-great-grandparents were a merchant, Johnson W. Welborn, of Clinton, Mississippi, who was born in 1825, and a house slave, whose name and date of birth are unknown. Welborn, who was also a captain in the Mississippi infantry, had a total of five children with my great-great-grandmother, four with another slave, and several with his legal wife. When they were of age, he sent several of his offspring to be educated at Fisk University in Nashville, Tennessee, a most unusual move. Whites in the South did not educate the children their slaves bore them and usually didn't even allow them to learn to read and write. My father's mother, whom I call Nan, told me that these children pleased their father by resembling him and being fair-skinned.

Two of the children, Walter, my father's great-grandfather, and Eugene, escaped from Clinton during the conscription riots that were widespread through the South after the emancipation of the slaves in January 1863. Walter and Eugene, financed with money their mother had somehow saved, purchased train fare to Washington, D.C. They also should have shared in an inheritance from their father, Johnson Welborn. But Walter, Eugene, and their siblings had no legal rights to collect inheritances. Welborn's white wife and children collected, according to the law of the day.

Happy to escape from Mississippi, Walter and Eugene were joyful on the train ride to Washington. Their mother had disguised them in Confederate soldier uniforms and they had carried it off because of their fair coloring. They were so light in complexion, they could have "gone to the other side," according to Nan, but Walter Welborn, who looked exactly like his white father, chose all his life to identify with his black mother.

Nan, like others of her generation, never talked much about this heritage. So while my father always knew where he came from, who his people were, no one really explored it with him because to those who had lived it, slavery was a topic best left alone. Recalled Nan, "My family never talked about Mississippi and slavery. In those days that was like a disgrace. They felt ashamed to have come from that kind of segregated environment, even though they couldn't help it."

In Washington, Walter began his new life as a free citizen. A short time later, his status improved considerably when he married Elexine Beckley, daughter of a socially prominent, educated, and well-to-do Washington family; both she and her parents had graduated from high school, no small accomplishment for blacks in those days. Elexine and Walter had five daughters, but she died on August 6, 1900, giving birth to my great-grandmother, Ruth Alma Welborn, Nan's mother.

Ruth, raised along with her sisters by their father, Walter, had blond hair and hazel eyes, and looked like her grandfather, the white merchant. In 1918, Ruth graduated from Dunbar High School, at the time, the best high school of the three in Washington, D.C., that were available to black children. Ruth always had an academic orientation, so she chose Dunbar, which was for students who had college aspirations; Armstrong High School offered auto mechanics, carpentry, and electricity, while a third D.C. high school had accounting, typing, steno, and other business courses. When Ruth graduated, she decided to join the Naval Reserve instead of attending college and became a petty officer in a special unit, the Yeomanettes.

While vacationing in Atlantic City, Ruth met Jerome Bonaparte Osborne, a young man with a job in the Veterans' Administration, most likely in a menial position because, generally, those were the only jobs open at that time to black people. They fell in love, married, and, a short time later, on September 13, 1921, had Gloria Elexine, my grandmother Nan. She was born in Freedman's Hospital, now part of Howard University, where twenty years later, her own child, my father, would also be born.

Ruth's marriage to Jerome was short-lived and they divorced when Nan was only four. Ruth then went to work for the U.S. Postal Service. Eventually she saved enough money to build a two-family house on Sherman Avenue in the northwest section of Washington on a small piece of land that her father, Walter, had left her; great-grandmother Ruth lived on one floor and rented out the other.

Jerome remained in his and Ruth's house on Fairmont Street, and most of the time Nan lived there with him because he had legal custody of her. It's not clear why, since Nan always said she wanted to be with her mother, but the courts had ruled otherwise. When Nan was eight, Ruth remarried a man named William "Bill" Davis; he was a black narcotics agent, a rarity during the late 1920s. Nan said she was jealous that he was with her mother and she was not.

Nan grew into a beautiful woman. She resembled her mother, and both had the kind of beauty that attracted stares wherever she went. With her perfect skin, shiny hair, and graceful bearing, she was exceptionally striking.

Life in the segregated city of Washington during the twenties and thirties was all about color: Color determined access. For Nan's generation, the grandchildren of slaves and slave owners, color determined whether or not one would have access to movie theaters, restaurants, stores, and other public places. As a black woman, Nan was not permitted into movie theaters; she could shop but was not allowed to try things on. If she tried to eat in a restaurant, she wouldn't be served. She quickly discovered that she could gain the access she wanted because some people assumed she was white, based on her light complexion; she didn't correct them. Because she was able to, Nan spent part of her life passing for white.

Many of her friends did the same. But the young women had to be on guard all the time because stores had "spotters," hired to monitor shoppers to see if any of them were black people passing for white. Nan recalled that People's Drugstore, now part of the national CVS chain, employed spotters. Once, after visiting her mother, Ruth, who was being treated for hypertension in a V.A. hospital, Nan and a girlfriend went to the hospital cafeteria for lunch. "We had already been served, when our waitress came back to the table and said, 'Sorry, you can't eat that here. We don't served coloreds.'" Someone had identified the women as black, a race outlawed from eating in the V.A. hospital cafeteria. "I asked the waitress, how did she know what race we were with all the foreign people in Washington. But we still had to leave," Nan said.

When I was younger, I found the idea of black people passing for white upsetting and confusing. Hearing stories such as this one from Buddy Wilkinson, Dad's godfather and Nan's first cousin, makes it more understandable: "People who were fair could do things that people who were not fair could not. For example, I'm dark but my mother was very light. We all lived in a segregated area and you didn't leave it. But when these [fair] people wanted to shop, to go to the department stores, to theaters, they would just go. They could go. I couldn't go. We used to laugh about it because it was kind of funny to us. The white folks didn't know those folks were Negro or colored; they just had no idea."

Many years later, in New York City, in the fifties, Nan was hired by Steuben Glass and worked in their Fifth Avenue store, selling delicate, expensive crystal. Steuben had an unstated but understood policy, as did many companies at that time, that only whites were to be hired as salespeople: Had the company known that Nan was black, she would have been fired. Because of this, my darker-complexioned father, then a teenager, could never stroll into the store to meet his mother. They were forced to meet a distance away so Nan's coworkers wouldn't see them together and wonder who Dad was. At the time, Dad was embarrassed by his mother's behavior and felt that she had no pride in her race.

Although my father didn't always agree with Nan, his love

for her was boundless and he was a dutiful and loyal son. They were close and spoke at least once a week after he grew up and left home. Dad thought nothing of running up to Nan's New York City apartment for a quick visit or to help her out. The Wednesday before my father's death, he was in New York taking care of my grandmother. She had been in the hospital, so he had gone there to consult with her doctors, then bring her home. He shopped for groceries so she'd have a full refrigerator, filled her prescriptions, and made certain she had everything she needed before he left for Washington. No matter what was on Dad's upcoming agenda, even a trade mission to Croatia, he always considered Nan and took care of her.

My Grandfather, Bill Brown

In 1904, my great-great-grandfather Gilbert Dorsey Brown Sr. took his family, in a buckboard, from Plains, Virginia, to settle in Bressler, Pennsylvania. Bressler was a small mill town and Gilbert Sr. would toil in the steel mill all his life. One year later, the oldest son, Gilbert Jr., married Nancy Nickens. Nancy's family, with its fourteen children, had moved to Bressler from Markham, Virginia, some years earlier.

Gilbert Jr. and Nancy, my great-grandparents, had twelve children, three boys and nine girls; William, or Bill, my father's father, called "GD" for Granddad by me and my brother, Michael, was born on January 31, 1916.

That same year, Gilbert Sr. used savings from his mill earnings to purchase a farm in Linglestown, ten miles from Bressler. On the farm, the Browns raised corn, wheat, and potatoes, had peach and cherry orchards, and kept horses, mules, and chickens. All of the Brown children and grandchildren helped out on the farm.

Gilbert Jr. and Nancy's home on Main Street in Bressler nurtured and raised their large family in only a few rooms but with an open, loving spirit. The Browns believed in sharing what they had; there were almost always guests at mealtime—friends, neighbors, relatives. This open-door policy led to GD's own generosity of spirit when he was an adult, always insisting that there was "room for one more" at the table. Wherever he lived, he had relatives visiting or living with him; in later years, he generously took nieces and nephews on vacations or paid for them to attend summer camp.

In addition to the food raised on the family farm, GD's family lived on the fruits of their own garden—asparagus, apricots, cherries, strawberries, plums, grapes, and peaches—and on the pigs and chickens they raised.

Great-grandfather Gilbert Jr. was well-read and an ardent follower of current events in his beloved *New York Times*. Relatives recalled his personable, easygoing way of relating to people, which he apparently passed down to GD and to my father.

Great-grandmother Nancy, who was called Grandma Brown by the family, had a wide range of talents. She was a green-thumb gardener, neighborhood caterer, inventive cook (she created an unparalleled potato bread), unlicensed doctor, and creative seamstress. She began by designing and sewing clothing for wealthier neighbors, then opened a dress shop with her daughter, Libby, on Front Street in the center of town.

Gilbert Jr. remained vigorous into old age, working at the steel mill until he was seventy-five. But Grandma Brown developed high blood pressure and heart problems while still young. Cousin Bobby recalled scraping salt off the pretzels she loved to eat. When my father was born, in 1941, he was brought to his bedridden Grandma on a pillow so she could see her new grandson. She died four months later, on December 14; she was fifty-six years old.

Gilbert Jr. and Grandma Brown's son, William, or my GD, graduated from small, predominantly white Swatara Township High School in Bressler, then went off to attend Howard University in Washington, D.C., where he was a basketball star. He graduated in 1941 with a bachelor's degree. In business matters, I understand that GD could be rough and tough, but to me he was always warm and gregarious. Just like my father.

Dad was like his father in many ways. For example, GD had a reputation for looking well dressed and impeccable at all times. He told my father that appearance was critical to success, so one should always look clean, neat, and well-groomed. Taking this lesson to heart, Dad incorporated perfect grooming into his daily life and made it a practice to be dressed neatly, pressed, and shined, on every occasion. According to Buddy Wilkinson, "Ron developed at an early age an impeccable taste for his personal being that he kept with him all of his life." As a teenager, he learned how to iron and sew, and in the army he learned how to spit shine his shoes. Throughout his adult life, if a button fell off a shirt, he sewed it back on immediately, and if a crease wasn't sharp enough, he ironed it deeper. One of Dad's personal rules was to never loosen his collar and tie, no matter what. I did hear that once, during a fourteen-hour plane ride to Africa, he relaxed the rule and loosened his tie. Although he was an immaculate dresser, Dad never gave clothing or dress any thought or time, other than the time it took to make certain he looked neatly groomed. That he was always flawlessly turned out led to a perception that he was an expensive dresser. But in Washington, people who are obsessed with clothing do not buy their suits off the rack, as my father did. The made-to-order shirts he purchased long before he could afford them were Dad's only foray into custom-made clothing. He had discovered that they fit better, making his appearance smoother and neater. This was an essential part of the lesson Dad internalized: Appearance was integral to success and a conscientious appearance was a sign of respect to oneself and one's associates.

GD's influence can also be seen in my father's desire and ability to lead. In Harlem, GD was a political and social leader, involved in community service and New York City Democratic politics. He was president of Howard University's Alumni Club of New York City, and was on a dozen or more boards and committees in the Harlem and New York City communities. He knew everyone. Occasionally, GD gave speeches on relevant and current topics, although his rhetoric could not compete with the orations of the full-time soap-box speakers who dominated the intersection of 125th Street and Seventh Avenue. This was the street corner where Dad's childhood home, the Hotel Theresa, was located. These impassioned Harlem orators filled the air in all seasons with their sermons and lectures and exhortations. My father heard many of them, including some who urged listeners to travel to Africa to find their roots.

My Father, Ronald Harmon Brown

Nan and GD met when both were students at Howard University, and even though Jerome Osborne liked GD, he was so strict that he would not allow his daughter to date. When Nan was eighteen, she quit college and eloped with GD, then twenty-four. They were married in Manassas, Virginia, on July 17, 1940, then traveled to GD's family home in Bressler, Pennsylvania. The Brown family gave the newlyweds a large garden party to wish them well. In years to come, GD and Nan would visit Bressler often. Nan was popular with her in-laws. GD's sisters especially loved the "city gifts," such as fancy dresses, that she brought them when she visited.

Nan and GD lived in Washington right after their marriage because GD got a job with FDR's Federal Housing and Home Finance Agency. Three months after they were married, Nan became pregnant with my father. She followed the doctor's orders exactly, so afraid that something might go wrong that she never deviated from his instructions. "If the doctor told me to eat one peanut a week, I would eat one peanut a week," Nan said.

Ronald Harmon Brown weighed in at six pounds, six ounces, on August 1, 1941, at Freedman's Hospital. GD, Nan, and "little Ronnie" visited Bressler regularly and, as the years passed, the Brown relatives found Dad to be an amazing child. He read a newspaper by the age of five and had an uncommon way of talking, saying "going" instead of "goin'," and "jumping" instead of "jumpin'." At Thanksgiving and other family holidays, Dad would amaze his cousins in Bressler by showing off the French he was studying at Hunter Elementary. Despite his precocious behavior, none of his cousins resented him. Instead, they loved him. Recalled Bobby Jones, "Even as a youngster, he made you feel that you were the only person he wanted to talk to. . . . When you were with him, he focused on you and only you."

In the twenties and thirties, Washington, D.C., with its government jobs, provided a safe harbor for emigrating southern blacks; an emerging black middle class was composed mainly of these southerners. In Washington, individuals with aspirations could find secure, well-paying jobs in the post office or other branches of the civil service. These newcomers to Washington were upwardly mobile and determined to make for their children a better life than they had had. They created and enforced a rigid set of standards for this next generation, rules that governed everything from behavior to education, from dress to speech. Parents expected nothing less from their children than excellent grades and manners, high school diplomas, and, in many cases, college degrees. There was no juvenile delinquency; it would have been unacceptable to these parents, most of whom were only a generation or two removed from their slave ancestors.

This rapidly growing middle class assumed its children would become professionals: doctors, lawyers, dentists, teachers. There was a narrow range of professions open to black people in that day and, as a result, many in the new middle class often had difficulty securing jobs, no matter what their degrees. The high school Nan had attended, Dunbar, benefited from the institutional racism of the day. Although many of Dunbar's faculty members had advanced degrees from major universities, they couldn't find work elsewhere and were forced to accept jobs as high school teachers.

As did other black middle-class parents, Nan understood that her son had to be exceptional to be successful in a racist world, so she pushed Dad, applauding his efforts, encouraging him to be the best. A group of mothers, had joined forces in 1938 to form Jack and Jill, a club that would ensure their offspring, many of whom attended predominantly white schools, would maintain their connection to the black community. Dad was a member of Jack and Jill, and the club was an important force in his childhood as it was for my generation and, now, the next generation. My brother's sons, Morgan and Ryan, are members. Mothers meet once a month while the children enjoy trips to the pumpkin patch in October, making sandwiches for local soup kitchens, and dozens of other cultural events and outings.

When Dad was about six months old, in January 1942, his family moved to Boston when GD was transferred there, helping families find federally funded housing in Boston as he had in Washington. The Browns' home in Boston was a detached house on a quiet street in Roxbury, a mostly black neighborhood. Theirs was a typical middle-class life with Dad a happy toddler and my grandparents busy socially. GD was outgoing, making friends easily wherever he lived, a quality my Dad inherited.

When he was four, my father attended kindergarten at St. Mark's Nursery School, and although most tots that age came home from school dirty and disheveled, Nan recalled that Dad came home almost as neat and clean as when he had left in the morning.

Once, when Dad was about four, he saw a neighbor pass by the Browns' front window. He must have heard his parents describing her as messy because as she approached, he called to Nan, "Mommy, here comes Mrs. Jonas looking like a devilish mess!"

In 1947, when Dad was five, GD's job transferred him to New York City and the family moved to 595 East 167th Street in the Bronx. Six months later, when GD was hired to manage Harlem's famed Hotel Theresa, a thirteen-story landmark marked by graceful carvings and arches, located at the intersection of 125th Street and Seventh Avenue, my father's life changed forever.

To my surprise, I've discovered that the Theresa did not admit blacks until 1940. But after it opened its doors to its own community, it became Harlem's mecca, *the* home away from home for black entertainers, sports heroes, politicians, and other public figures. Part of the reason for this was the hotel's location in the heart of Harlem, just down the block from the world-famous Apollo Theater. Then there was the other reason: If you were a black man or woman seeking a hotel room in New York City fifty years ago, it was easier to stay where you would not have to deal with discrimination.

The Theresa provided shelter for civil rights leaders Dr. Martin Luther King Jr., Ralph Bunche, Roy Wilkins, Bayard Rustin, Benjamin Mays, E. Franklin Frazier, and Mordecai Johnson. Politicians such as Adam Clayton Powell Jr. used the Theresa as a central meeting place. And perhaps the hotel's most notorious guest, unwelcome at every other hotel in New York City, was Fidel Castro.

In the late 1940s, a story in *Ebony* about the Hotel Theresa stated: "To its famous registration desk flock the most famous Negroes in America. . . . Joe Louis stays there. . . . So does Rochester and the Hollywood contingent . . . all the top bandleaders . . . Negro educators, colored writers and the Liberian and Haitian diplomatic representatives. Big men in the business world jostle top labor leaders in the flowered, mirrored lobby."

When Richard Nixon was campaigning in Harlem during the 1952 presidential campaign, he stopped at the Theresa. Dad, eleven, met Nixon and shook his hand. My father always told a funny story about this meeting: "From that moment on," Dad said, "I knew I would never vote Republican. I became a Democrat, with a capital 'D.' "

Although a handful of the Theresa's guests maintained permanent quarters there, most used the hotel on a short-term basis, including all the great performers who worked down the street at the Apollo Theater. My father met them all: Nat King Cole, Dinah Washington (who had a suite next door to the Browns' apartment), Jackie "Moms" Mabley, Ray Charles, Billie Holiday, Ruth Brown, Duke Ellington, the famed emcee of Birdland, Pee Wee Marquette, writer Ralph Ellison, and dozens of sports heroes.

Reflecting about the talented and influential folks who frequented the Theresa and dined and danced in its rooftop Skyline Ballroom, Dad told me, "If you could have your wedding at the Skyline, you were top-shelf." The bar in the lobby was a nightly hangout spot while the ballroom featured dancing, music, and comedy by the very best in American entertainment: Count Basie, Lena Horne, Billy Eckstine, and Milton Berle.

The Brown family lived in a modest-sized but elegant apartment on the top floor of the Theresa: two bedrooms, one bath, a living room, and kitchen. Since Nan did not like to cook and GD cooked only occasionally, the Browns had most of their meals in the hotel dining room. At mealtimes Dad would go around the hotel looking for his father, but GD was generally too busy to eat with his family, so meals were usually Nan and Dad alone. My father loved hotel living: He cajoled the cooks into providing him with endless treats and all the hotel employees made a fuss over him. Congressman Charles Rangel was then working as a desk clerk and often let Dad help out. If he got an urge for an ice-cream soda—or any other treat he wanted—he'd go into the coffee shop for it. Living in the Theresa, and being an only child, Dad was spoiled; he was a little kid in an adult world and many hotel guests paid special attention to him. Some of them took him to shows, plays, baseball games, and other sporting events that most boys his age had no opportunity to see. Or guests would provide complimentary tickets to GD for a variety of events and he would take my father along.

GD once went to see Joe Louis in a championship bout at Madison Square Garden. Since it was cool weather, he wore a big, heavy coat. He wrapped his very, very skinny son inside the coat and sneaked him in, since underage children were not allowed into fights. My father was thrilled and never forgot it.

Sometimes, friends of GD's and Nan's who were staying in the hotel would go up to their apartment to have drinks and socialize. Most of the entertaining, though, was generally done by GD, not Nan, downstairs in the hotel dining room, the bar, or the Skyline Ballroom. For years, GD hosted marathon poker games in the apartment—which were basically illegal gambling—and my father would hang around and serve drinks, collecting tips from the players. The players were either hotel guests, professionals from the Harlem community, or GD's buddies from the Guardsmen (a private club) and Omega Psi Phi (a black fraternity). The games began on Friday night, with the guys playing cards, smoking, consuming quantities of scotch and bourbon, and taking catnaps in between hands. When Monday morning arrived, somehow, they all went off to work.

Nan stayed far away from the poker games and it's clear that she disapproved. These games may have contributed to what lay ahead for my grandparents: a painful divorce. Another contributing factor may have been the different roles GD and Nan played at the Theresa: GD's job as manager of the Theresa kept him busy all the time. But my grandmother had little to do and wasn't that interested in the hotel. At one point Nan opened an exercise salon across the street, but that was short-lived.

The family had a television in the living room and if my father watched at all, it was sports. As an adult, Dad was an intense fan; he never just watched a game, whether live or televised. He became involved, yelling and hollering, whistling and cheering, berating the ump and challenging rulings. This behavior began early. When he was thirteen and a passionate Brooklyn Dodgers fan, after his team blew a World Series game, he grew so enraged that he threw a vase at the television set hard enough to break the glass.

From his bedroom window at the Theresa, my father could look west down 125th Street to the Apollo Theater and, far west, to the distant George Washington Bridge and New Jersey. His room, decorated with sports memorabilia and an enormous autograph collection, had bunk beds, the cause of catastrophe when friends slept over. Dad always slept in the bottom and gave his friends the top bunk; when they fell asleep, they would often fall out of bed, causing no end of havoc.

Cousin Bobby Jones recalled that Dad would not just get an autograph from the hotel guests. He requested they be personalized; he kept some in books and others on scraps of paper. He solicited autographs from all the celebrities at the Theresa, but his favorites were sports heroes such as Sugar Ray Robinson, who owned a beauty parlor and barbershop on the next block. Dad was intrepid, determined to have the finest autograph collection ever. Nothing stopped him. When the great Ray Charles was going through a heroin withdrawal, GD and cousin Bobby slipped him into the hotel through a back entrance and took him in the freight elevator up to his room. My father, thirteen, popped into the elevator and asked for an autograph from the singer, who was near collapse and literally foaming at the mouth. When Bobby said, "Ronnie, this is not the time," Dad withdrew.

For a while, my father had an autograph hustle going. He discovered that his classmates would pay him up to five dollars each for autographs of sports figures, especially Joe Louis, Roy Campanella, Jackie Robinson, and Sugar Ray Robinson. The hustle was short-lived.

"Little Brown, come here," said Joe Louis to my father. Little Brown was his name for Dad. "Didn't you ask me for my autograph a few times before?"

Dad admitted that he had.

"Well, what are you doing with them?"

"I've been selling them to some of my schoolmates," said Dad. And that was the end of that entrepreneurial endeavor because Joe Louis never gave him any more autographs.

A friend of GD's, Ed Boyd, worked for Pepsi-Cola and that led to my father's doing a bit of modeling when he was six. Dad was photographed reaching toward a carton of Pepsi held by his "mother" in a scene depicting a typical African-American family at home enjoying Pepsi. It was apparently the first time the company had marketed directly to the black population. The ad was so successful that it was used on billboards and displayed in many Harlem grocery stores and other shops. Nan and GD were excited over my father's role in the ad, and he received a small payment for modeling.

My father's childhood friends were always eager to visit him at the famous Theresa Hotel. Dad would lead them through the lobby and public areas, but eventually they'd end up on the roof to play Dad's favorite game: filling balloons with water and dropping them on pedestrians below. When my grandparents found out, they made my father understand that he could unintentionally hurt someone—a baby in a carriage, for example—and he stopped.

An only child, Dad often played with his best pal, his beloved dog, Flash, a huge Doberman. Flash was an unlikely pet for Dad, but he had convinced Nan to buy him when they were at the 1950 Westminster Kennel Club show at Madison Square Garden. A Doberman with a recent litter had won best of show and Dad, nine, fell in love with one of her puppies. He begged and begged, and, although Nan didn't think a hotel was a suitable place in which to raise a dog, she gave in. She forgot how big that puppy could grow to be.

As Flash grew bigger and bigger, Dad's love grew proportionately. He was crazy about his dog. Flash's care was Dad's responsibility but, as do most children, he had to be reminded frequently. Nan would warn, "If you don't feed that dog . . ." and Dad would finally feed his pet. Eventually, Flash grew into such a large, powerful animal that he couldn't be walked on the street because pedestrians were terrified of him. He couldn't even go in the elevator because of the look of horror on the faces of passengers when they saw him. My father ended up "walking" Flash on the hotel roof—unsanitary, but easier all around. Ferocious as he looked, Flash was actually mellow and was my father's constant companion for the next seven years.

The roof was Dad's second home; in addition to running with his dog, there was a small basketball hoop up there and my father would shoot hoops, either alone or with friends. He and his friends played stickball, too, but lost many balls to the street below.

A favorite pastime was fooling around with the hotel elevator, an old-fashioned hand-operated machine. The regular operator was always careful that passengers got off in line with the hallway floor, but when my father "drove" the elevator, passengers were in for a rough ride. This was an early sign of my father's lifetime incompetence behind a wheel: From the day he got his driver's license, he was the world's absolute worst driver.

To my father's academic- and success-oriented family, school was all important. After my grandparents' friends, educators Kenneth and Mamie Clark, tested Dad at age five and found he had a high IQ, they suggested he apply to New York City's premier public school, the Hunter Elementary School for Gifted Children. Hunter, located at Sixty-ninth Street and Park Avenue, tested my father, then accepted him and he attended the school from first through sixth grades, graduating in 1952. Nan and GD were jubilant, but not surprised at Dad's acceptance to this difficult school. From the day he was born, they expected nothing less than brilliance and great achievement from him. During his years at Hunter, he was studious and willingly did all his schoolwork. After sixth grade, while girls could stay on and go through high school at Hunter, boys had to transfer. Dad spent seventh through tenth grades at Walden, a private prep school in Manhattan. Both Hunter and Walden were predominantly white and had only a handful of black students when Dad attended.

Dad was adventurous, fearless, and loved to travel even as a child. He benefited from summers spent in the country, at Y camps in upstate New York, and from family summer vacations at Oak Bluffs on Martha's Vineyard. His family often took trips to visit friends or relatives. Dad was a bit of a daredevil, always looking for fun, never afraid of anything, whether a physical challenge or an emotional adventure. Once, my grandparents took him to visit friends who lived on Maryland's Chesapeake Bay and Dad, about ten, was walking along a wall on the edge of the water. He wasn't paying too much attention, and fell in. A friend of Nan's pulled him out, and Dad, instead of being frightened that he had almost drowned, emerged laughing. A Detroit couple, friends of my grandparents, invited Dad to visit them and their son, who was the same age as my father. Nan was nervous about her child traveling to Detroit by himself, but adventurous Dad had no fears and convinced his mother to allow him to take a plane there, on his own.

Dad showed his competitive and tenacious nature early, in games and sports. He and his friend Billy Harris played one-on-one basketball in Central Park on the weekends, and along with another boy, Billy Perry, they had their own mini-Olympics at New York University's old uptown campus on University Avenue. They'd run track-and-field events, including sprints, high jump, and long jump, competing against one another as intensely as if battling for the gold. All his life, Dad hated losing and loved winning. He gloated if he won, but only for a short time. If he lost, his disappointment was also of short duration.

The year 1956 was a turning point for the Brown family. GD lost his job after a bitter dispute with the Hotel Theresa's owners and the family moved to White Plains, a half hour north of New York City. At the time, White Plains had a small, sophisticated black community that included other Harlem expatriates. For example, Moms Mabley and Cab Calloway both had homes there. GD and Nan rented a yellow split-level house with three bedrooms and a small yard on a quiet street. My father, by now a serious jazz fan, decorated his bedroom with posters of the Modern Jazz Quartet.

At the Theresa, the family had enjoyed a comfortable lifestyle, but in White Plains circumstances were much reduced and they had to tighten their belts. GD tried a variety of ways to earn a living. He started a beauty supply business, selling curling irons and other equipment to beauty parlors; he sold

Walter Welborn, Dad's maternal great-grandfather, who posed as a Confederate soldier to escape the South

Nan, 1925

Nan and her mom, Ruth Osborne

Ruth Welborn Osborne and Jerome
Osborne, Dad's maternal grandparents

William Harmon Brown
Sr. (GD) with Dad

Nan and Dad, circa 1947

GD and Nan, circa 1950

Dad playing football on the roof of the Hotel Theresa, 1949

Nan and GD in lobby of Hotel Theresa, 1955

GD at his beauty supply booth, circa 1948

Dad flexing his muscles at
Hotel Theresa

Dad (*right*) at Tom Thumb Ball, 1949

Dad shaking hands with Richard M. Nixon outside the Hotel
Theresa, 1955

Nan (*left*) with coworkers at Steuben, circa 1962

insurance and also managed a couple of small Bronx hotels. None of it worked out.

It was a tough period for my father. After spending four years at Walden, on the upper East Side of Manhattan, Dad, fifteen, had to transfer to White Plains High School. He had a difficult time leaving his Walden friends and was miserable at White Plains. He still got involved in sports, running track and playing basketball; he also had many friends, both black and white, because he had an amiable personality and got along with most people.

Then Dad had to face the emotional trauma of losing Flash. After the family moved, one day, for no apparent reason, the dog snapped at GD. And that was the end of Dad's pet. GD immediately found him another home despite the fact that my father was devastated. It took him a while, until he left for college, to get over Flash. (History does repeat itself, because many years later, the same thing happened to me and Michael and our dog Thunder. Our family had just moved when, for no reason, Thunder snapped at Dad. Reacting just as his father had so many years earlier, my father decided Thunder needed a new home. And that was that.)

The only bright spot in White Plains for my father was that he had discovered girls. He repeatedly disobeyed his nightly curfew, imposed on him by GD. Night after night, when his parents fell asleep, he would slip out a large basement window that came out on ground level. He just had to see his girlfriend Toni: the daughter of photographer Gordon Parks. One night, cousin Bobby, who was staying with the Browns, caught Dad climbing out the window.

"Where are you going, Sonny Junior?" asked Bobby.

Dad, unfazed, said, "I'll be right back." And went on his way.

In 1957, after a year in White Plains, GD was rehired as manager under the Theresa's new ownership, a corporation, and the family moved back to Harlem. Their old apartment on the top floor had been remodeled and made larger, with four bedrooms and two bathrooms. Both Dad and GD were happy with the move but Nan was not. In White Plains, she felt she had escaped from the fast-lane lifestyle that was part of the Theresa, and she resented returning. But because GD's various businesses had not earned enough to support his family, he had no choice but to take back his old job. Living at the Theresa meant free room and board and that would help the family finances considerably.

A short time later, in January 1958, Nan and GD separated and Nan took a room at the Y. At the time, my father, sixteen, had transferred for his last year of high school to Rhodes, a private school at Fifth Avenue and Fifty-fourth Street in Manhattan. In their divorce agreement, GD was given custody of my father, since he worked in the family home. Nan was given liberal visitation rights. For Dad's last semester of high school, he lived with GD and two cousins, Nick and Bobby Jones, who came to live in the hotel.

At Rhodes, he was a B student, concentrating on math and science because he intended to study medicine. He was also a member of the debating club, the student government, and played varsity basketball. He was not a star, playing only occasionally and warming the bench more often than not. He was still in a minority—one of ten black students in a class of eighty-five—but, unlike the other black students, he got involved in activities after school. Recalled his classmate John Nailor, "Ronnie was always willing to put in the time and extra effort on things that interested him. He had this strong conviction that this was what he was supposed to do. For example, pitch ball. There was no such thing as telling him 'You can't do this.' He might think about it, but he was always going to pick up the challenge."

Dad seemed to lose interest in academics during his junior and senior years in high school, maybe because of the shifting from school to school or the tensions at home. Nan was afraid his negative attitude toward school might mean he would forgo college, which, to her and GD, would have been unacceptable. My grandparents introduced their reluctant scholar to Dr. Al Moron, president of Hampton Institute (now Hampton University), a historically black college in Virginia. Dr. Moron worked magic on Dad, telling him that graduating from college was the only way to succeed, and inspiring him with visits to the beautiful Hampton campus. Dad expressed a renewed interest in education and applied to college.

Senior year in high school, Dad spent a lot of time with his friend Billy Perry, alternating between looking for girls in Billy's home community of St. Albans, Queens, and seeking more sophisticated pursuits at the Hotel Theresa and its environs. Billy described that year as "heavy partying," and apparently Dad never passed up a party, whether in Queens or Harlem; sometimes they'd start on Friday night and end on Sunday morning. (If only I had known this during my own high school days!) Even though my father was a "lightweight" drinker—one or two drinks was his limit—he was a serious party-goer. The scene at the Theresa during Dad's last year in high school was, as Billy recalled, "party time. . . . You wonder how Ronnie got any studying done there."

Nan, living at the Y, would often call on Dad to come and see her. His friends recalled that at times he would disappear, and they found out later that often when they thought he was "missing," he was actually with his mother. He spent his time with Nan trying to ease her through increasingly serious periods of depression.

This is when Dad grew up: participating in the older social scene at the Theresa, dominated by Nick and Bobby, and taking on responsibility for his mother. Part of his new seriousness manifested itself in new behavior, such as a daily habit of reading *The New York Times* over coffee in a diner on 125th Street. There he was—a skinny, baby-faced high school senior with big ears, sixteen years old, reading the *Times,* handling his mother's problems, and socializing with adults. That's when Dad, in all likelihood, developed his ability to handle any situation with assurance, and his talent for being at ease in any environment.

But he was still a teenager, and with his friends he acted his age. John joked that, based on conversations he and Dad had in economics class, it was clear my father had no understanding about anything as complex as the U.S. Commerce Department. And Billy said that Dad's much-quoted question after his appointment to commerce secretary—"So what does the commerce secretary actually do?"—came as no surprise based on years of knowing Dad.

One day he saw a pretty girl at school and told John he wanted to date her; John warned him off, saying she was the girlfriend of a local gang leader. But that didn't deter my father, and after he asked her for a date her thug boyfriend and his gang showed up to "get" Dad. As my father and his friends exited the school building, the gang blocked their way. They could have gone back into the building, but Dad sized up the group and walked toward them, shutting the school door behind him. He was wearing a funny hat, which they grabbed off his head, and, the next thing, fists were flying and a fight was on.

Dad, who was as inept with his fists as he was behind the wheel, survived somehow and stood there, a little grin on his face, his funny hat in his hand. He was not at all perturbed. Something as adolescent as a fight over a girl could never get to him. Said John, "He had too much Westchester, too much Mom, and too much Theresa Hotel in him."

Summers during high school, Dad always had a job, often secured with GD's help. One year he was a messenger for the black radio station, WLIB, and another summer he was a messenger for the New York Social Services Department. Remembers Hal Jackson, the Harlem disc jockey, "This little devil was so neat. Even as young as he was then, he would always wear his little shirt and tie and jacket in the studio."

When my father was a month shy of fifteen, in July of 1956, he and my mother attended a party given by a club, the Centurions, although they didn't meet each other that day and would not meet for another two years. The Centurions were similar to Jack and Jill, only geared toward teenage boys; teenage girls, like my mother, belonged to the Laureliers. Club members socialized in New York City and, during summers, in Sag Harbor or Oak Bluffs, where some of their families had summer homes. A friend from his teenage years, Tommy Williams, recalled that Dad crashed that party but was allowed to stay because he "looked like he belonged." Described by Tommy as "sprightly and fun," Dad was a "string bean of a fellow." But keeping the ratio of boys to girls two to one was most important. Tommy said that Colin Powell was at the party, too.

∼

In the fall of 1958, when my father left for college, he left Harlem forever, except for a brief stay with GD in 1962. But he never forgot his roots. In 1992, Dad returned to visit while he was in New York for the Democratic convention. He took me, Michael, and Mom on a tour of the Theresa, now an office building; then he led us to his old playground, the roof.

"This is where your Daddy lived," he said, with a big smile. He talked about the water-filled balloons, about playing ball and running with Flash. He pointed out Harlem landmarks, and the view of the Apollo Theater from his bedroom window. He talked and talked as we stood on that rooftop that so evoked his childhood. Then we went for lunch at Sylvia's, the famous soul-food restaurant on Lenox Avenue between 126th and 127th streets, two blocks from the Theresa. Sylvia's wore a banner that day: WELCOME HOME DNC CHAIRMAN RON BROWN. Dad, as always, relished everything on his plate: fried chicken, collard greens, candied yams, and macaroni and cheese.

As we left the restaurant we were surrounded by Dad's aides, who were trying to steer Dad directly to the car. A man hanging out on the corner yelled out. "That's Ronnie Brown. He don't need no security in Harlem. Ain't nobody gonna bother him. That boy is home."

It had been thirty-seven years since Dad left home, seeking and finding success and influence in Washington's halls of power. But those years and those successes made no difference and he remained true to his beginnings. He remained a native son, a child of Harlem.

～

My father never talked about his parents' divorce. Since Nan's parents, Ruth and Jerome, had also divorced, his parents' split-up was a second generation of divorce. This background led to his own resolution that when he married it would be a bond of steel that would last forever. Dad's incredible closeness with Mom and with me and Michael was, I think, the result of his great need for stability.

Nothing in his childhood had remained the same; the schools, the neighborhoods, his parents—everything shifted, so Dad grew up seeking what he hadn't had: security and continuity. As a man, he created the life he wanted and needed. In our family, Dad was our tree, rooted to his wife and children as we were rooted to him. He was always there for us, always.

Until.

The only time Dad ever said anything mean to Mom was when he went on cleaning rampages, episodic attacks of why-is-this-house-such-a-mess? One Sunday morning, I am in the kitchen, drinking OJ and watching C-SPAN, smiling as I hear him stomping around the top floor of the house.

"Alma! I asked you this morning to throw away these goddamn newspapers and magazines from the floor! Why do you insist on keeping everything?"

Then I hear him in my room, which truly was a mess. Within seconds, he's downstairs in the kitchen, still yelling at Mom, who can't hear a word since she's all the way downstairs in the laundry room. But that doesn't deter Dad. As he storms into the kitchen, I get busy fussing at an imaginary stain on my shirt.

"Tra, your room is a mess! How can you stand it? You can't even walk in there without stepping on something!"

I ignore him; I know these tirades are short-lived. He stomps into the pantry, grabs a big green plastic garbage bag, and stomps back upstairs. I can hear him stuffing things into the trash bag. When Mom comes into the kitchen, she asks what Dad's ranting about and I say, "He's on a cleaning rampage. You'd better make sure he's not throwing away anything important."

At that moment, Dad yells to us, "Whatever is on the floor is going into the trash."

Mom rushes into action, races upstairs, and convinces my father that a Chanel purse is not trash.

Half an hour later, with the trash stowed neatly in the garage, Mom is standing in front of the sink. From behind, Dad slides his arms around her waist and kisses her neck. She giggles.

Just another Sunday.

THREE

Alma

BY the time Dad graduated from high school in June 1958, he had chosen Middlebury College in Middlebury, Vermont, over Brown, Bowdoin, Bates, and Williams, other schools to which he'd been interested. He was following his parents' suggestion that a New England college education was best. Middlebury was a small, rural, coed institution as far away as possible, both geographically and socially, from Harlem's Hotel Theresa.

Some of his high school friends questioned my father's choice, since Middlebury placed an emphasis on the study of languages, not one of Dad's strong areas. Plus, when Dad enrolled in September 1958, the number of black students in the entire student body, including him, was three. But Dad chose his college based on a romanticized all-American image of an old-fashioned, peaceful, rural New England town with a green, ivy-covered college campus in its midst. As unreachable as that idealized New England campus was during the fifties, and as unreachable as it is today for most Americans, its appeal is undeniable and Dad fell for it.

Middlebury was a typical New England college of the 1950s:

It had stricter rules for women students than for men; more than 99 percent of the students were white; and there were no black faculty members. Dad was the only black student in his class—and, unfortunately, there were no black women students. My father had no qualms about entering a world totally opposite to the one he'd grown up in. In Harlem, he had lived in an all-black world; almost all of the people he'd met at the Theresa were black. He experienced almost no racism in school, even though all the schools he attended were predominantly white. If he felt any discrimination, he never allowed it to stop him from fully participating in sports and other school activities. He had white friends and black friends and the facility for getting along with most people. In terms of summer jobs, GD had interceded and helped him get interviews; Dad always worked in his own community and so never experienced in-your-face discrimination. He seemed to have glided through his youth, sheltered and protected from the cruelties of racism.

He started classes at Middlebury one month after he turned seventeen, the youngest student in the freshman class. Middlebury was an expensive private college. Although my grandparents lived comfortably, there was not a sufficient college fund for my father, so he helped pay for tuition and room and board with his earnings from his summer job, student loans, an ROTC stipend, and money he made as a waiter on campus.

Freshman year, my father waited on tables in Gifford Hall; he ate his meals there, also, although he lived in another dormitory. The best part of being a waiter was that he got to eat early and was allowed to eat as much as he wanted; for my father, unlimited quantities of food was as near to heaven as one could get on earth. Another student/waiter, Tommy Meehan, recalled how much Dad ate and his enthusiasm about mealtimes. Tommy and Dad's friendship, based on a mutual enjoyment of sports, music, playing cards, and talking, became a lifelong relationship. Six months after Dad's death, Tommy paid tribute to him at Middlebury's Fourth Annual Nicholas R. Clifford Symposium, which, in 1996, honored my father. The symposium was a two-day conference on diversity in education, global economics, and other themes from my father's career.

My father handled adversity at Middlebury as he did throughout his life, with calm and optimism. But he was starting on his List of Firsts, a list that would grow with every one of his lifetime achievements. At Middlebury, he was the first black member of his fraternity, Sigma Phi Epsilon, a national organization with local chapters on campuses around the country. He also had a dating problem. Sophomore year, Dad had two dates with Bonnie, a white student. When he stopped calling her, he never explained why. A quarter century later, at their class's twenty-fifth reunion in 1987, my father finally told Bonnie why he never called back. He had been called on the carpet by Dean of Women Elizabeth B. Kelly, whom the students called "Ma," about those two dates. Ma Kelly was a relic from another era who made more difficult the lives of the young women students she was supposed to assist, discouraging them from pursuing advanced degrees, even interfering with some of their applications to medical school. She told my father that Bonnie's parents were "concerned" about their daughter's dating a black man, that he was not supposed to date white students, and that he should stop immediately. Because she made such an issue of it, Dad decided it wasn't worth bucking convention and never called Bonnie again.

Although the emphasis on campus was casual activities, with groups of girls and boys going to parties and football games, studying, and riding around in cars together, Dad didn't go through college without dating. During his junior year he dated a Middlebury student, Anne; he was still seeing her the summer between junior and senior years, the summer he met my mother.

But during my father's freshman and sophomore years, being rushed by a fraternity was the most important thing. In late January, Dad and Tommy Meehan, along with twenty others, became pledges of Sigma Phi Epsilon, or Sig Ep. It was the sports fraternity—not a total jock house, but most of its members played a variety of varsity sports such as track, hockey, football, and skiing. (A sign of the times was that skiing was the only varsity sport available to women.)

Sophomore year was difficult because Sig Ep had a "white-Christian clause" and although several Jewish members were previously initiated without problem, when Dad pledged, representatives from the national charter were on campus. They noticed Dad and issued a warning: The chapter was not allowed to initiate a black person. But most of the Middlebury chapter wanted my father and had to choose between him and their national charter. Some older members were concerned. Who would pay for the fraternity house? How would the fraternity pay its debts without the support of the national?

Sig Ep's pledges and brothers were in favor of flouting the national's rules. Dad had successfully made it through the pledge process, so how could they abandon him? The national brothers were traditional Joe College types, whereas Middlebury's chapter was more casual. As Tommy Meehan explained, "For us, the decision was easy because if you knew Ronnie, you wanted to be with him."

Ultimately, the chapter stood by my father with a unanimous vote and he was initiated into the fraternity in the fall of his sophomore year along with the others in his pledge class. The college was also supportive, issuing a statement that backed the chapter. At the same time, the national took away the chapter's charter and it became an independent fraternity. In appreciation of my father's ability to stay strong despite the racism of the national's white-Christian clause, and in recognition of his later accomplishments, the fraternity awarded its 1991 Citation to my father. Integrating the fraternity went on Dad's List of Firsts, and I am certain he loved every minute of it.

That same year, Dad reached an academic impasse when chemistry formulas and French verbs did him in. He had begun college with a joint major in biology and chemistry, encouraged by his parents to pursue a career in medicine. But organic chemistry broke him and he quickly changed his focus from the natural sciences to the social sciences. Before this, Dad had been a decent student, but despite all his efforts, he could not pass organic chemistry. At the same time, he also failed French. According to the college's academic policy, if a student failed two courses in any one semester, the college and the student had to part ways. Dad was officially dropped on February 8, 1960, a day or two after the second semester began. Since Middlebury allowed students who had been dropped to present arguments for readmittance before an administrative committee, my father immediately requested a hearing. The hearing was held three days later, on February 11, with Dad and twenty other students explaining why they should be readmitted. On the committee were Ma Kelly; Samuel S. Stratton, president of the college; the ROTC instructor, a colonel; and several professors and administrators. Dad, using all his considerable persuasive powers, convinced the committee that he did indeed have the right stuff for Middlebury. He was readmitted on the spot, as were ten other students. Needless to say, Dad vowed never again to fail a college course.

This vow didn't help him the next semester, though, when he tackled Spanish, having given up on French. He failed. It was not until he took Spanish at Hunter College during the summer of 1961 that he managed to pass a language course. He earned mainly B's during the second semester of junior year and both semesters of senior year. He even passed intermediate Spanish. Dad graduated in June 1962, with a major in political science. His best grades throughout college had been earned in politics courses, especially those with an international or comparative component.

Throughout college, Dad worked as a busboy rather than a waiter after that first year because Middlebury had built a new cafeteria-style facility. He also spent a lot of time playing sports and was a "gym rat," according to Tommy Meehan. He ran the quarter mile and the mile relay in track during his freshman, sophomore, and senior years. He played intramural football and basketball all four years.

Politics was in the air during Dad's junior year: JFK and Nixon were running for president. Dad passed out flyers for Middlebury Students for Kennedy, whose cochair was Tommy Meehan's future wife, Maurin. But when Maurin drove to Burlington to see Kennedy at a campaign stop, Dad and Tommy were too busy playing Frisbee to go. But my father preferred the Democratic candidate, having been influenced by GD and impacted by both the legacy of FDR and the Truman era in which he grew up. At his father's knee, he learned about social justice and injustice, about the need for people to get their fair share, about the inequality that existed between those that had and those that didn't. Partly because of his Harlem upbringing and partly because of GD's liberal viewpoint, Dad evolved into a progressive Democrat.

At Middlebury, most of Dad's energy went into having a good time and, of course, learning. Junior and senior years, he lived in the Sig Ep house. Senior year, he shared a third-floor bedroom with four beds and a sloping ceiling with Tommy Meehan, John Chegwidden, and John Hornbostel, until John Hornbostel got married in November and moved out. Music was a big topic in that room because John Chegwidden knew the lyrics, composer, singer, and backup singers of every rock-and-roll hit of the day. Dad frequently challenged John on some of the finer points, and the room would rock and roll with their heated discussions on such earthshaking questions as who wrote "Book of Love"? and who was first to sing "Tears on my Pillow"? They also played many games of cards—cribbage, not poker, because Dad didn't gamble. He loved to dance and introduced Chubby Checker and The Twist to the Vermont campus. My father also is remembered by his college friends as immaculately turned out even then; Tommy Meehan recalled that my father would send new shirts out for laundering and pressing before he'd wear them; a trait he picked up from GD.

In addition to academics, sports, fraternity, and parties, Dad participated in ROTC. It was mandatory for all the boys at Middlebury for the first two years, but Dad enrolled for the last two years as well because he planned to join the service when he graduated.

～

Some of Dad's misadventures sprang from his certainty that he was mechanically inclined and street-smart. Neither was true. He had no mechanical aptitude at all and invariably got into trouble when he did anything that required street-smarts. One of his friends from New York, Johnny Nailor, recalled one summer when Dad was living with GD at 10 West Lenox Terrace in Harlem after GD and Nan were separated. Dad had an old Ford that he drove on occasion, but whenever possible he would get his friend Gaylord to drive for him, since he recognized what a bad driver he was. Gaylord, an eccentric, single-minded young man, died young during a second tour in Vietnam, for which he had volunteered; this occurred during the era when a majority of men went to extreme lengths to avoid even a first tour.

Johnny Nailor, who today is an orthopedic surgeon, said my father always blamed him for a knee injury Dad suffered when he was about eighteen. Dad, Johnny, and Gaylord were having a few beers and relaxing one evening at Johnny's parents' house in St. Albans, Queens, when Johnny had to leave but suggested Gaylord and Dad stay on. Later, my father and Gaylord went out, but when they returned, since Johnny had forgotten to leave them the key, they had to break into the house. Since my Dad was not Mr. Dexterity at such endeavors, he ended up falling down a hole and hurting his knee, an injury that bothered him for the rest of his life.

Gaylord and Dad bickered, according to Johnny, squabbling over trivia: Are we going to buy two bottles of beer? Or three? They never disagreed over who would drive, though. Once, on one of their road trips, my father had forgotten to check the car to make sure it was ready for the road. Something in the engine blew and he and his friends, with Gaylord driving, returned home from Labor Day Weekend on Martha's Vineyard, very slowly. They couldn't do more than twenty-five miles an hour. Dad, being Dad, didn't get rattled but burrowed under the coats in the backseat and went to sleep. His friends thought he was dead; every few hours, they'd check to make sure he was still breathing. Dad slept peacefully while Gaylord drove home for twelve slow hours.

Another Labor Day Weekend was more memorable, for on Friday night of that weekend in 1959, my mother and father met at a party at Butch Parks's house in Sag Harbor. My mother, Alma Arrington, had many friends in Sag Harbor with summer houses, both boys and girls. The night my parents met, she was nineteen and about to begin her junior year at Fisk University in Nashville, Tennessee; Dad, eighteen, was entering his sophomore year.

That night, Dad, along with Gaylord and Johnny, had

crashed the party. Mom noticed him and said to her friend Tommy Williams, "Who's that over there by the record player?"

"That's Ronnie Brown. You don't know Ronnie Brown? His father runs the Hotel Theresa." And he went and got Dad and brought him over to Mom.

When my father told the story, he would say, "So Tommy came over to me and said, 'Alma wants to meet you.' "

Of course, Mom claims she was just curious and never said she wanted to meet Dad. Although she did think he was cute— skinny but cute. At the time, Dad was about six feet tall but weighed only 140 pounds. After they were introduced, Dad asked her to dance, a slow dance to a Sam Cooke song. While they danced, they talked about their colleges. Later, they danced The Bop, a fast dance. They talked and danced all evening. When Mom heard Dad went to Middlebury, she said, "Where is that?" She was shocked that he went to school in Vermont, a place that seemed foreign to her.

"That's one of those white schools up there, isn't it? What's it like?" Mom asked.

Dad's response was in character: "It's cold. It's so cold the mucus in your nose freezes." When he told her there were more cows than people in Vermont, she was sold; she found him funny and interesting. He liked her also and they spent most of the weekend together, making sure they went to the same parties at night. During the day, Saturday, they went to the beach, where Dad offered to teach Mom how to swim. They played in the water, kissing a bit, but nothing too heavy. Dad's friend, Stanford Moore, had a convertible, so they all piled in and drove around, picking up friends, acting silly, ending up at the beach. When the weekend was over, my parents exchanged phone numbers but neither one of them thought anything serious, such as, "This is it." They both had other relationships; Dad was seeing Anne, from Middlebury, and Mom had a boyfriend, Ivan, a much older guy who was a medical student at Meharry Medical College. Meharry was across the street from Fisk. When she compared the two, Dad and her boyfriend, Mom thought Dad was young in age, but mature in attitude. She found his warmth and charm endearing. Many of the guys Mom was used to dating were on the GI Bill, had served in Korea, and were in their middle to late twenties. They were also serious party animals, and drank hard liquor. Dad drank a little beer, was clean-cut, maybe even square. But she liked him. As for Dad, he thought Mom was fine, one of the finest women he'd ever seen. He particularly loved her legs and her smile, and complimented her all the time about her "great big pretty legs," or her pretty face.

A major attraction between my parents was that they both cracked each other up; each found the other's stories about school and friends hilarious. And even though they went to different types of colleges, they both came from the same middle-class environment. Both Mom and Dad, when they were kids, were in Jack and Jill, he in the Manhattan chapter and she in the Brooklyn chapter. All the men in their families belonged to social clubs for adults, such as the Guardsmen, the Gaylords, the Alphas, or the Boulé, while the women were in either the Links, the Girlfriends, or the Smart Set.

These national black fraternities and social organizations played a large role in the lives of families such as ours. My maternal grandmother, whom I call Mere, belonged to a social club, the Yadrutas, which is Saturday spelled backwards. She was very well educated, earning both undergraduate and graduate degrees from NYU. My mother's father, Martin Luther Arrington, whom I called Bop, belonged to the Alpha Phi Alpha fraternity, which he joined when he attended West Virginia State. GD was an Omega Psi Phi at Howard University and also belonged to the Guardsmen, while Nan belonged to the sorority, Delta Sigma Theta, and was a founding member of the Smart Set. It's likely, since they were part of a relatively small group, that my grandparents on both sides either were acquainted with or had heard of each other. Because of this common background, when Mom and Dad met, they felt secure with one another, as if they had known each other all their lives.

After that weekend, they both went back to college, having promised to write to each other. It was not until Thanksgiving, though, that my mother received the first letter from my father. She remained at school in Nashville for that holiday and didn't return to New York City until Christmas. She and Dad spoke on the phone during that Christmas break but the conversations were far from romantic; they exchanged news about classes, friends, and plans for the next semester. Mom had brought her boyfriend, Ivan, to New York with her for Christmas and she mentioned that to Dad when they spoke on the phone. They ran into each other at a Jack and Jill party, where Ivan, older and out of place, had a miserable time and pouted the entire evening. When Mom and her boyfriend were ready to leave, as Dad used to tell it, she pointed a finger at him and said, in front of Ivan and the others, "Call me tomorrow." Which, of course, he did. But for the remainder of that vacation, they only conversed on the phone and never saw each other.

From January until the end of the semester, my parents wrote back and forth, their letters growing more romantic, less chatty: "I really miss you; I hope we can spend more time together. I can't wait to see you." And they spoke on the phone often. Back then, dorm or fraternity-house residents shared a single hall phone. When Dad and Mom spoke on the phone, he would go into a little closet nearby, close the wooden door, prop his feet up on the wall, and monopolize the phone for hours.

During the summer of 1960, after months of letters and phone calls, they finally began to date. My father had a summer job as a clerk in the courthouse on Centre Street in lower Manhattan, while Mom was working as a playground teacher in a city recreation program in the Bronx. They met after work, went to dinner or a movie, then Dad would escort Mom home on the subway to the Crown Heights section of Brooklyn.

Their first date was memorable. They went to the Village Vanguard to hear the late, great jazz pianist Thelonious Monk, double-dating with Dad's friend Freddy Ressler and his girlfriend. At the Vanguard, Dad was hip and he was cool. He was so into jazz that he kept time by tapping on the tabletop. Mom was bored, though, and not impressed; she was a rhythm-and-blues and rock-and-roll fan.

After the performance, they went to Freddy's apartment on Central Park West. There, Mom discovered, to her horror, that she had gotten her period. She felt comfortable with my father even though it was their first date, so she told him about her predicament. He offered to go buy her sanitary napkins. "Are you sure you can handle this?" Mom asked him.

Dad, casual, competent, and unruffled—as he would be for the rest of their years together—said, "Sure, I go for my mom all the time." Later, they drove home, dropping Freddy's date off first. Then, with Freddy driving and Mom and Dad next to him on the front seat, they headed toward my mother's house. My father fell asleep instantly and Mom chatted with Freddy from Manhattan all the way to Brooklyn. Mom assumed, since Dad was asleep, that he wasn't very interested in her. When they arrived at her house, Mom had to poke Dad to awaken him so she could get out; he walked her to the door and asked, "What time do you want to get together tomorrow night?" He assumed that it was okay to fall asleep, assumed she had liked him, assumed she wanted to see him again. And he was right.

Mom quickly discovered that Dad's habit of falling asleep at odd times and in odd places such as in cars, in people's houses, and in theaters did not mean much. It would be a lifelong habit, which old friends understood but that could be embarrassing when he fell asleep in front of someone he barely knew.

My father's total incompetence around cars—or any piece of machinery—was evident on another date. Dad was driving GD's big, fat, gray 1955 Chrysler New Yorker and, after dropping off Mom, headed toward Harlem. After he crossed the Manhattan Bridge and nosed the car up the West Side Highway, he fell asleep. A bump awakened him and he discovered he had hit a car at the very moment its driver was being handed a ticket by one of New York's finest. The policeman went crazy and came at Dad with nightstick raised. Dad, backing away, said, "My gas pedal got stuck, officer. You know I wouldn't run into you if I could have avoided it." Since no one had been hurt, the officer let him go. But when he told Mom the story, it made her think about the wisdom of his driving home at night when he was tired. Or about his driving at all.

If Dad didn't have GD's car, he traveled by subway, which he called "the iron horse." Many times that summer, he'd travel from his home at 10 West 135th Street to his job in lower Manhattan, then up to the Bronx to meet Mom after work, then to

Brooklyn to take her home, then back to West 135th Street. They saw each other almost every night; Dad practically lived at Mom's house but was never allowed to sleep over. As Mom remembered, "I asked my mother if he could sleep over and she said, 'No. He came on the subway. So he can go home on the subway.' "

It was a different time, and young couples like Mom and Dad often got married young. Many of my parents' friends married as soon as they graduated from college.

That summer, as was their tradition, Mom's parents rented cabins in Chenango Falls, New York, along with some other relatives. My father drove up to spend a long weekend with my mother and her family, sleeping in a cabin next to hers, with her aunt, uncle, and cousin. This time, he drove his own Simca, a small, foreign car that gave him considerable trouble. GD had bought it for my father "very used" when he began his junior year in college. That weekend, Dad drove the Simca four hours from New York City to Chenango Falls without stopping once because if the car was turned off, it wouldn't restart. During the weekend, he couldn't actually drive the car because once it was started, he had to keep going. So everywhere my parents went, they traveled with the family and never had any time alone. They had no complaints, though; they were young and enjoying life and each other.

By this time, both had ended their other relationships, Mom's with Ivan and Dad's with Anne, and Mom had already met GD and Nan. Dad invited Mom to spend a day at the beach with his parents so they could all get to know one another. On a sunny day, the Brown family drove out to Brooklyn to pick up Mom. By this time, GD and Nan were divorced, but Nan turned to Mom after she got into the car and said, "Did you know that today is our anniversary?" Mom thought it was strange but didn't say a word, and all four of them had a great day. In my mother's family, divorce was almost unheard of and here Dad's parents were not only divorced but spending the day together celebrating their anniversary. It was a wonderful day, though, and we have the pictures they took hanging in Morgan and Ryan's room at my parents' house.

After the beach, GD and Nan came in to meet Mere and Bop.

All four parents got along well; Bop made drinks and they chatted. Because of his parents' divorce, Mom always felt that Dad gravitated to her family, which seemed more stable. "He was at our house all the time," said Mom. "He loved to eat and my mother cooked every day; my grandmother cooked every day. There was always a big Sunday dinner. When he would come home after work, my mother would say, 'Get your chair, Ronnie. Come on, sit and share what we have.' He was very fond of my parents."

Although Mom and Dad were never alone together for any extended time that summer, they grew closer and closer and, sometime in August, expressed their love for each other. In September 1960, they returned to college and another year of letters and phone calls began. They saw each other during Christmas vacation and the relationship became more intense. When Mom returned to school, after storing her things with Ivan, her ex-boyfriend, during the break, she discovered that he had read her letters from Dad. "Who's Ronnie Brown that misses you so much? Who's Ronnie Brown that can't wait until you come home this summer?" Ivan asked her. My mother was furious.

In February of 1961, Dad invited Mom to Winter Carnival, a college weekend of hockey games and parties. Even though she found Vermont strange, and a college campus filled with nothing but white people most unusual, she and Dad had a wonderful weekend.

The following summer, Dad and Mom got even closer. She recalls that Nan was then working at Steuben Glass, and when they would pick her up from work, they would have to stay in the car. "She didn't want us to come in because she didn't want anybody to see that her son was black." The first time she accompanied him to pick up his mother, they waited for a while, then Mom suggested Dad go in and look for Nan. Remembered my mother, "He said, 'No, I can't go in because my mom is passing. She'll come out when she's finished.' " At the time, he was being matter-of-fact and accepted his mother's actions. My mother also didn't say anything, but it bothered her. Many years later, after they had been married for a while, and the civil rights movement had changed the landscape of the country, my mother finally expressed her feelings. Nan, complaining to Mom and Dad that she had not received a promotion, mentioned race. Mom blurted out, "Well, Gloria, if they knew you were black, you probably would have been promoted." She was still afraid to be herself, still avoiding black customers, thinking one of them might recognize her.

Mom graduated in June 1961 but remained in Nashville for six weeks for the Fisk University Race Relations Institute, a respected and well-known seminar on race issues. She had always wanted to take part and felt this was her last chance. After that, she returned to New York, where she and Dad attended several of their friends' weddings. Once again, Dad had a summer job clerking in the courthouse before going back to complete his senior year, while my mother was about to begin her first post-college job as a teacher at the Marcy Day Care Center in Brooklyn.

My parents' conversation now began to focus on a future together. Dad would inject the phrase "when we're married" into every conversation and they even planned a name for their first son: Michael. Eventually, they made plans to marry the following summer, in August of 1962, after my father had graduated and completed his requisite six-week ROTC training. The following Christmas Day, my mother and father were sitting in the living room of the Arringtons' house. Mere was in the bedroom, and Bop was in the basement. Dad said, "I have something for you." Then he pulled out a small, square velvet box tied in a red Christmas ribbon. Mom, thrilled and surprised, said, "You have my ring, the one I wanted!" Meaning the orange blossom–design diamond solitaire that she'd fallen in love with after seeing it in a bridal magazine.

Dad opened the box and put the small but beautiful ring on Mom's graceful hand, with its long, manicured nails. Dad thought it might be too big but Mom quickly reassured him that it was perfect. It really was too big, but she didn't want him to take it back, even to get it sized. Then Mom screamed and Mere came in and saw the ring and admired it. Dad got all formal and said, "Mrs. Arrington, I've asked Alma to marry me." So she got all formal, too: "Well, you need to go talk to her father." Dad trotted downstairs and had this conversation with his future father-in-law:

"Mr. Arrington, I'd like to marry Alma."

"You have a job?"

"Well, not exactly. But I'm going in the army so I'll have a job for two years. And then I plan to go to law school."

"It's all right with me, if it's all right with Alma."

Mom, listening at the top of the steps, yelled down, "It's all right with Alma!" The family had drinks and toasted the engagement and then my grandmother said the magic words: "When do you all want to get married?" My parents told their plan for an August wedding and everyone agreed that was a fine idea. My grandparents loved my father, and seven months would give Mere time to plan the wedding.

Nan may not have been as pleased. My mother is a beautiful brown-skinned woman, and years later she told me she thought Nan might have preferred it if Dad's wife had been white. Nan did express satisfaction that my mother and her family were well educated and came from the same familiar middle-class circles as did Nan and GD.

During those last few months before their wedding, Dad finished up his courses at Middlebury and Mom lived at home, teaching nursery school and planning her wedding. Dad was home often on vacations and for weekends. All was going well until a weekend in May when my father invited my mother to Middlebury for Spring Week. Mom drove up in her own car and, when she arrived on Friday night, checked into the guest house on campus where she would be staying. She had begun to get ready to meet my father when, suddenly, she passed out. When Dad arrived, she was lying on the floor suffering the worst pain she had ever experienced. He took her to the infirmary first, where the nurse took a quick look and sent them on to Middlebury General Hospital. There, the doctors told Mom she had a ruptured appendix and needed surgery immediately; Mom was hysterical, sobbing in pain and fear. Dad called Mere, who immediately left for Middlebury. During the operation, the doctors discovered the real cause of her agony was an ovarian cyst that had ruptured. When Mere arrived, the doctor told her that he had managed to save my mother's ovaries but she might never have children. My mother was paralyzed with grief; it was three months before her wedding and, suddenly, she was hit with the news that she and Dad might never have children. She was devastated. My father handled the news as he always handled any crisis. He told Mom not to worry, that they didn't have to have children, that they could adopt. "Don't worry about it. Don't worry. You just get well." She sobbed and he soothed, but he really meant it; he could adapt to just about anything.

After ten days, Mom was well enough to travel and, when she returned home, visited the family gynecologist, who prescribed hormone treatment for six months. Mom was diagnosed with endometriosis and, because of the scarring from the operation at Middlebury, she indeed might not have children, the family doctor said. Dad continued to be optimistic and continued to calm her, telling her over and over that it would work out and they would have children; if not, they would adopt. Nothing seemed to dim his spirits.

A month later, Dad graduated from Middlebury College with Nan, GD, Dad's cousin Nick Jones, and my mother in attendance. When my parents drove to Vermont for the ceremony, Dad was nervous; he was still uncertain as to whether or not he would receive a diploma. He had not yet found out his final grade in Spanish, and since languages had been his albatross at Middlebury, he was worried. But he passed Spanish with a C, graduated, and celebrated with everyone at the Dogteam Restaurant in the center of town. The restaurant was known for its warm cinnamon buns, which Dad loved almost as much as he loved Mom.

After graduation, Dad went to Fort Devens, in Massachusetts, for six weeks of ROTC basic training and Mom put the final touches on their wedding plans. A wedding announcement with my mother's photograph ran in the *Amsterdam News,* New York's black newspaper, but Nan asked her not to send her picture in with the notice going to *The New York Times*. She was still passing and didn't want her white friends to know that her son was marrying a black woman. Mom and Dad went along with Nan, but my mother was not pleased. The *Times* had earlier run an engagement announcement, also with no photo. Dad didn't get angry at his mother. Her behavior was always something he accepted. Early in life my father showed his tolerance: When something was not to his liking but he had no control over it, he simply accepted it. That's who he was when he and Mom got married and that's who he was for the twenty-eight years I knew him.

On August 11, 1962, my parents were married at 4 P.M. at St. Phillip's Episcopal Church on Decatur Street in Brooklyn. The bridal party consisted of seven bridesmaids, clad in short-sleeved mint green dresses and mint green pillbox hats, a maid of honor in yellow muslin and a yellow pillbox; a ring bearer, a flower girl, and seven ushers. Mom wore a traditional white wedding gown, short-sleeved and off the shoulder with a white Jackie Kennedy pillbox and veil. Dad and his ushers wore formal morning suits with striped pants. Tommy Meehan says that Dad's godfather Buddy Wilkinson "specifically recalled Ronnie's wedding and his own young son who was with him at the wedding, asking why Ronnie had this wide smile on his face all the time. His godfather explained to his son that he would understand when he was in his twenties, if he was lucky enough to be marrying a woman as beautiful, as bright, and as personable as Alma."

My parents' wedding went by the book: the bridal magazines that were so popular with young women then. Mom followed their schedule: what to do during month four, month three, month two, down to W-Day for wedding day. And Dad wore his morning suit because that's what my mother told him to wear.

They had parties and wedding showers and a rehearsal dinner. After the church ceremony, there was an elegant reception at the Towers Hotel on Joralemon Street in Brooklyn Heights, with guests enjoying tea, sandwiches, cookies, and punch. Neither one of my parents ate anything, being too excited and table-hopping, kissing friends and relatives, and dancing. They spent their wedding night at the International Hotel at JFK airport because the following morning they had a 6 A.M. flight to San Juan, Puerto Rico, for their honeymoon. Mom recalls donning her wedding-night negligee: white, lacy, floor-length, with a matching robe. When she walked into the bedroom, Dad asked, "Are you hungry?" Of course, he was starving. They ordered from room service and Dad wolfed down a couple of cheeseburgers before he and Mom shared their wedding night champagne. Then they lifted their glasses and toasted each other and a long, happy life together.

I'm amazed by what my parents had already accomplished when they were my age. I realize that it was a different era, but I can't imagine being married, set in my career, and finished with having children by the age of thirty. I could never have married in my early twenties, as did Mom and Dad, not only because there was no one I wanted to marry but because I was still too self-absorbed and irresponsible to deal with another person's needs. At that age, the word "compromise" was not yet in my vocabulary.

Dad struggled hard: working during the day, attending law school at night, paying off student loans, raising children. Michael and I wouldn't know struggle if it knocked us in the head. Sure, we know disappointment and sadness, but not struggle. We never had to work growing up; we worked summers because we wanted to, because it was interesting. We didn't need an after-school job to help pay for a new bike, or a trendy coat. We didn't work our way through college waiting tables to help pay tuition.

Much to my parents' credit, though, we were taught the value of work. I worked every summer from the age of thirteen on. In high school and college, Michael and I didn't sit around letting life pass us by. We followed their example. We played team sports, we clerked on Capitol Hill, and we volunteered at nursing homes and for civil rights organizations. We traveled and discovered new people and places. Sometimes, I would tease Dad and tell him I needed to travel more in order to "find myself."

"Oh please, Boli, you'd be bored in about two seconds," Dad would respond. He was right. It's impossible for me to do nothing, to wait for life to happen. I have to grab it and live it.

But I have my struggles, although they are far different from the ones my mother and father had at my age. Accepting my spirituality without overanalyzing it is a struggle. Learning to be comfortable in my own skin is a struggle. Discovering that I can maintain a healthy skepticism without becoming a cynic is a struggle.

Trying to get others to realize that, like Dad, I am always right is a struggle. Accepting that some of the things I enjoy most are bad for me is a struggle. Learning that I can actually be friends with non-Democrats is a struggle.

Accepting that it's okay for me to live a happy life without my father is a struggle. And realizing that I'll never hold his hand again, until I get to heaven, is the most difficult struggle of all.

~ *F O U R* ~

Starting Out

THE morning after my parents' wedding, they flew to San Juan, Puerto Rico, for a two-week honeymoon, courtesy of GD and Nan. Their first week, at the Dorado Beach Hotel, was beautiful and romantic, and they especially enjoyed their ocean-front cabana. The second week, they were scheduled to stay at the El San Juan Hotel, but after my mother found it unattractive and not clean enough, Dad called a friend of his mother's, who lived in St. Thomas in the Virgin Islands, just east of Puerto Rico, who invited them to spend their second honeymoon week at her house. (Their hostess was the sister of Dr. Al Moron, who had helped my father renew his academic orientation during his senior year in high school.) My parents hopped a commuter plane to St. Thomas and spent another romantic week, dancing and dining each night at a waterfront bar, Sebastian's.

When they returned from the Caribbean, Mom and Dad spent a night at Mere and Bop's house in Brooklyn. Then they moved into GD's apartment in Lenox Terrace in Harlem, at 10 West 135th Street, where they would live for two months—they thought—until Dad received his army assignment. Now that he had graduated from college, my father, a second lieutenant, had to satisfy his ROTC commitment and serve two years in the army. He expected to join an artillery unit at Fort Sill, Oklahoma, but when the army called my father in to retest his eyes, his sight was determined to be not up to artillery-caliber. Since the next available unit with a junior grade officer opening was in Transportation, he had to wait six months for that class to begin, in March 1963.

As a result of this snafu, Mom and Dad lived at GD's for six months, sharing the three-bedroom apartment with, in addition to GD, three cousins, Nick, Bobby and Billy Jones. Nick, best man at my parents' wedding, is my godfather. Mom and Dad took GD's bedroom, GD took a smaller room, and the cousins shared the third bedroom. GD didn't mind the smaller room as he spent a lot of time at the apartment of his girlfriend, Peggy Jones. Peggy was a doctoral student with a young daughter, Leslie, and she was twenty years GD's junior. Seeking a sense of independence, my parents filled their room with rented furniture they had selected and spent much of their time, when they were home, in that room.

As soon as Dad found out he had six months to wait for his army tour, he applied to and was accepted by St. John's Law School, a quick process in those days because there were no standardized test requirements. He had an interview at the New York City Department of Social Services (DSS) after GD, who knew everyone in city government, arranged it for him. He took the job offered, as a caseworker, eager to begin earning a salary. During the day, he handled his caseload of families, making home visits and writing reports to determine the amount of welfare benefits the families would receive. From August 1962 through February 1963, he attended law school four nights a week, getting home after 10 P.M. Monday through Thursday; days, he worked for DSS.

Mom recalls being thrilled to be living in Harlem—Lenox Terrace was on the corner of Seventh Avenue and 135th Street—and in an apartment house. Except for college, she had lived all her life in a two-family house in Crown Heights. She loved everything, from the elevator to the stimulating neighborhood. She never knew who would be in the elevator with her: a world-famous entertainer, a Harlem big shot, or a no-torious gambler.

Mom was working at the time as a teacher in the Lenox Ter-race nursery school. When Dad was at law school, during week-day evenings, she would spend time with a former roommate of hers from Fisk, Faith Berry, who lived with her husband, Buddy Gist, at 10 West. This young woman would stop at her own apartment to change from shoes to slippers, then go down-stairs to visit my mother, still dressed in work clothes but wear-ing those slippers. For some reason, this impressed my young mother as "cool." She also liked the camaraderie she glimpsed when the residents of the building would take the elevator, drinks in hand, to visit friends on other floors.

During this six-month period, my father took charge of do-mestic duties. My mom, having grown up with a mother and grandmother who enjoyed cooking and cleaning, never both-ered to learn how to do housework. Dad was familiar with the domestic arts, having lived with GD during school holidays throughout his Middlebury years. Since there were no women in that apartment, if they wanted to eat—and they all loved to eat—they had to cook. Dad taught my mother how to shop for food, clean, wash dishes, and do laundry. At the supermarket, he would give her a lesson in picking out meat and produce, but she displayed no interest at all, so he ended up shopping weekly for meat at a wholesale market in the Bronx. Mom did have some culinary skills: She was a whiz at opening cans and defrosting frozen foods, and could make a mean salad.

The first time my parents entertained, Dad said, "I'll vacuum. Do you want to pick up in the living room?" My mother was shocked; her own father had never done more than sit down at the table and wait for his meal. But my father could even sew buttons on his jacket! After they straightened the apartment that evening for their soon-to-arrive company, my mother mixed onion soup mix with sour cream and opened bags of chips while Dad got the drinks and mixers organized.

During the week, my father's schedule was backbreaking, a preview of the rest of his life because he would always work extra-long hours and make extraordinary efforts throughout his career. In the morning, he commuted from Harlem to the

Department of Social Services office in lower Manhattan. Then, during the day, he traveled back uptown for on-site visits to his Bronx cases before returning, in late afternoon, to the office. After work, he'd take the subway across the Manhattan Bridge to St. John's, then located in downtown Brooklyn.

After school, he'd take the A train to 10 West, where Mom would have ready "a little dinner," her term for the meals she was learning to cook, which he loved to eat: liver with bacon and onions, lamb chops, pork chops accompanied by frozen string beans, broccoli, plus rice or baked potatoes. When she was feeling brave, she tried out exotic recipes from her Chinese cookbook. "Oh, this is new, honey. This is tasty," said an appreciative, supportive husband. As long as the portions were large enough, he never turned down a meal that my mother had cooked.

After dinner, Mom watched television in the living room, staying out of Dad's way while he studied in the bedroom. When he finally turned off his reading light at two or two-thirty in the morning, they would go to bed. Dad's lifetime habit of sleeping only four or five hours a night began at this time because he would have to be up by seven to get to work.

My parents' relationship was peaceful, because both were easygoing. They had only one fight while living at GD's, which my mother said "lasted about as long as a minute." She cried and they quickly made up. For all their thirty-four years together, my parents had a smooth, loving relationship. Recalled Maudine Cooper, Dad's colleague at the Urban League in the 1970s, "I'd be in Ron's office at the Urban League talking about the next project, and we'd get this phone call. Alma was home and didn't want to cook and Ron would say, 'Oh, that's all right. We'll have some scrambled eggs or something. No big deal.' I never saw negativity in their relationship, which was maintained as very private. When I saw the two of them in public, she was there for him and he was there for her."

Although neither of my parents earned very much during this period, they were satisfied that Dad's career was moving along; he was in law school and not wasting time while waiting for his army assignment. He often discussed his cases with my mother, expressing sympathy for the families he handled; he was particularly bothered about one woman with six young children and no husband who had no place to leave her children while she sought work. In 1962, day care was an unknown concept. Dad was frustrated that the city's welfare allotment wasn't sufficient for this woman to feed herself and her children. Mom said he never looked down on his clients, telling her he understood that people sometimes cannot overcome the obstacles of their situations.

Dad's supervisor at Social Services was an understanding boss who allowed him to leave early if he had exams at law school. During this first semester at St. John's, my father didn't form close associations with his peers as he would do years later when he returned to finish school. Only twenty-one and a newlywed, he would leave immediately after class, anxious to get home to his bride.

When he wasn't studying, he and Mom went to the movies, to dinner, or to visit friends, usually Mom's friends, and as time went on Dad became friendlier with them than he was with his own friends. On weekends, my parents would stroll through the Harlem neighborhood to a favorite restaurant for dinner, either El Caribe for Cuban food, Dante's for steak, Well's Fried Chicken and Waffles on 125th Street and Seventh Avenue, or the famous bar the Red Rooster.

While they walked, they talked. Often it was about my father's aspirations, including his goal of becoming the first black president of the United States. He was drawn to politics. As a child, growing up in Harlem, he was surrounded by politicians, including Percy Sutton, Basil Patterson, and Bob Weaver, all of whom at the time were in positions of influence; Sutton was Manhattan borough president, and Weaver and Patterson were in state government. Mom didn't scoff at my father's aspiration because, to her, he was brilliant and capable of anything and she had not yet discovered the heartache that was sometimes part of being in public service.

Sundays were family day and my parents would either go to Brooklyn for dinner with her parents or they'd stay at home for one of GD's special Sunday dinners. The family would be joined by Nick's girlfriend, Fran; GD's girlfriend, Peggy, and her daughter, Leslie; O. T. Wells, a funny, interesting lawyer who lived in the building, and his wife, Jean; Faith Berry and Buddy Gist; and anyone else GD ran into and brought home for dinner. The guys did all the cooking and the women cleaned up. Dinner conversation was politics, the civil rights movement, race issues, and entertainment—who was performing where. When Nick's girlfriend became pregnant, then later gave birth, the baby was the focus of much conversation. These dinners were stimulating and exciting, Mom recalled. "Sunday was a big time for everybody in Bill Brown's apartment. He was the kind of person everybody gravitated to, and he'd say, 'Come on, come on. Yeah, we have enough,' so you never knew who else was going to be there."

The sound of Sunday afternoon football could be heard through the chatter and laughter. And the food! "Real food for real people," my father once said. They had rib roast or pot roast or roast chicken, with potatoes and string beans, in quantities large enough even for Dad.

Occasionally, my parents would visit Nan, who was then living on West Fifty-seventh Street in Manhattan. She was working and had an active social life, but if she were free, Dad would suggest to Mom that they stop there. Once or twice she made them dinner and Mom recalled that she served creamed spinach along with advice: "Now make sure you give Ronnie creamed spinach. He just loves creamed spinach."

In February, Dad had completed a semester of law school and he and Mom prepared to leave for Virginia to begin his tour of duty in the army. My father took a leave from St. John's with the understanding that he would return to finish his law degree. He quit his job at DSS and Mom left her job as a teacher. They packed their personal belongings, returned their rented furniture, said good-bye to relatives and friends, and prepared to go off on their own for the first time.

Together, they were ready to take on the world.

My brother Michael said it was zero degrees on Thanksgiving weekend, 1989, when he and Dad, with hammer and chisel in hand, helped thousands of ecstatic Germans knock down the Berlin Wall. "Everyone was so excited," Michael said, "that most of them weren't wearing shirts." People stood on top of the wall, dancing, singing, and drinking German beer, of course. Michael and Dad, wearing overcoats and gloves against the cold, hammered away and collected pieces of the wall to bring home to me and Mom. As they chipped and chopped, they were so carried away by the emotions surging about them, Michael recalls, that they both cried.

Dad, at the time chair of the Democratic National Committee, was on a trip to Germany sponsored by Democrats Abroad and had invited Michael along to visit the house they'd lived in when he was born. The day after the Berlin Wall came down, Dad and Michael drove to the army base near Kassel, Germany, where my parents lived during Mom's pregnancy and after Michael's birth. At the house, Dad knocked and a woman answered. "I was based here in the sixties and we used to live in this house," my father said. "This six-foot-five fellow you see next to me was only twenty-one inches long when we brought him home from the hospital." She smiled and invited them in; Michael believes that she recognized Dad as chair of the DNC.

Dad took my brother from room to room, giving a play-by-play commentary on everything they had done in that house. "This is where I changed your stinky diaper. . . . This is where you threw up on me. . . . This is where you cracked your chin on the table." Michael was amazed. I was born in Brooklyn and my maternal grandparents still live there, so I've often seen the hospital in which I was born, the apartment in which I lived when I was a baby. But this was the first time Michael was able to see where he had begun life.

Dad knew how special this was for his son. "Step into the doorway," he said to Michael. "I want to take your picture here so I never forget this moment."

FIVE

In the Army

F ROM 1963 to 1967, while intense civil rights battles were being fought at home, my parents were on an army base in Germany, far away from the action.

My father's first assignment in the army was a short stint at transportation school in Fort Eustis, Virginia, a tidewater town. The army provided on-post housing for Dad only, so my parents had to choose between living outside the post, in an all-white suburb close to Fort Eustis, or two hours away in Hampton, the site of a black college, Hampton Institute. Living in Hampton would require Dad to drive two hours each way, every day, to the base. But in Virginia, in 1963, before the civil rights movement had put a dent in discrimination, Mom wasn't comfortable living in an all-white community. A third alternative, that she remain in New York City while my father attended transportation school, was not acceptable to the newlyweds, so they decided to live in Hampton. Dad always wanted to do whatever would make Mom happy. That's the way they were together. Nan called a friend, the sister of Dr. Al Moron, about an apartment for my parents. Dr. Moron's sister knew of a small one-bedroom at 336 Wine Street, and my parents agreed to take it, sight unseen.

On his own, my father would have felt fine living anywhere, including all-white Fort Eustis, but on the drive down south, an upsetting experience supported Mom's viewpoint and made Dad certain they had chosen the right place to live. They left New York City in early March 1963, in their snappy new '62 navy-blue Mercury Comet convertible with light blue leather interior, packed with everything they owned: clothes, books, records, and wedding gifts.

Several hours after they left, they stopped for lunch at Shoney's Big Boy, a drive-in restaurant in Newport News. My mother often ate at the Shoney's in Nashville while she was at Fisk University and knew they offered the fast food Dad loved. Shoney's was a pre-McDonald's drive-in that served meals on trays that hooked onto the car window. That day, the waitress came out, took my parents' order—two burgers, fries, a Coke, and apple pie for Dad and a burger and Coke for Mom—then leaned over and said, "Okay, but you're gonna have to eat in your car down the road." My parents must have looked confused, because she added, "I can't bring a tray out." They were even more confused. "I can't serve you with a tray," she repeated. "I'll put your lunch in a box and you have to take it and eat it down the road."

"Down the road, because why?" Dad asked.

"Because you can't eat here," said the waitress. "It's not me, I'm from Ohio."

Finally, he got it. Black customers could only eat out of sight. Dad said, "Never mind," and drove away, fast. "Ronnie was just beside himself," my mom recalled, "because this was his first slap 'Hello.' He said, 'We are not going to eat any of this shit,' and we drove and drove and finally got to Hampton and found the black part of town."

Although Mom had anticipated that they would encounter bigotry in the South, Dad had no idea. After a sheltered childhood at the Theresa, surrounded by the warm acceptance of his community, then years in top-notch schools where his charm and wit won him friends of all backgrounds, Dad was unfamiliar with discrimination. He was shocked by the experience at that drive-in restaurant. But he was also aware that he was a black man living in a white world and, at that point, was happy that Mom had insisted they live in the black community of Hampton.

They headed there, found a restaurant and ate, then went directly to their apartment at 336 Wine Street. They slept on cots the proprietor had set up for them. The next morning they rented a burgundy faux leather living-room set, a bedroom set, a dining table and four chairs, and a refrigerator. For the next three months, my father awakened at six every morning to make the two-hour drive to Fort Eustis and often didn't get back home until nine at night. My mother was lonely but she'd walk into town, visit the university, or visit with the downstairs tenants, who were teachers in Newport News.

Twice a week, Mom drove Dad to Fort Eustis in the morning, came back home to dress, then went into town for the afternoon until it was time to pick him up at the post. Occasionally, she would drive him to the base and spend her day there, shopping at the supermarket-like commissary or the PX, which sold clothing and shoes, furniture, and other household items. On weekends, my parents were together, either in town or at the officers' club on post. They talked on the phone to friends and family back home, watched television, and grew even closer to each other. Neither one of them made any friends at Fort Eustis, but Mom's parents, Mere and Bop, visited twice and her college roommate, Alma Harris, also visited.

Dad was protective of Mom even in those early days, never wanting anything to upset her, if he could help it. A few mornings, when they awakened, they saw black dots on the floor, which my mother would sweep up, all the while asking Dad what they were. And every day, he'd say, "You must have spilled the peppercorns." Since she had total faith in my father, she accepted that, even though, in the back of her mind, she knew she hadn't spilled the peppercorns three days in a row. Dad, who knew what the black blobs really were, quietly got a mouse trap and set it. One night, while they were in bed, Mom heard a "pop."

"We got him," Dad said and got up to dispose of the mouse. That's how my mother discovered what those tiny black items really were.

Only a short time after Dad left New York for Fort Eustis, GD got remarried without telling him and without inviting him to the wedding. In late March, GD called to announce that he had just married his girlfriend. Although Dad knew and liked Peggy, he blamed her for his being left out of the wedding. Initially hurt and angry, Dad was eventually able to adjust and accepted what had happened, and by the time he returned to New York City after transportation school, he was able to see his father and Peggy and ignore any negative feelings about not having been invited to the wedding.

When Mom and Dad came home, they stayed with Mere and Bop for two weeks before they left for Dad's two-year tour overseas. The army had given my father an option: a hardship tour—so named because soldiers couldn't bring their families—or Germany with Mom, in exchange for a commitment to a third year in the service. (ROTC normally requires a two-year tour.) At the time, Dad was considering making the army his career and finishing his law degree while in the service so he had no problem with serving an additional year.

My parents left for Germany in June 1963, and Dad reported first to Geissen Post, then to Rothwesten, a small post outside the city of Kassel. There, they joined other young officers and their wives in their army-issue houses, cozy and comfortable, which bordered a small park.

As the post's motor officer, Dad ran the motor pool, overseeing several hundred army cars, trucks, and tractors and supervising about seventy German civilians who maintained them. He was also responsible for vehicle authorizations and requisitions and participated in monthly training weekends, where he slept in foxholes and performed maneuvers.

Each evening, Dad would come home from work at about five and Mom, just learning to cook, would practice her new skills on a tolerant and always hungry husband. Dad had only one requirement: large portions. If he had enough, he'd eat anything, even hot dogs and beans. This combination was actually one of his favorites, and a snack he enjoyed throughout his life, so Mom served it often, always with large side dishes of sauerkraut and plenty of rolls.

My parents loved their three years in Germany. While Dad was at work, Mom took care of their quarters and socialized with other young officers' wives. Evenings, they'd listen to mystery serials on Armed Forces Radio or Dad would read thrillers, especially those by a favorite author, Ian Fleming. And they went out often. Sometimes, my mother would get a ride to the officers' club on a Friday night and meet Dad for happy hour and dinner. On one such evening, she picked up a strange habit: Watching the colonel's wife, Mrs. Maudlin, cut a hamburger in half before she ate it, my impressionable young mother was so taken with the older woman's sophistication, position as post commander's wife, and reputation as a world traveler, that she never again ate a hamburger without first cutting it in half. Dad also had some role models; he looked up to Colonel Maudlin, whose graciousness and wide-ranging knowledge were qualities he admired. He also admired down-to-earth folks and generally exhibited an I-never-met-a-man-I-didn't-like attitude.

Some of the young couples my parents became friendly with became lifelong friends, including Chuck and Marilyn Alston and Pete and Dot Cherry. My parents and their friends got together often to play bridge and have parties. My fun-loving father, "a skinny little devil," according to Chuck Alston, worked hard and played hard, even back then. He loved to dance, especially to favorites by the Supremes, Martha and the Vandellas, and the Beatles. Dad just loved "Please Mr. Postman" by the Marvelettes and never seemed to tire of it. Chubby Checker's The Twist was popular, and although it was considered daring by some my father—who'd introduced the dance at Middlebury—and Mom twisted away at house parties and at the officers' club.

My parents and the other young officers and wives played a drinking game, "7-14-21," in which they rolled dice to determine which of them would name the elaborate and awful concoctions that the other players would have to consume. One night, the "drink" was brandy mixed with peppermint schnapps and it did in my father. Staggering out of the Alstons' house, he unsuccessfully tried to navigate their gate and ended up marooned on a picket fence. After Mom and the Alstons found him there, moaning, head on one side and feet on the other, Mom helped him home as he vowed never again to play 7-14-21.

In Germany, Dad added to his List of Firsts: He was the only black officer on his post in Kassel. There was no apparent prejudice against black people in Germany, although my mother was stared at all the time. As Marilyn Alston remembered, that was because black women were rare there and my parents were "a gorgeous couple." She said, "We made a good-looking foursome. Hot. We'd go downtown and we just strutted our stuff." Sometimes the two couples would instigate trouble by "switching" for a few minutes, with Dad holding hands with Marilyn, and Mom and Chuck arm in arm. They'd laugh hysterically at onlookers' shocked reactions to these two interracial "couples." Once, in a downtown Kassel beer house, when several German citizens began pointing at Mom, apparently because they had never before seen a black woman, Chuck Alston, who was fluent in German, told them off.

Michael

My mother, who had been diagnosed with endometriosis when she had surgery during her visit to Middlebury College when Dad was a senior, had since been on hormone therapy. She remained uncertain whether she could conceive, since the surgeon in Vermont had been pessimistic. After my parents married, they used no birth control, with Mom fearing the worst but hoping for the best. Dad remained optimistic and reassured her that they would be able to conceive and would have children.

When they were in Germany, she discussed her reproductive problem with friends who told her about an infertility clinic at the American Army hospital in Frankfurt, a two-hour drive from Kassel. They had been married only a year but my anxious mother decided they needed the clinic's help. Dad, as always, went along with her and they went to the clinic to be tested. After the results were in, Mom was prescribed Enovoid, a birth control pill that she was to be on for three months, then off for three months; its purpose was not birth control in Mom's case but to regulate her reproductive cycle. She was instructed to take her temperature daily to determine if she was ovulating. She followed directions to the letter and, if it turned out that she was ovulating, she would call Dad and issue the command: "Come home now." He always complied.

Although it was early in their marriage to go to these lengths, Dad never suggested that Mom relax and wait a couple of years. Years later, my parents would laugh at how he would race home after Mom's call, yelling to coworkers, "Gotta go! I'll be back." The clinic doctor had also instructed Mom in the many ways to aid conception, all of which my parents followed.

One time, my mother decided they should adopt one of the many "brown babies" that were available for adoption. These were the children born of relationships between black GIs and white German women. Dad refused and was quite firm about his refusal. After the Middlebury surgery, he had comforted Mom by saying they could always adopt. But at this point, he was absolutely certain they would conceive their own baby.

"No," Dad responded to Mom's suggestion. "We are going to do everything that doctor tells us to do and have our own baby." Now that conceiving was a challenge, my father's can-do attitude took over. He was determined to get Mom pregnant.

And six months later, she was.

It was in July when he asked her, "Did you get your period yet?"

She replied that it was late but added that she refused to call the doctor until at least a month had passed; she didn't want to jinx it. When she had some episodes of morning sickness at the end of September, she became certain. They went to see the doctor in Frankfurt, who confirmed it, and he was almost as excited as my parents. Because of his obvious happiness for them, my mother wanted him to deliver the baby when the time came.

The details of my brother's birth reveal much about my mother's fortitude and my father's bad-driver syndrome. It was because of that syndrome that my mother gave birth to Michael under primitive conditions instead of in a modern American hospital as she had planned.

Mom had been going for prenatal checkups at the American hospital in Frankfurt; like the clinic, the hospital was two hours from the post. Sometimes she went alone; other times Dad accompanied her and they would make a day of it, going shopping, visiting the command post. As soon as she had her first contraction, sometime during the night of March 3, Dad said, "Well, we're not going to Frankfurt." Dad, panicked, admitted he feared driving on the autobahn, a superhighway with no speed limit, with Mom in the car about to have a baby. Nervously, he said he was afraid she'd give birth in the car. When Mom's water broke, Dad called Dick Guglieri, a friend, fellow officer, and a physician, although not an obstetrician. Over the telephone, Dick timed Mom's contractions. He may have hesitated when Dad said, "Alma wants to go to Frankfurt," because Dad relayed that Dick didn't think Frankfurt was a good idea. Dick suggested they call the German hospital, only eighteen miles from the post. This hospital relied on the traditional method of childbirth, what we call natural childbirth, and did not prescribe painkillers to women in labor. Expectant mothers who were to deliver there generally attended classes on natural childbirth. Mom did not want to deliver naturally and did want painkillers. She asked Dad if it was he or Dick who had said going to Frankfurt was a bad idea. Dad just smiled and never answered.

Determined to have the baby in the modern American army hospital in Frankfurt, my mother was upset with this change in plans and attempted to change his mind, but did so gently. She encouraged him: "Honey, we can make it. I know we can." But Dad knew Mom and he knew himself. He knew my mother could take more than he could. He knew she could take whatever the German hospital gave her better than he could take driving on the autobahn for two hours, with her beside him, having labor pains.

In the end, they went to the German hospital and, regardless of Dad's opinion of Mom's strength, her experience there almost broke her spirit. She arrived at the hospital, made up and manicured as usual, ready for anything—but not what was to come. They quickly took her away from Dad, undressed her, and put her into a hot tub. They timed her contractions, dressed her in a nightgown, and brought her into the white, sterile delivery room.

Mom quickly discovered the worst about having a baby in a German hospital: There were no stirrups on the delivery table. She had to hold her own feet and ankles, all the while screaming at the top of her lungs since she had not been given anything for the pain. After six hours of contortions and pain on the delivery table, the doctors told her to push, and when the baby's head emerged, they finally gave my mother a painkiller. But it was too late. Michael's head was out, the hardest part was over, and she had done it awake and aware. My brother's birth, on March 4, 1965, at five in the morning, was one of Dad's favorite stories. He found the humor in the situation, then dramatized and exaggerated to make it even funnier: "They took Alma away from me and I didn't know where they were taking her. I just sat in this cold waiting room by myself. Nobody came out to tell me anything. I saw one person and he smiled at me when I said, 'My wife—one like me,' meaning our color. No one spoke English at all. I waited and waited and finally someone came out, gave me her bloody nightgown, and said, 'It's a boy. Come this way.' " Mom and little Michael were waiting in a large beautiful single room, where Dad was allowed to stay as long as he wanted.

Another of my father's funny stories was a sarcastic description of the oh-so-foreign practices in this hospital. Mom was due to get an injection to dry up her milk because she wasn't going to nurse. The hospital staff's idea of sanitation was to leave the needle filled with my mother's medication lying exposed on a table, waiting to be contaminated by any germ floating around the hospital.

Later, when my parents found out that Stadt Krankenhaus, or State Hospital, was the name of the hospital, it made some practices understandable: It was a state-run institution for German citizens who were used to ways different from ours. A stoic hausfrau might accept having a baby while holding her own ankles, but my middle-class American mother did not.

On the other hand, Mom's room was clean and pretty and

Dad could visit at any hour. Mom was a major attraction for the hospital staff, as was Michael, and Dad once again added to his List of Firsts: His was the first black baby born in Stadt Krankenhaus. Everyone came in to see the baby, who was adorable in addition to being a "first." Also, because the hospital allowed new mothers to remain for a long eight days while they recuperated, Mom enjoyed a wonderful rest. If she was sleepy, the nurses would take the baby out; and they brought him back when she was ready for him.

The American army hospital in Frankfurt would have limited Mom's stay to three days in a double room but she would have received anesthesia, painkillers, or both. In contrast, she had endured natural childbirth without practice in breathing or information on what to expect, and because of hospital regulations no fathers were allowed in the delivery rooms to offer their wives emotional and physical support. No staff member in the room coached or encouraged Mom, not even in German. And no one's hand was available for holding. (Of course, she couldn't have grabbed a hand since her own were serving as stirrups.) And she gave birth in a room full of strangers whose only English word was "push."

Thirty-plus years later, although she admits there were some good points at the German hospital, such as the aftercare, Mom remembers all those hours of holding her ankles. Earlier, during her pregnancy, Mom heard from other wives on the post who had opted to have their babies at the German hospital. They talked about how wonderful it was because one could stay eight days in a great room, with unlimited visits from husbands. Mom had not heard a whisper from any of these women that they'd had to hold their feet and ankles during delivery. I believe that had she known about this bit of information beforehand, she would have *walked* all the way to Frankfurt.

After Michael and Mom were back in their house on the base, Mom would say to Dad, "Ronnie, you know I wanted to go to Dr. Jones, my doctor in Frankfurt." Not angry, but just letting him know he had broken his promise to take her to Frankfurt. He always had the same answer: "No, you might have had the baby on the autobahn while I was driving. And Dick said going to Frankfurt was a bad idea." The truth is that he was twenty-three years old, it was his first baby, and he was scared.

Michael was a happy and even-tempered baby and became the pride and joy of the family, being the first grandchild for Mere and Bop and for Nan and GD. GD was excited, but Nan was not really ready to be a grandmother. She was an extraordinarily beautiful woman and as a chic forty-three-year-old divorcée she was quite busy with her social life.

Trouble at Home

On November 22, 1963, my parents were at the Alstons' playing bridge, listening to the radio. Suddenly, a news flash came on and an announcer, in a hushed voice, said that President Kennedy had been shot. This was followed by a solemn pronouncement that the young president was dead, assassinated. My parents and their friends were numb. Then all four began to cry, their sadness heightened by a sense of isolation, as if the tragedy might have been easier to bear if it were shared at home, with millions of other Americans. Stunned, they talked about how it could have happened, why it happened. Later, my father planned and organized the base memorial service for the slain president.

The assassination of President Kennedy was the most awful event of the three years my parents were in Germany, 1963 through 1965. But this was the beginning of tumult and unrest at home, a time when the civil rights movement heated up and became a war, when the counterculture was born, when the opposition to the war in Vietnam divided America. Both Mom and Dad felt sharply removed, aware they couldn't directly contribute to the struggle undertaken by southern black people, a struggle that, in the coming decade, would forever change the country.

My parents were awed when they heard the news about the March on Washington, on August 28, 1963. About three hundred thousand people had gathered in Washington in the greatest mass meeting in civil rights history. But not until they received that month's copy of *Ebony* from Mere and saw the photographs of the March did Mom and Dad realize the event's enormity. As they gathered to hear the Reverend Martin Luther King Jr. and other civil rights leaders speak, the minds and hearts of the people were united and the March became one of the great moments in American history. Although they kept the magazine on their coffee table so they could share the photographs with friends, although they talked and talked about the March, my parents felt isolated. Not only were they in another country, but they were in an isolated section of that country. Television programs were in German, of course, so they relied on radio and *Stars and Stripes,* the armed forces newspaper, and since it had to cover international news as well as U.S. news, the paper gave only minimal coverage to the March. My parents had followed the movement from its beginnings during the 1950s. But the enormity of it was made real by the photos in *Ebony.*

My father felt left out of the civil rights movement. People were going on Freedom Rides, marching and demonstrating, risking life and limb for the movement. He could do nothing and it bothered him. When Mom was at Fisk, she had participated in lunch-counter sit-ins in downtown Nashville's Woolworth's and her picture had even been on the cover of an issue of *U.S. News & World Report* detailing the sit-ins. My mother had seen and talked to some of the Freedom Riders who had traveled through Nashville. Dad, in Vermont for four years, a state where the movement in the South was basically ignored, realized now, in 1963, how uninvolved he'd been. In their little house on the Kassel base, Dad said to Mom that he regretted not going to a black college. When they dated, in letters, he would always ask about the movement, what was going on, who was doing what. Now, in Germany, he realized just how out of it he had been and still was. Recalled Mom, "Years later, he said the two things that he regretted were that he didn't get a chance to participate in the sit-ins and that he was sent to Korea instead of Vietnam."

My father was never stationed in Vietnam, despite the war that was then going on, and it bothered him. He didn't think that perhaps he was avoiding serious injury, even death. And his sadness over not being at lunch counters, in marches, or on buses in the South was not mitigated by relief that he would not be jailed or beaten up. My father would never drive down a lonely country road, be pulled from his car, have his bones broken, then be murdered and left to lie by the side of the road—as was James Chaney. He would not feel the fear of a young man walking alone into an all-white University of Mississippi—as did James Meredith.

In his feelings about missing the sit-ins and protests of the early civil rights movement and about missing the war in Vietnam, my father demonstrated one aspect of his personality and character. Both the South and the war in Vietnam offered Dad a chance to take risks and do good at the same time. In Vietnam, he could have served his country where he thought he was most needed. In the South, he could have helped his brothers and sisters gain equal rights and a seat at the table. These two American adventures, divisive and difficult, were among the most significant events in this century. The Vietnam War's spawn, the antiwar movement, and the civil rights movement led to enormous social, political, and economic changes. By being in Germany and "out of it," Dad was missing a chance to make history.

But then there was another side to Dad, the part of him that sought a safe and secure life, whether in the army or elsewhere. On the other side of the world in Germany, far from the action at home, my father was building a life with my mother, looking ahead to a family and a successful career. This part of Dad would try to change the system and improve things for black people by working on the inside. He was not a revolutionary, risking stability and security, but would push toward his goals by hard work and intelligence, by wit, charm, and grace.

Going Home

Tours of duty were the subject of endless speculation and analysis on an army post. Couples with children discussed which posts had good schools, or the best shopping. Some posts would be condemned, others praised. My parents began to speculate about Dad's next assignment in the winter of 1965. Whenever he went to his command post, or headquarters, at Geissen, Mom would quiz him about whom he had seen and what he had heard because there were constant rumors about who was being transferred where.

By this time, their house was filled with crates of furniture they had purchased earlier that year. All the young couples at the post traveled to Denmark and bought the sleek, light furniture that country is known for. Mom and Dad, looking forward to filling a New York apartment with "the teak," as they called it, spent four months in their little house with the huge crates. Shortly before they left Germany, they shipped the teak home; there are still several pieces of it in my parents' house.

In late spring of 1966, after Dad had served his three-year tour in Germany, he remained in the service, still considering it as a possible career. He briefly contemplated resigning and even sent in a request to be released from active duty; but after that request was denied, Dad accepted spending at least one more year in the service because he still was not certain that he really wanted out of the army. He had been successful as an army officer, winning a National Defense Service Medal and an Army Commendation Medal. All of his evaluations had been positive, almost effusive, in their praise of Lieutenant Brown. Here is a sampling of his army evaluations from 1964 to 1966: "A fine young officer with a warm personality . . ." "always cheerful . . ." "responds well to changing situations . . ." "capable of a superior performance . . ." "an ability to organize, delegate authority and make proper use of his subordinates . . ." "in the upper 10 percent of officers . . ." "accepts advice and criticism without bitterness and is sincerely interested in self improvement . . ." "possesses a fervent desire to do a good job in all his endeavors."

Dad received notice of his next assignment, Korea, and was given leave to return to New York in June until the assignment began in August. Mom and Michael were to remain at home during Dad's one-year tour in Korea because officers assigned to a hardship tour, such as Korea or Vietnam, were not permitted to bring their families. Although Dad had to serve a year away from his family, he had no regrets. He still thought the service might be the right career for him and, in addition, he and my mother had loved their years in Kassel: the friends they made, living in a European country, and the army lifestyle.

Because my mother had expected Dad's hardship tour to be Vietnam, since her understanding was that most junior grade officers (captain and below) were being sent to that war-torn country, she was thrilled that he was to go to Korea instead. Later, my parents learned that as many officers at the time were being sent to Korea as to Vietnam. It was simply the luck of the draw. But Dad's reaction was mixed. He wanted to be an officer in Vietnam for the action and for the war's historical and military importance. Vietnam was where every officer he met was on his way to, or from. "I'm an officer in the U.S. Army, Alma," he told Mom. "This is what I do. I'm supposed to be on the front lines." But at the same time, he was relieved; he understood the horrors of war.

As their departure from Germany grew close, my parents' friends threw a series of farewell parties for them and they had a wonderful last few weeks in Kassel. Happy to be going home and looking forward to seeing their families, Mom and Dad were sad to be leaving the close friends they'd made on the post. Mom has said you make friends quickly in the army because it's never clear how much time you'll have in the same posting. Mom and Dad grew so close to one couple, Robyn and David Pitman, that they were Michael's godparents.

With fourteen-month-old Michael and a few personal possessions, Mom and her first lieutenant left Germany on a direct flight to New York in July of 1966. Everyone they loved was waiting for them at the airport: Mere and Bop; Mom's grandparents, who were called Grandpa and Boo Boo; Nan; and GD and Peggy with Leslie and their son, Chip (William Jr.), Dad's new half brother. Mom and Dad expected to see Mere and Bop at the airport but were surprised and thrilled to see everyone, all the family members they loved most. They exited the plane and walked onto the tarmac and, as they headed toward the terminal, they could see their family inside, waving from the windows, waiting for them. Michael had walked down the stairs of the plane, and although Mom's parents and Nan had visited them in Germany, none of them had seen the little guy walk.

It was one of life's perfect moments, everyone laughing and smiling and together.

It was such a wonderful homecoming that whenever my mother recalls it, she cries, her heart breaking with knowledge that such moments are short-lived and rare. Today, many of those people are gone: Mom's grandparents. GD. Bop. And my father.

After lots of hugs and kisses, the group headed to Brooklyn for a big dinner at the Arringtons' house with Mere and Bop as hosts. It was fun watching Michael and Chip, only eight months older, playing like two little brothers. Then, after a huge meal and family reunion, everyone else went home while Mom and Dad and Michael slept over. The next morning, my parents headed for their new co-op apartment, a generous gift from Mom's parents that was greatly appreciated. Mom and Dad were eager to establish their new life in New York City in the two months before Dad had to leave for Korea.

The apartment at 21 St. James Place, across the street from the Pratt Institute, a noted fine arts college, was in University Towers, which had been built during the years my parents were in Germany. The sixteenth-floor apartment had two bedrooms, with a terrace off the living room, a dining area, and a tiny, windowless kitchen.

Over the next few days, they furnished and fixed, thrilled to finally have their own apartment rather than army quarters. Dad was anxious to get it all done before he had to leave for Korea so he could picture Mom and Michael there, waiting for him to come home. They first arranged for "the teak" to be delivered and then accented the simple Danish furniture with wedding gifts and items they'd purchased in Europe: pictures, knickknacks, and ashtrays—important, since at the time, everyone smoked. Mere helped my parents get the apartment ready hanging pictures, putting away all of my brother's toys and clothing, fixing everything so the apartment was livable. Mom insisted on keeping the house filled with fresh flowers; there were vases of them everywhere.

Mom and Dad filled the refrigerator and stocked the cabinets with canned goods and other food items they purchased at the commissary at Fort Hamilton in Brooklyn. They bought chairs for the terrace so they could sit outside and began to enjoy their new home. By the time my father left for Korea, in August, their little nest was feathered and secure.

Dad, who was promoted to captain during the period between his postings in Germany and Korea, handled it well when he had to leave because of his philosophical acceptance of most things that came his way. Mom also took this first prolonged separation in stride because she had Michael and the new apartment. Intrigued and enchanted by the city of her birth, Mom found it newly stimulating after her three-year absence. At the same time, the city also offered comfort and security because the places and people, the language and customs, were home. Even though she missed her husband, my mother was happy, taking care of Michael and reacquainting herself with old friends and family.

Once Dad arrived at his posting in the Thirty-eighth Replacement Battalion in Korea, my parents spoke weekly on the phone and wrote daily. Every day they were apart, they mailed out short, chatty letters about what they were doing. Dad's letters, about the country he was in and what he was doing there, were never reflective because he was not like that; he was too busy living his life to analyze it. A letter might begin, "I saw my first four-star general today" and go on to tell about the experience. Mom developed a ritual of writing every evening about Michael and her experiences and interactions that day. In Korea, Dad lived in a BMQ, bachelor men's quarters, a simple environment for single men or men without their families, and had little social life.

As Commandant of the Eighth United States Army KATUSA (Korean Augmentation to the U.S. Army) Training School, my father continued learning how to command and lead. He was responsible for training all Korean soldiers assigned for duty with the Eighth Army. One fifth of the U.S. Army at that point was made up of Korean soldiers, and every American dignitary who visited the country toured the training school. Concluded an April 1967 army evaluation of Dad's work, "Captain Brown has built the school into one of the most unique and outstanding schools of the United States Army . . . In spite of a shortage of personnel and funds, he converted the KATUSA School Recreation Facility into one of the finest in Korea. He rewrote the curriculum of the school as to provide the greatest learning opportunity for all KATUSA soldiers. Captain Brown distinguished himself in the field of Korean-American relations."

My father served as an escort officer during LBJ's visit to KATUSA from October 31 through November 2, 1966, and received a letter of appreciation from his commanding officer for the "major and essential contribution" he made to the presidential visit.

When Dad first left for Korea, both he and Mom expected him to be home for either Thanksgiving or Christmas. But in September he called with bad news: "Honey, I'm not going to be able to come home for Thanksgiving. I'm too far down on the list." They hoped he would manage to be home for Christmas, though.

While she waited for my father, my mother was active with friends and family and even did some work for the Republican party! She ran into Butch Forster, a friend of Dad's from Middlebury College, at a friend's house, and he convinced her to donate some time to the Young New Yorkers for Rockefeller, who was then running for governor of New York. Mom thought making phone calls, sending out mail, and answering phones at the Rockefeller headquarters sounded interesting. So Mere baby-sat for Michael while Mom went to work for the Republicans.

Mom and her family had traditionally been Democrats—with the exception of her grandmother Ann Madison (Boo Boo), who was a registered Republican, although she didn't vote any particular party line. Her family had been active on the local level in district politics since the 1920s with Boo Boo hosting candidate forums and fund-raising teas at her Brooklyn home.

When Dad called to tell Mom about Thanksgiving, she told him about working for Rockefeller. "You're working for a Republican!?" Dad was surprised, but not angry. Later, Mom realized that what she thought was "fun" was actually serious volunteer work for a Republican. Even worse, on Election Day, she had actually voted for Rockefeller.

There was disappointment on both sides of the world when Dad learned, sometime during the fall, that he would also have to remain in Korea for Christmas. He mailed dozens of Christmas toys for Michael and gifts for my mother and his other relatives, then called home on Christmas morning. He spoke to Michael, then almost two: "Did you like the truck? Did you see the other toys? Do you like them?" The conversation was one-sided but it made both Dad and Michael happy. When he spoke to Mom and asked if they were going to Boo Boo's for "that good old food," greens and sweet potatoes, the down-home cooking that he loved, she could hear the longing for home in his voice.

Mom spent New Year's Eve with her friends Marilyn and Roger Whiting; they were good friends, and, not too far in the future, Marilyn would be my godmother. My mother took Michael, went to their party, and spent the night. The next day, Dad called her and they chatted about the party: who was there, what they ate (of course, Dad would want to know that) and drank; whether "Big Fella," his nickname for Roger, was the bartender.

Then my father learned that he would receive two weeks R&R in February. Mom, excited about seeing my father after so many months, also had a plan. She told her friend Ardath Hill that she wanted to get pregnant while he was home on leave so the baby would be born while he was still in the service so maternity and childbirth costs would be covered by Uncle Sam. At that time, my father had begun talking about leaving the service. (Mom is a good planner.)

My father arrived in New York just before Mom's birthday, which is Valentine's Day, a day they always spent together from the first year they were married. My mother told no one about Dad's homecoming and early on the morning he was due to arrive took Michael and picked up my father at the airport. Then, they drove straight to the Arringtons' house to surprise them. Dad called GD and Peggy, who then lived on Riverside Drive in Manhattan, and Nan, all of whom were so happy to hear his voice. Then my parents went home and spent the day, with their own little family, enjoying each other and their apartment. During Dad's leave, he saw all the relatives but spent a lot of time with Mom, being "romantic every minute possible," as my mother recalls.

And that's when I was conceived. About a month after my father had returned to Korea, my mother missed her period and was starting to feel nauseous in the mornings. She went to see a black woman doctor, Josephine English, whom Mere had recommended. After Dr. English corroborated Mom's suspicions, she wrote the news to Dad in her daily letter. He called on Sunday before he received the letter, so she told him. Ecstatic, he talked about when the baby was due—November. Remaining in the army was still a consideration, so they discussed aiming for a stateside assignment and talked about how the baby—I—would be born in the United States.

As it turned out, I was born on credit. Despite my mother's planning to give birth with the army covering the costs, Dad left the service and the three-month grace period for army insurance expired in September, two months before I was born. My father, who had just qualified for his very first MasterCard, took a three-hundred-dollar cash advance, paid the hospital, then paid me off in installments to MasterCard.

It was a joyous time, and even though they missed each other they knew they'd be together in a few short months and looked forward to that and to the addition of a new baby. I feel lucky that I was that baby, lucky that I was born into my parents' loving family.

We are an affectionate family: lots of hugs and kisses and hand-holding. I remember how Dad, Mom, and I would sit close together, watching a game or movie, with Mom and me having foot wars over who would get to prop her legs on Dad's. And Dad had a practice of holding me and Michael down while he planted the wettest, sloppiest kisses on our cheeks. These kisses were made even more uncomfortable by the scratch of his mustache on our faces. Just as we would raise our palms to dry our faces, Dad would say, "Don't you wipe off your father's kiss."

Michael, who now has his own four-year-old twin boys, has admitted that he gives these same wet kisses to Ryan and Morgan. "I tell them I love them all the time," Michael says. "I hold them. I make them feel special, just like our father made us feel special."

Dad and I had our own ritual, three special kisses: the nose kiss, the butterfly, and the frog. I don't remember when it started, only that it never ended. In the nose kiss, we'd lightly rub our noses together. Next, the butterfly kiss: We would flutter eyelashes to eyelashes, right eye to right eye. Last came the frog kiss. I'd put my tongue in my cheek and puff it out like a frog and he would do the same, then we'd press our cheeks together.

Those kisses. Each one made me feel warm and loved and connected to his heart.

SIX

The Urban League

WHILE he was in Korea, in December 1966, Dad received a letter from St. John's Law School stating that he would lose the credits he had earned if he didn't reregister by June 1967. My parents' conversations now focused around the future: Should Dad return to New York and go to St. John's? Or should he stay in the service? They had often discussed the option of making the army his career. Both Mom and Dad loved the army people they'd met as well as traveling and living in different places. And although my father's salary while he was stationed in Germany was only $220 a month, the perks were appealing: pleasant living quarters, an active social life, and Christmas parties where they mingled with the post's highest-ranking officers. Army life is also very stable and secure; barring unusual circumstances, no one loses a job or is "downsized."

Dad relished the dignity and respect he received as an officer. When he was promoted to captain shortly before he left for Korea, he became a "five percenter," one of those officers who rise up in rank very quickly. Dad told Mom proudly, "I'll be a captain when I get to Korea!" This was a turning point; if Dad remained in the service, he would move up to field grade officer—major, then colonel—which was a lot to give up.

On the other hand, he and Mom knew his second hardship tour would likely be Vietnam. At the end of 1966, thousands of young army officers like my father were facing head-on the horrors of the Vietnam War. Mom was afraid for Dad's safety and thought he should leave the service and return to law school. All of these factors played a role in my father's ambivalence over whether to stay in the army or become a civilian. "Is this where we want to spend our lives?" my parents would ask each other.

Then, in mid-January, Dad and Mom made their decision: Dad would seize the day, take whatever the future brought and leave the service. On January 19, 1967, he applied for a release from active duty, which was granted, effective in six months. Dad came home from Korea in May and had to move fast in order to enroll in summer school at St. John's. He had less than a month to have his discharge papers signed and stamped by the army bureaucracy. Nan called a colonel friend of hers who mapped out for Dad exactly where he had to go and whose signatures he needed. He and Mom went to Washington and spent two days literally walking his papers through the Pentagon. They went from office to office getting the papers signed and stamped. While in D.C., Mom and Dad stayed with his grandfather, Jerome Osborne. Dad also applied for student loans to pay his law school tuition and looked for a job. He had a family to support, including a new baby, me, on the way.

Once again, Nan came through. Her friend Isobel "Izzy" Chisolm, director of the National Urban League's Guild, which was the women's auxiliary of the organization, arranged for Dad to contact Malcolm Puryear, deputy director of the Urban League under Whitney Young. At the time, Dad was unaware that Mr. P.—Malcolm Puryear's nickname—and Nan had already met, introduced by her friend Rose, who was Mr. P.'s secretary. Nan told him that her coworkers at Steuben Glass wanted to invite Dad, Mom, and Michael to a party they were planning to celebrate her recent promotion. She was in a panic because they all believed her to be white. Although she never said she was white, she had left blank the question about race on her application form. Nan's colleagues assumed she was white and some of them would make derogatory comments about black customers in front of her. In the end, Nan had the party canceled to avoid any conflict.

On the day of his job interview at the National Urban League headquarters, my father's youthful appearance was countered by his immaculate grooming, Puryear recalled. He interviewed Dad and joked that he would knock my father down to size for his next interview, with Whitney Young, since Young had only been a sergeant in the army while Dad had been a captain. The same day as his interviews, my father was offered a job, which he accepted. He would be a trainee adviser in an on-the-job training program in the Bronx, identifying jobs and industries with openings and setting up training programs for people interested in those positions. In the job-training program, which was financed by the U.S. Labor Department, neither rules nor standards were lowered for job applicants, and thousands of permanent jobs were filled by the League's job trainees.

My father was familiar with the National Urban League and its affiliate offices all over the country. It was an important social service agency whose primary purpose was to help black people secure jobs, training, education, and housing. The fifty-year-old League had been revitalized when Whitney Young became director in 1961. Never afraid to take on new challenges, Young opened up new lines of communication between black America and corporate America. A sociologist and former dean of the School of Social Work of Atlanta University, he had dedicated his life to the issues of the urban poor. Under his leadership, the League had developed into a civil rights organization of significance, establishing Head Start and job-training programs and centers for tutoring. (Decades later, in 1995, when my father helped save federal affirmative action, his words echoed those of Whitney Young, who had earlier warned that preferential treatment of blacks, although controversial, was necessary after centuries of institutionally sanctioned oppression and poverty.)

My father viewed the Urban League, with its mandate to train and educate black Americans and work for civil rights, as a perfect fit for him. He recognized the need to work within the system in organizations such as the League and the NAACP even though some of his friends were joining antiestablishment groups. Dad's friend Courtland Cox recalled that when he joined the Student Nonviolent Coordinating Committee (SNCC), he viewed the Urban League and the NAACP as behind the times. "They were the older people," he said. "They were staid and they all wore ties." SNCC and CORE (Congress of Racial Equality) members were on the front lines, desegregating public accommodations, gaining voting rights, protesting and organizing and marching. It wasn't until later that Courtland realized how essential the Urban League was to the civil rights movement: "SNCC finally understood that we had to involve ourselves in national politics if we were going to give ourselves the cover—I mean physical cover—we needed so that we could function in the South. Because if we functioned in the South in isolation without involving the nation politically, [the results could have been disastrous]."

When Dad came home the night he was hired at the Urban League, he was jubilant about his job and, later, even happier when he received a grant from the League to help pay his law school tuition. He told Mom how relaxed the interviews had been. (Dad always told me and Michael he enjoyed opening doors for us, as Nan and GD had done for him. But he made it clear that once the door was opened and we were inside, the rest was up to us.)

That month my father also returned to St. John's Law School. Early in the fall semester, Dad met his future study group buddies. Mike Sloane saw Dad, the only black student at night school, and went over and started talking to him. Then Dad and Mike were joined by Bob Taylor and Steve Sinagra and the four—black, Jewish, Italian, and WASP—formed a group that studied and socialized together for the next three years. Dad's group studied together almost all the time—when they weren't at their day jobs, of course. They would arrive at school by six and talk for a half hour before class. After class, Dad and the other guys "shot home." Dad to Mom and Michael, Mike and Steve to their wives, and Bob to his girlfriend. On weekends, they met in Steve Sinagra's large house on Long Island, spending five or more hours a day on Saturdays and Sundays, studying, talking, socializing. They brought along their families for potluck suppers; Mom's specialties were potato salad and baked beans.

As they were forming close friendships, the four men constantly joked around. Recalled Bob Taylor, "If I was restive, he'd say, 'Bob, these are basic concepts.' Basic concepts, that was his line. And we always used to say to each other, 'You're *numero uno*,' meaning top friend." Dad always checked out Bob's dates, never failing to make comments: "He'd talk about what my date's face looked like, how she dressed, her physical attributes, how friendly she was. He was cute—he felt a need to comment and liked to give his stamp of approval."

As relaxed in law school as he was in life, my father didn't worry about grades. If he hadn't studied, he just caught up, and went on. And although law school was highly competitive, the competition never affected Dad; he was disciplined and maintained good grades but did his work at his own pace. In June 1968, Dad received the highest grade in his jurisprudence course, winning an award certificate and a copy of the textbook. The following year, for earning the highest grade in poverty law, he also received an award and textbook.

Dad loved to tease and when he "got the book" he never let his friends forget it: "Who got it? Remember, it was me," he would joke. He didn't like to make negative comments but he loved sarcasm. For example, if someone got on his nerves, he would take the high road and ignore that individual. But given the chance he would make a sarcastic crack about some aspect of the person.

A highlight of law school was a course in legal research and writing taught by former New York governor Mario Cuomo. Mom recalls Dad telling her that he loved Cuomo's humorous, stimulating course. He would often stay after class to chat with the professor. Dad always said that Cuomo was his best teacher, inspiring him and guiding him to strive for excellence.

∾

The fall of 1967 was hectic, not only because of my father's new job and his return to law school, but also because of my impending arrival. During Mom's pregnancy, she and Dad had selected the name Barri for a girl, so I would have been Barri Brown. But at the last minute, they chose to name me Tracey Lyn, which, of course, I've never liked. The night before I was born, my parents were up watching election returns, thrilled that Cleveland's Carl Stokes was voted in as the first black mayor of a major American city. At midnight, Mom began getting contractions, and as she and Dad timed them, both of them were much calmer compared to when Michael was born. The drive to Brookdale Hospital was only twenty minutes, so Dad wasn't worried and Mom knew her experience could only be better than it had been in Germany, so she wasn't that worried either.

At 2 A.M., Mom decided it was time to go to the hospital, so they woke Michael and called Mere, who was to watch him, and Mom's obstetrician, Dr. Josephine English. They brought Michael to Mere's, then went on to Brookdale, where Dr. English took Mom in and dismissed Dad: "We'll let you know when we know something."

My birth was so different from Michael's. This time, the doctor asked Mom, "Have you decided what you would like me to give you?"

"Anything so I don't feel what I'm feeling."

Dr. English administered ether and Mom fell blissfully asleep until, seconds after I was born at 5 A.M., she heard Dr. English calling to Dad, "It's a girl!" I was all pink and white, but the doctor reassured my parents: "Don't worry. She'll brown up." Dad always joked that he was not sure I was really his baby because of how light I was. Eventually, this became the Birthday Story, which he created, acted out, and retold each year.

While Mom and I were at Brookdale, Dad could see me only through the nursery window because, unlike at the German hospital, no visitors were allowed in rooms with newborns. It wasn't until I was two days old and was taken home from the hospital that Dad was finally able to hold me.

In our two-bedroom apartment, I slept in a bassinet in my parents' room while Michael, two, had his own room. Dad would get home from school at about 10 P.M. and have dinner; then he'd study for a few hours. When he went to bed, at 1 or

2 A.M., my gurgles and cries kept him up, so my parents put my bassinet in the hallway and put me on a feeding schedule that fit in with Dad's schedule. Mom fed me during the day and evening and Dad gave me my 1 A.M. and 5 A.M. bottles, napping on the couch in between studying and feedings. Since he also changed me and put me back to sleep, Dad and I bonded immediately and he loved me from the beginning. Obviously, it was mutual: I've been Daddy's little girl all my life.

~

In early 1968, my father was promoted to assistant to Mr. P., the deputy executive director of the League. Dad was asked by his boss how he saw himself in ten years and answered, "As a lawyer." Because the Urban League was committed to helping its employees acquire college and advanced degrees, Dad was given permission to leave work two hours before night school began and received two days off to study for exams.

Dad founded a chapter of the Black Law Students Association (BLSA) at St. John's, although initially he was the chapter's only member. (There are BLSA chapters at most law schools.) Later, as other black students enrolled in the school, they joined the association; one new member was Dad's old friend Butch Forster.

In addition to school and work and taking care of a new baby, Dad was right alongside Mom as they began throwing their famous Christmas parties. As long as I can remember, my parents threw wonderful bashes at Christmastime, inviting a cross section of people, black and white, old friends from Brooklyn and Harlem and new friends from law school and the army. They served huge amounts of food, including ham, various dips and cheeses, and plenty of liquor to wash it all down. Dad, still incredibly skinny, loved the holiday food and ate everything from pigs' feet and chitlins to *soufflé Grand Marnier,* his portions larger than anyone else's. Everyone expressed amazement at the amounts he put away without getting fat. At another family tradition, our annual soul-food dinner in Sag Harbor, at Tommy and Audlyn Williams's house Dad would consume his usual seconds, thirds, and fourths. Then, at friends Ernie and

Ardath Hill's house, he'd have his bedtime snack: a few more pigs' feet, a little piece of chicken, and some potato salad for good measure.

On one trip out to Sag Harbor, in the summer of '69, Dad again showed that he was much less mechanically inclined than he thought he was. Mom and Dad were driving with Ernie and Ardath to attend his old friend Johnny Nailor's wedding, when they ran out of gas. They pulled off the highway, and Dad decided to siphon from a friend's car enough gas to get him to a gas station. Using a hose, he began to siphon the gas but ended up swallowing a mouthful. He missed the wedding and spent the night in the Southampton hospital instead. And as a result he had esophageal problems for the rest of his life. Although he had surgery twice, his damaged esophagus always bothered him. He sometimes had difficulty swallowing and the food would get stuck in his throat. When this happened, he would quietly get up from the table, go into the bathroom, and with the help of his finger, regurgitate the food. Amazingly he would return to the table and continue eating. It was a serious problem though and we all worried, but Dad never let it slow him down.

∼

The years Dad was in law school, 1967 through 1970, were years of turmoil in America. Radical groups and movements, including the Black Panthers, the Free Speech movement, the New Left, and the women's movement, gained large followings and polarized the nation. Dad was involved through his work at the Urban League, the Black Law Students Association, and the books he read. Recalled Dad's college roommate Tommy Meehan, "Ronnie's bookshelves were filled with books about the black experience and the problems and lack of opportunity for minorities in America. By then, Ronnie was actively involved in civil rights and social issues. And he had chosen to focus his life on making America a better place."

When the Kent State shootings occurred in May 1970, practically every campus in the country erupted in protest. At ultraconservative St. John's, student protests, including some led by black power groups, forced the administration to sit down with student leaders and listen to their demands. These demands included that the university hire more black faculty members and work to increase enrollment of black students. My father met with black power organizations and with St. John's administration and was one of the law school students who helped negotiate these demands.

As Malcolm Puryear's assistant, Dad had revamped the League's travel budget. Before Dad took over this job, travel by League employees was disorganized and costly. For example, if the regional League office in Los Angeles needed help, someone would fly from Washington to L.A. at great expense. My father placed a huge map on his office wall and marked each city that had a League office, using different-colored pins for each League representative who was currently traveling between League offices. By keeping track of where all employees were traveling, Dad could send someone who was at a nearby League office, rather than dispatching someone from Washington or New York. He saved the Urban League a considerable sum of money. He realized that staffers would not be pleased losing some of their travel but felt confident he could convince them that this new policy would benefit the Urban League. And he did; everyone who entered his office angrily left peacefully.

Dad was promoted on January 1, 1970, to Youth Specialist, Program Administration, and for six months coordinated all programs for young people, and designed and supervised the development of educational programs. Six months later, Dad received his law degree from St. John's and was again promoted at the League; he became program associate in the Consumer Protection Project, administering programs and organizing workshops for urban consumers.

Around this time, Mom and Dad decided to buy a house. They soon found one they liked, and in September 1970 we moved to 559 North Columbus Avenue in Mt. Vernon, a Westchester suburb a half hour north of New York City. We lived in a large white house with wood plank floors and a huge backyard that was set on a steep hill. My parents, whose taste was strictly seventies, wanted their place to be hip looking and decorated it accordingly. Years later, we would laugh over the decor in the Mt. Vernon house: red shag rug in the family room, black walls and fake leopard carpeting on the main stairs, and smoky mirrors in the dining room. Michael and I had an orange and yellow playroom, enhanced, my parents thought, by a flat, indoor/outdoor orange carpet.

In Mt. Vernon, I went to nursery school and Michael was in elementary school. Mom walked me one block every morning to where a little red school bus picked me up for Tiny Town Nursery School. Dad or Mom would help Michael across busy North Columbus Avenue, then he and a group of neighborhood kids would walk three blocks to Pennington Elementary School.

Dad passed the New York Bar in February 1971 and was working hard at the League with regular nine-to-five hours, so we saw a lot of him. When he arrived home in the evening, Michael and I would jump up and down, screaming to tell about our day and what we had done. We barely let him put down his briefcase before we'd leap on him. Mom was then working toward her master's in American history and, along with the late Dr. Betty Shabazz, taught teen mothers at Mt. Vernon High School. Mom would make dinner while Michael, Dad, and I played our own version of tackle football, rolling around on that red shag carpet, Dad still in his suit. Our gigantic German short-haired pointer, Thunder, with his white spots and floppy ears, rolled around with us, barking joyfully.

Finally, after about fifteen minutes of this bedlam, Dad would extricate himself and go upstairs to change. Then we'd have dinner and afterward we'd watch television together on the red shag. Traditions in our family last forever, and when I was little in Mt. Vernon, we began a tradition that continued into my adulthood: me taking naps in my parents' bed and asking for stories before I fell asleep. I am embarrassed to admit it, but this tradition ended only a short time ago, after my father died. I used to love Dad's stories. They all began "Once upon a time" and were always about me. For example, "Once upon a time, there was this girl and her name was Tracey. She had this huge kingdom, and she was the ruler of this kingdom. People would come to this kingdom because she was so nice." The stories were never deep but always had me as the brave and true leader of a city or country, either as the king, queen, prince, or princess.

On the rare occasion that Dad came home from work after Michael and I were in bed, he always came into our rooms to kiss us good night. Weekends, the family would be together, either at home or visiting friends or relatives. Most nights, Mom and Dad both put us to sleep. Michael was tucked into bed in his vast navy blue bedroom, so large it had an echo; I slept in a tiny yellow room the size of my brother's walk-in closet. If I stood up too quickly, I hit my head on the shelves above my bed. Michael and I shared our "Brady Bunch" bathroom because it opened into both our bedrooms.

It was in this bathroom that our sibling rivalry led to a terrible battle; I was five and Michael was seven. Early one school day as I was getting dressed, Michael walked up to me, wielding scissors, and cut off one of my ponytails. I let out piercing screams while he held my braid over his head in a gesture of victory. As a result, my parents wouldn't let Michael play outside or watch television, and gave him the worst spanking he'd ever had. Mom used her hand but Dad used Michael's plastic Hot Wheels tracks; my brother stayed home from school that day. My hair grew back and Michael healed, but neither of us ever forgot that particular fight.

Washington

A year after we moved to Mt. Vernon, the Urban League was altered forever with the death, on March 11, 1971, of Whitney Young. Vernon Jordan, then executive director of the United Negro College Fund, became the new director in January 1972. Dad was promoted twice: first to director of the League's Consumer Protection Project; then, at the age of thirty, he became the League's general counsel. For the next eighteen months, he reviewed the League's projects and programs to ensure that laws and regulations were properly observed. In connection with this work, Dad commuted often to Washington, D.C., and in October 1973 was named director of the National Urban League's Washington bureau.

Only three years after we had moved to Mt. Vernon, we moved again. This time to Washington, D.C. Mom and Dad bought a three-story white brick house with chocolate brown shutters at 7935 Orchid Street, in northwest D.C. Dad's new office, on Freedom Plaza at the corner of Thirteenth Street and Pennsylvania Avenue, was only a short drive away. Tommy Meehan and his wife had tried to convince my parents to live near them, in Bethesda, Maryland, just outside of D.C. But Dad wanted to raise me and Michael in the city. He had been born there and he also "wanted to be personally and directly involved in the issues being confronted . . . by African-Americans and other minorities," Tommy said.

When it was time to leave Mt. Vernon, Mom and Dad went ahead with the moving trucks, and they had the house almost set up when Michael and I arrived a few days later. We had come from New York by train, accompanied by Mere and Bop. We loved our new neighborhood, where there was little traffic and almost every house had children our age. It was a child-centered area, about 70 percent black, where we played kickball and touch football and tag and made many new friends.

I was almost six and Michael was eight. A month after we arrived in Washington, I began first grade and he entered third grade at Shepherd Elementary School, five blocks from our house. In the mornings, we sometimes had breakfast with Dad in our pumpkin-colored breakfast nook, but more often he would be getting ready for work while we ate. Weekends were different because he cooked breakfast every Saturday and Sunday: corned beef hash and eggs, or pancakes; he also made grits and scrapple for us and any of our friends who'd slept over.

Before school, Mom always did my hair, which was thick and long and difficult to manage. But once, when she was out of town for her job at the National Black Child Development Institute, Dad had to do it. He brushed and combed, trying to tame my unruly mane, but ended up making me two ponytails in the wrong places: One stuck out in front of my head, like a unicorn's horn, and the other sticking out in back. And it was the day of my second-grade class picture. Mom was so upset when she saw me that evening. As long as I can remember, Dad teased me about my hair, saying that it had begun to "crink up" from the holy water the minister used when I was christened. The day after my christening, Dad said, my hair started to curl and curl, tighter and tighter. He joked that when I had children, I had best see that no holy water was ever sprinkled on their little heads.

~

As head of the National Urban League's Washington bureau, Dad's job was to act as liaison between the organization's national programs and projects and U.S. government agencies. The Washington bureau was integral to the League's funding, lobbying, and influence on key issues such as equal opportunity. Patterned after a corporate office, the Washington office of the League became proactive as Dad worked to establish a League presence on the Hill. He wanted legislators to view the organization as a force. He testified on the Hill, drafted legislation, led letter-writing campaigns to legislators, and reenergized the League's research department, which conducted and published studies on issues that affected black Americans and the urban poor. Most of the League's research, studies, and published papers, originated in the Washington bureau.

Dad brought attention to the League's most important issues, including civil rights legislation, unemployment, subsidized housing, and access for the disabled. By reaching out and networking, Dad enlarged the League's contact base to include senators, congressmen, Cabinet heads, and White House staff. Recalled Vernon Jordan, then president and CEO of the National Urban League, "Ron was all over the place. . . . There was no place where [the League] was not present. Whether it was the Leadership Conference on Civil Rights or some labor deal, we were there, and we were there to a large extent because of [Ron's] energy and understanding of what we had to do."

Two decades before my father was appointed U.S. secretary of commerce, fifteen years before he was elected chair of the Democratic National Committee, he began to build a constituency and a reputation, and to gather a bright, loyal staff who would remain with him for the duration of his life. He delegated authority, trained his staff members to function at their highest capacity, and was always clear about his goals for himself and his subordinates. He told them, "I want everybody on Capitol Hill to know who Ron Brown is." He saw himself as a messenger and advocate for the League and for policies to advance the well-being of African-Americans and the urban poor. Dad felt that the only way to achieve these goals was to have access to decision makers.

When Dad gave testimony on the Hill before standing committees of the House and Senate, he communicated the Urban League's positions on issues that affected African-Americans, citing examples and statistics that he'd often learned just before he testified. Dad had the ability to take in information, then present it in an understandable manner to an audience. But in order to do this, he needed the best and the brightest staff, people who could brief him completely and correctly.

Dad ran the Washington office in an open-door style and was always accessible to staff members. As an administrator and manager, Dad displayed his usual even temper and calm demeanor. If he became upset or angry, it lasted only a short time and generally was directed at a situation, rather than an individual. He showed the most anger at injustice and, while he attempted to correct the injustice, the anger remained but its display was always short-lived.

My father displayed a lifelong inability to interact with his staff on negative issues. If someone had to be fired or criticized, he had someone else do it. He liked people, liked pleasing them, and was always nonconfrontational. Bob McAlpine, who worked under Dad at the League, recalled one summer day in 1976 when a young intern wore shorts to work. Dad, disturbed that she was dressed so unprofessionally, asked another staff member "to attend to her" and request that she go home and change.

Another time, he was upset because another intern brought him a sandwich without mustard. Since everyone knew not to mess with Dad's food, the young woman obviously wasn't listening when he asked her to get him a corned beef on rye with mustard. Dad went out of his office, peered at the intern, and said, "I need some mustard." She said, "Mm-hmm."

He waited a moment, then said, "Now."

"Oh, you want me to go back downstairs and get it?"

"Yes," answered Dad.

When his secretary, Lajuan Johnson, came in, Dad asked her to speak to the intern, who "doesn't know what she's supposed to do." He may have been annoyed, but he couldn't reprimand anyone.

Betty Adams, Maudine Cooper, and Tom Mitchell were assistant directors of the Washington bureau who appreciated Dad's management style and sense of humor. Betty remembered arriving at the League office on her first day of work, late, racing into the parking garage. "I zoomed past a car and took a spot it probably would have taken. As I stepped out of my car, I saw that the other driver was Ron, my new boss. I was horrified until he called out, smiling, 'Well, I have not been bogarted like that since I left New York City.' "

Later that morning, Dad held a staff meeting in his office. He was standing near his desk, talking on the phone; when Betty arrived, she sat down on a chair near the desk. When he got off the phone, he said, "That's my chair."

"Yeah," Betty thought, "and that's your sofa, that's your desk, that's your bookshelf." She didn't move. He waited a while. Finally, he said, "I sit in that chair during these meetings." So then she moved over and Dad started the meeting. "I want to welcome Betty Adams to the staff. But, I don't know," he said, laughing. "First, she bogarted me in the garage and then she tried to take my chair."

Dad's management style led to close personal relationships with his staff. When Betty was ambivalent about returning to graduate school, he encouraged her. When she walked in one day and told him that she had decided to put it off, Dad said, "I knew that."

"A while back you said you didn't know who would care for your plants while you were at school and I realized you weren't ready to go back to school," he teased, adding that she was allowing her plants to dictate her life. Ultimately, Dad's support and influence helped Betty make the decision to return to school.

Bob McAlpine, recalling his interview with my father twenty-four years ago, said that as soon as he met Dad, he knew he would end up working for him. "Just the way he stood up and extended his hand. We shook hands in the old African-American style of the 1960s. We must have flipped back and forth five or six times."

"I'm looking for someone to advance the policies, goals, and objectives of the National Urban League on the Hill," Dad told McAlpine. "Someone who enjoys interacting with people, wants to spend a lot of time with people in their offices, in the hallways." Bob's mandate, should he be hired, would be to get Dad before congressional committees so he could deliver the League's message and affect legislation.

In the middle of the interview, Dad got a call from Maudine Cooper, who had recommended Bob for the job. When he hung up, Dad said, "I've got to hire you because Maudine says don't let you leave without a commitment."

During his years as Washington bureau director, my father testified on the Hill more and more often. Bob McAlpine would learn about a scheduled hearing and notify the appropriate staff members that Dad was available to testify. Maudine Cooper prepared his testimony and finalized arrangements. Then my father would be informed and prepare for his speech. He usually received the material either the night before or very early in the morning; he would read it, make minor changes, and go before a Senate or House committee fully prepared to speak and answer questions from committee members.

After a few years as head of the Washington bureau, Dad was well established as the Urban League's voice on Capitol Hill and was more and more in demand as a speaker before national organizations. But as his prominence grew, he never forgot his mission. Bob McAlpine, who years later would make a speech about Dad, "The Making of a Star," at a National Urban League regional conference, believed that he succeeded because the issues he focused on were "issues he understood. He felt the pain, the grief and was able to see the plight of the black community in his mind."

By 1978, Dad was so sought after as a speaker by congressional committees that he was on a collision course with his boss, Vernon Jordan. Dad was a powerful leader and spokesman both in Washington and with local Urban League affiliates, occasionally appearing at fund-raisers for them as the keynote speaker. Vernon told him, "Now, I don't come to Washington messing with your turf. You shouldn't be out here with those affiliates, doing fund-raisers. I should do [their] fund-raising dinners." After that comment, my father agreed to check on Vernon's availability before he went outside the area of his direct responsibility, the Washington office.

As Dad became a more visible leader in the Urban League hierarchy, people would call him to get the official League view. The word was out that Dad was a dynamic speaker, so the affiliates often called on him to speak. Dad didn't want any negative feelings, though, so he turned down most invitations. But by then it was too late. The competition between Dad and Vernon had begun.

The Saturday Club

When we first moved to Washington, Mom and Dad developed an exciting and varied social life, participating in many events, spending time with a wide range of friends, and joining a number of organizations. Dad became part of an informal network of African-American professionals that included men such as Bob Johnson, who later founded Black Entertainment Television. According to Bob, "We black men sort of formed an ole boys network, an unofficial fraternity of people who were trying to be the best they could be. That meant going to the places where other players were going to be."

There were parties on all the holidays, including New Year's Eve galas given by the Consorts, an organization of professional African-American men. There were annual New Year's Day parties thrown by an old family friend, Evelyn Boyer, with tons of food and football games, and other family friends that we see to this day. Dad and his oldest friend, Charlene Drew Davis, "met" when they were born in the same hospital, on the same day. Charlene told me recently that she last saw my father at Evelyn's New Year's Day party in 1996. Mom was helping with the cooking and cleaning up, recalled Charlene, while Dad was helping the food disappear.

In September 1973, Dad and Mom met Vinnie and Diane Cohen at an open house for parents at Shepherd Elementary School. Vinnie, a partner at the law firm of Hogan and Hartson, was immediately attracted to a unique quality of Dad's: "He would really focus on you when he was dealing with you," Vinnie said. "He didn't look away to see if somebody else more important was around." My parents and Vinnie and his wife, Diane, had dinner together often, with Dad as the cook during the early years. "Ron has to see the food," said Diane, "even when he's not actually eating. He's like a person who thinks, 'I don't want to run out of food.' So he'd look in the refrigerator all the time."

In 1976, Mom organized the Couples Club, a group of ten couples, including Vinnie and Diane, who took turns hosting monthly events such as a boat ride, a trip to the racetrack, or a simple party. Dad and Vinnie grew to be close friends. They joked around constantly. "You're my lawyer," Dad would say.

"I ain't your lawyer," Vinnie responded.

Dad was adamant: "Yes, you're my lawyer."

The repartee went on until Vinnie said, "How am I your lawyer? Lawyers get retainers." But, in truth, he was my father's personal lawyer and, along with my mother, is the executor of Dad's will.

Dad and Vinnie joined the Saturday Club, a group of African-American men who played pickup basketball every Saturday morning. The club was great for me and Michael because all of the fathers brought along their kids to watch the games, and then we would all go out to lunch. The Saturday Club was supposed to be about basketball, but since the group was composed of achievers and superachievers, including former secretary of the army Clifford Alexander, the conversation was as important to the members as the game. Mom and the other wives loved having their Saturday mornings free, so would urge their husbands and children not to miss a session.

The club, which started a few years before Dad joined in 1975, had half- and full-court basketball and used a gym at the old Marjorie Webster College. Later, they used the gym at Rabaut Junior High School at Second and Peabody streets in Northwest. Dad, Vinnie, and the others would arrive by 9 A.M. and play or warm the bench, discussing world affairs and politics all the while.

The Saturday after Christmas 1977 stands out in my mind. Michael was twelve and I was ten. We entered the gym proudly showing off our new polyester warm-up suits, orange for me and green for him; the suits had white stripes up the sides and our names emblazoned across the back in huge white felt letters. We ran and jumped and played high-energy games of tag with the other kids, all of whom we knew either from Shepherd Elementary or from Jack and Jill.

That Saturday, we had lunch at Lum's, beloved for its video games, hamburgers, hot dogs, french fries, and free refills of root beer, a favorite of Dad's and mine. There were only two rules for these Saturday lunches: one, leave the dads alone; and two, don't get hurt because then the dads would get into trouble with the moms.

Vinnie, who'd been a college basketball star, described my father as "a good player [who] understood the game but liked to play it his way. . . . He really wanted the thrill of the game so he'd try for long jump shots." He described Dad's defense as "matador-style." As the other team's player went by, he would kind of wave at him and let him by. Vinnie recalled Dad as a good sport when he lost, because at the Saturday Club camaraderie was more important than winning.

As we got older, some of the boys, including Michael, joined in the game. I was a teenager by this time and had lost interest in the Saturday Club and in basketball. Years later, when Dad's career became more demanding, he played less frequently, and when he became secretary of commerce in 1993 he stopped completely. But he always paid his annual dues in hopes that one Saturday morning he'd be free and could drop by and shoot a few hoops.

~

No matter how busy my father was during his years at the Urban League, or at any other job, he always made time for me and Michael. When I turned seven, in 1974, we began a family ritual that continued for years, my annual birthday slumber party. On the Friday night closest to my birthday, ten friends would sleep over. Mom and Dad would take us to eat at Shakey's Pizza on East-West Highway in Bethesda, Maryland, just over the D.C. line. There, for some reason I can't fathom today, we'd scream hysterically as we watched the pizza dough being tossed. Dad would try to manage us, urging us to keep our screams down to shouts, if we could. After pizza, we'd go back to the house for cake and presents. I'd get to sit in Dad's seat at the head of the table, with my friends all around, while he brought in the cake and placed it in front of me. After I made a wish and blew out the candles, he'd cut portions and hand them out while Mom served fruit punch. My friends and I slept in the attic on the floor, covered with sleeping bags; but we didn't do much sleeping and several times during the night, Dad would have to come up to quiet us down.

The fun continued at breakfast the next morning. Some of the girls would have to leave early but my remaining guests and I would pile in Dad's car for breakfast at the McDonald's on Georgia Avenue in Northwest. Dad always tried to get our orders beforehand so we wouldn't be in such a mess when we got there; but that never worked and we were as unruly at McDonald's as we'd been the night before. Eventually, we'd get our food and quiet down. Dad would sit with us and chat, teasing us about everything from our clothes to boys. When my friends finally left, I would already be looking forward to next year's slumber party.

∾

During Dad's twelve years at the League, he always attended the annual summertime National Urban League's conventions, which were held in a different city every year. They were family affairs, so Mom, Michael, and I accompanied Dad, and while he worked Michael and I had as much fun and made as much mischief as we could. When I was ten and Michael was thirteen, during the summer of 1978, the convention was in Los Angeles.

We stayed in a two-bedroom suite and my brother and I often invited the other kids, children of Urban Leaguers, up to our room when Mom and Dad weren't there. We'd close the curtains, turn out the lights, and play hide-and-seek. We also played a game we must have been genetically predisposed to: We filled balloons with water and launched them out the window, watching with joy as they splashed on the ground or, even better, hit people. Someone found out where the balloons were coming from, because Dad marched into the room and delivered a stern lecture about how we might have hurt someone. Not once did he mention that he had done exactly the same thing at the Hotel Theresa when he was a boy.

Leaving the League

My father's last three years at the Urban League were marked by an increase in his responsibilities and new prominence as a spokesman for the national organization. In 1976, Dad was promoted to deputy executive director for programs and government affairs. At the same time, he took over Clarence Mitchell Sr.'s position as legislative chair of the Leadership Conference on Civil Rights. A coalition of more than 135 civil rights organizations that was founded by A. Philip Randolph, the Conference worked to bring about legislation on behalf of women, people of color, the disabled, and other disenfranchised groups. Mitchell, the NAACP's Washington lobbyist, had moved from legislative chair to chair of the organization. So beloved by members of Congress that they called him the 101st senator, Mitchell sponsored Dad for his new post. My father remained legislative chair of the Conference for almost a decade.

Together these two positions gave Dad new forums and more leverage. Dad continued to make the League's Washington bureau an even stronger representative of people of color, influencing federal policies to improve the lives of poor people and other groups.

Dad was expected to stand up for his community and publicly disagree with policies that were not helpful to African-Americans, be they Republican or Democratic policies. During

President Jimmy Carter's administration, Dad took issue with several policies, including one that would have removed the Civil Rights Department from the Department of Justice and set it up as a separate federal agency. Dad and other civil rights leaders concluded that if the Civil Rights Department were to be moved out of the nation's enforcement agency, civil rights violations might still be studied and perhaps uncovered but they would likely not be properly penalized. And civil rights laws would not be properly enforced. Dad and the others decided this would not benefit people of color and issued a statement opposing the change.

Another issue on which Dad differed with the Democratic administration was the Hawkins-Humphrey Full Employment Policy, which would officially be known as the Full Employment and Balanced Growth Act of 1978. This bill, which set a target of 4 percent unemployment, stated that all practical means should be used to promote maximum employment and production. Dad endorsed the legislation, but at one point the Carter administration was lukewarm toward it. It also did not have the full support of labor. Betty Adams, Dad's deputy director, suggested the Urban League Washington bureau sponsor a hearing on the legislation, bring in experts, attract the press, and draw attention to the need for the bill's passage. This attention might embarrass certain groups and officials into supporting the bill, Betty said. Dad agreed with her and met with senior White House staff, lobbying them for increased support of the legislation.

The hearing was sponsored by the National Urban League and by the Congressional Black Caucus, the Black Trade Union, and other organizations. Despite all their efforts, the bill did not pass at the time, though it finally did pass in 1978. Many of those who worked on getting this legislation passed belonged to the Black Forum, a group that Dad and others had established. It comprised staff members from the Hill, the Urban League, the NAACP, and the Leadership Conference who met regularly to discuss pending legislation that would affect African-Americans.

∾

During Dad's last years with the League, he was named staff liaison to the League's Commerce and Industry Council, his first significant interaction with corporate America. Through the years, in every position he had with the League, he had opportunities to write, to speak, and to negotiate. He gained immeasurably from his years at the League and, as he said years later at a League conference, "I grew up in the Urban League."

By 1979, Dad's interaction with the Hill had led to his developing close ties with several legislators, especially Senator Ted Kennedy. This relationship would provide an opportunity for him when, after twelve years, during which he matured from a young ex–army officer into a spokesman and policy maker for a national organization, he decided to leave the League.

When I was a page on the floor of the U.S. Senate, I sometimes sat in the Democratic cloakroom during breaks and read The Washington Post. One day, an article by reporter Alison Muscatine skewered my father in connection with his position as board chairman of the University of the District of Columbia; UDC was then mired in controversy.

I was crushed. I thought my Dad walked on water and couldn't comprehend that anyone would disagree. I decided that this reporter should not get away with writing mean things about my father, so, without saying a word to my parents, I mailed her a letter in which I countered every one of her negative statements about my father. Two days later, when Dad came home from work, the first thing he said was, "Did you write a letter to the paper?" I admitted that I had and showed him a copy. He first laughed at my gall, then said that the reporter had called and suggested he was the one who put me up to it. My letter was news to him, Dad told her, but he was pleased I'd set her straight. Dad thought my letter was funny and endearing but asked me to give him notice next time so that he wouldn't be blindsided.

I inherited this tendency to be defensive from Mom. Dad used to joke that President Clinton should create a new Cabinet position for Mom: minister of defense. She was constantly protecting and advocating for Dad, the President, and the First Lady at every opportunity. Mom would call radio and television news talk shows to give her opinions. There is a twist, however: She never gives her real name. "Hi, this is Sally and I'm a lifelong Republican. I just want you to know that we Americans don't give a hoot how much money the Clintons lost or gained in Whitewater. We care about his education reforms and the jobs he is creating, the things that make a real difference in our lives." Or, "This is Jean and I think Ron Brown is doing a great job at the Commerce Department. The trade mission he just led to Mexico resulted in a contract for a U.S. company that created one thousand jobs for U.S. workers. Isn't that what we want our Commerce Department to be doing?" Today, she continues to call C-SPAN's on-air shows defending President Clinton on every issue that gets her going.

Mom would usually tell Dad about her calls, but sometimes he'd hear it on C-SPAN himself and then ask her about it. "I had C-SPAN on at the office and I heard a woman call in who sounded just like you. Was it you, honey?" Mom would smile and say, "Darling, I have no idea what you're talking about."

SEVEN

Inside the Beltway

BY the late seventies, Dad had been at the Urban League for more than a decade and he found himself less challenged and increasingly intrigued by the strategies of Beltway politics. Much as he loved the Urban League, much as he had learned there, he was restless. Mom felt that he couldn't contribute any longer at the League and urged him to move on and find new outlets for his talents and abilities.

Dad was not certain what he wanted to do. For a while, in 1978, when Walter Washington was up for reelection as mayor of Washington, my father thought about running for that office. Mom had fifty fits, certain that public office was not the right path for my father. But Dad saw the mayoral race as an opening in D.C.'s political establishment that he felt he could fill as well as anyone, that he wanted to fill. Several friends, including Vinnie Cohen and other Saturday Club members, thought he would make a good mayor and urged him to run: He got along with people, had charisma, was young, bright, dynamic, and not a career bureaucrat.

Eventually, after much discussion with my mother and considerable attention from the press, Dad chose not to run, in part because of the number of friends he would be opposing: Walter Washington had been a college roommate of GD's; Marion Barry and Sterling Tucker, two announced candidates, were friends of Dad's. Urban League president Vernon Jordan also helped Dad's decision by informing him that League policy precluded him from remaining at his job while running for office. So the mayoral race went on without Dad, pitting Washington, Tucker, and Barry against one another. Marion Barry won, and the rest, as they say, is history.

It's just as well that my father wasn't enormously engaged during this period because Michael and I were fighting more than ever and Dad was sometimes needed at home to separate us. The physical battles began when I was twelve and Michael was fourteen. Our dog, Fudge, a brown miniature poodle, was untrained and out of control and chewing up everything in sight, including my Christmas gift from Dad, a Casio watch. I so loved that watch, with its black face, red digital numbers, and shiny black wristband, that when I saw it lying in shreds on our carpeted staircase, I became enraged. Since Michael had received the same watch for Christmas, my anger illogically led me to the conclusion that he too should have his watch destroyed. I went into his room and cut his Casio watchband to pieces and crushed the watch. When he came home and saw it in bits, he was as upset as I had been; but I never told him what I'd done. To this day, I think he believes Fudge did it.

When Dad arrived home, he fussed and fussed: "You're the ones who are supposed to be taking care of Fudge and walking her!" Michael and I began arguing over whose responsibility it was to take Fudge out. Since my brother didn't know what I'd done to his watch, the debate over who was responsible for Fudge precipitated the battle to come. Although we'd been fighting for years, Michael's superior strength kept me from hitting back. This time, after he punched me in the face and chest, I leaped on him and began swinging. Then I chased him around the house with a hammer. He screamed and hollered and Dad came running. He grabbed and held me, and took the hammer out of my clenched fist. After that incident, my brother and I had a dozen or more violent battles during which Dad would literally have to pull us off each other as we were rolling around on the floor to restrain us.

After each incident, I would get a stern talking-to but my brother got spanked. Dad never spanked me in my entire life. And while Mom got annoyed by our constant fighting, my father would become deeply upset. "How can you treat each other this way?" he would ask. "You have a wonderful opportunity to share and be close. How can you treat this opportunity so violently?" Since he, like Mom, was an only child, he never understood how Michael and I got under each other's skin, how we knew exactly how to push each other's buttons. During these years, I wouldn't and couldn't concede that even though I hated Michael, I also loved him.

~

When Dad wasn't refereeing battles at home, he was fighting his own battles in the political arena. Having given up the idea of running for D.C. mayor, he sought another political post, as President Carter's appointment to head the Equal Employment Opportunity Commission (EEOC). His competition for this position was Eleanor Holmes Norton, then chair of the New York City Human Rights Commission. At the time, there was talk inside the Beltway that the President planned to merge the EEOC and the Office of Civil Rights. Washington insiders buzzed about the possible merger, which eventually did occur. In New York, the women's community was supporting Eleanor. Dad didn't campaign or lobby for Carter's nomination for the post because he felt that those who knew him would agree that he would make an effective EEOC chair. Of course, he felt conflicted because he knew Eleanor, liked and respected her, and, in a certain way, supported her. No matter who got the position, having an African-American serve at that level would be a "first." There had been very few black people serving on the national level at the pleasure of a president: only one African-American in the Johnson administration, Robert Weaver, and Bob Brown and Arthur Fletcher in the Nixon administration. Now, in the Carter administration, for the first time, African-Americans in large numbers were being appointed to key posts.

My father wanted to be part of this historic involvement of blacks in federal government. As Alexis Herman, now U.S. secretary of labor, told me, "Your daddy was always about history."

Eleanor got the nomination, not my father. According to Betty Adams and other insiders, she won because key black leaders, most of whom were men, said: "Let's take care of Eleanor now." She had paid her dues, contributed to the civil rights movement, and wanted to be EEOC head. These leaders did not keep secret that they saw no future for Eleanor beyond this, and expected her later years to be devoted to lecturing and writing. Whereas for Dad they saw a limitless future; he was young, up and coming, and the world was his oyster. They would find a better niche for him. President Carter, influenced by Vernon Jordan and other black leaders, appointed Eleanor.

My father was deeply disappointed when he learned from Vernon, who had "an inside track into the Carter administration," that he would not be given the assignment. Vernon said he had told Dad, "Ron, listen, don't get your hopes up." My father was dejected but immediately called Eleanor to congratulate her. That's how he handled letdowns; he just moved on. Said Betty Adams, "Vernon initially was supportive of Ron until he learned that Eleanor was campaigning for that position. Thinking, 'It's her time' and 'Ron will be okay,' he supported Eleanor. . . . Beyond their professional relationships, [Ron and Vernon] were each other's 'main man.' . . . Because he and Vernon had been so close for so many years, that added to the disappointment."

Vernon Jordan has never acknowledged the existence of a rift between him and Dad. "Whatever the disagreement was, it was not of sufficient import to cause some fracture in our relationship," Vernon said, adding that when he recommended Eleanor over Dad, he was doing what he thought was best for both of them. After that incident, my father and Vernon grew apart because Dad felt disillusioned by his friend and mentor.

Eleanor Holmes Norton, who was one of my professors when I attended Boston College, did not retire to lecturing and writing. She was elected to Congress in 1990 and remains the congresswoman from the District of Columbia to this day. She recalled that when she and Dad competed for EEOC chair, it was difficult because they shared the same circle of friends, and were old friends themselves. Eleanor had met Mom during the sixties before she met Dad. She and my mother belonged to Liaison, a New York City–based club of young black women who did community work. Eleanor, who recalled the EEOC competition as "very spirited," made it clear that she and Dad had long since gotten over their competition, that there were no bad feelings between them. "Ron Brown was head-to-toe a class act," she said. "There were several friendly, funny phone conversations during that period in which we talked about our friendship and about this contest and how crazy it was. When I was announced, Ron called and said, 'You are a tough momma—and I have called to say congratulations.' How often do you see that in this town?"

After this disappointment, Dad actively sought a new job. In the meantime, at the Urban League, he worked hand in hand with Eleanor on important congressional reforms; their goal was to get Congress to enact legislation that would remove congressional exemptions to certain critical private sector laws. Since 1935, Congress had exempted itself from twelve laws that affected all Americans, most importantly the Occupational Safety and Health Act and the National Labor Relations Act. It took fifteen years for Congress to act on this legislation. The Congressional Accountability Act finally passed in 1995 and went into effect on January 23, 1996, only a short time before my father's death. It had taken sixty years for the U.S. Congress to operate under the same workplace laws as the rest of the United States.

∾

In the autumn of 1979, Stephen Smith, manager of the presidential campaign of his brother-in-law, Senator Edward Kennedy, called Dad. He asked if my father would come to work for the Kennedy campaign. Although working for a campaign offers no job security, this was a way out of the Urban League and Dad was interested. Generally, it was Mom who would push Dad to leave what he was doing and move on and take the next step; when they talked about law school versus staying in the army, she had argued for law school. Now, Mom encouraged Dad to take Kennedy's offer. Vernon Jordan had named John Jacob as the League's executive vice president, making him Vernon's heir, so Mom felt that Dad's ascendancy at the League was over. She viewed the Kennedy campaign as a way for my father to become involved in Democratic politics, something that interested him. And even though it was a risky move for a man with a wife, two children, and a mortgage, since campaigns are well known for telling employees, "Sorry, buddy, but we just ran out of money," Mom urged Dad to go for it.

"I really pushed him to take that," she said, "because he had been [with the League] twelve years and thought a long time whether he should jump out and take this very risky position."

When Dad decided to resign from the League in December 1979, he called Bob McAlpine, the Urban League's congressional liaison, and said, "I'm leaving to be codirector of the Kennedy campaign." Bob was speechless. He could not imagine the League without my father. Or my father without the League. Recalled McAlpine, "I was mad. . . . I always thought if Ron got [a different job] he would take me and Maudine [Cooper] with him. Because he had made us feel that we were part of his inner circle, his team. We were like part of a wheel."

To Dad's great satisfaction, Maudine Cooper was named as his replacement as director of the Washington bureau; and when she left to work for D.C. mayor Marion Barry, Bob McAlpine took over in that position.

At Christmas dinner that year, Dad announced to Mere and Bop, "I'm going to work for the Kennedy campaign for president."

Bop asked in a concerned voice, "You are leaving your job to work on a campaign?" Meaning, how can you take such an insecure job?

"Yes, Bop," said Dad to his father-in-law. "I think it's going to be a good opportunity for me." Mom explained that it would be a challenge and that, in keeping with Dad's maxim never to leave a job until he had another lined up, it was a way for him to resign from the Urban League. Bop calmed down, and once again there was harmony at the table.

Just after Christmas, Mom, Michael, and I helped Dad pack

up his office at the Washington bureau. There was no going-away party and the national Urban League did nothing special for my father after his twelve years of service. Dad never showed his disappointment about this, but for the rest of his life, whenever he would see someone receiving a gold watch or being honored at a retirement party, he would say, "I never got mine." He was kidding around, but underneath, he felt hurt. He didn't dwell on it, though.

For years, Dad maintained contact with Bob and Maudine and other League staffers and they always had access to him, no matter where he was. If they needed advice, Dad helped if he could. Bob called Dad a few years later, when my father was in private practice. "Mac, what's up?" Dad asked, having long since nicknamed McAlpine. Could Dad help McAlpine's future son-in-law, Clyde Robinson, get an interview for a summer associate position at the law firm? Dad arranged it and so began a long association between my father and Clyde Robinson. Clyde was hired as a summer associate and became a full-time lawyer at the firm after he graduated from law school. In 1994, Clyde went to work for Dad at the Commerce Department.

Senator Kennedy

Senator Kennedy knew my father from watching him testify before congressional committees. When Dad went to work for Kennedy, most of his friends and coworkers at the League were supportive, seeing it as a chance for an African-American to work at the highest levels of electoral politics, a presidential campaign.

In a statement issued at the time, Stephen Smith described my father's duties: "He [will] be involved in policy decisions regarding issues and political strategy. . . . He [will] have the primary responsibility for coordination and leadership of Senator Kennedy's effort to attract strong support from black Americans." In other words, Kennedy was telling Dad, "Help make policy, but get me the black vote." But Dad's duties on the campaign evolved over time, changing according to what was needed. His initial responsibilities were civil rights issues, civil rights legislation, and economic development for urban areas. Said Senator Kennedy, "He was the new leader representing the younger voice in terms of . . . urban issues. He had ideas of his own . . . and was a compelling, articulate figure."

Dad first worked on outreach, concentrating on securing the black vote for Kennedy. In a memo to Stephen Smith and Paul Kirk, then political director of Kennedy '80, Dad wrote: "Although Carter does have considerable support, particularly among black political leaders, that support is soft and not based on the comparative records of the two candidates. Carter support is almost exclusively related to the powers of incumbency, which appear to be more important to blacks who have just begun to get access."

To increase black voters' support for Kennedy, Dad suggested, the campaign should focus on black churches and black ministers, utilize black news outlets, develop a piece emphasizing Kennedy's relationships with black personalities, publicize Kennedy's presence at conventions of black organizations, and, finally, create an event at which the candidate could speak directly to black leadership. Some of the early criticism leveled against Kennedy stressed that he had "no black at the top." That was no longer a problem, Dad wrote in this memo.

As early as 1980, the political strategies my father would use later in his career were evident when he wrote that "*all* sectors of the campaign, from advance, to press, to scheduling, [must] understand that mistakes and insensitivity toward blacks can make the best of plans worthless." Years later, when Dad led the coordinated campaign for the Democratic presidential election in '92, he would continue to stress that, in a campaign, everyone and everything must work together.

～

Carl Wagner, who would become a close adviser to Dad, recalled their first meeting in 1980 at Kennedy campaign headquarters on Twenty-second Street. Dad was memorable, Carl said, because his optimism never wavered even though the campaign was in trouble, lacked funds, and showed poor returns in the Iowa and New Hampshire primaries. Campaign workers were unpaid and burned out, but my father seemed to be always at peace. His "glass was always half full. And there was a generosity of spirit to him," Carl recalled.

When one staffer on Kennedy's Senate Judiciary Committee, Antonia Hernandez, had an argument with another staff member, she went into the hall to cool off. She saw my father, told him what had happened, then laughed as he gave her the Ron Brown solution to dealing with life.

"You know," he'd say, "we're all like turtles with really thick shells. In fact, we have two shells. An external shell that allows things to roll off our back. And an internal shell that gives us a lot of time to think about how we're going to get even."

As the campaign ran into more and more difficulty, Dad took on additional responsibility and was made deputy campaign manager. There were serious divisions in the Democratic party as a result of Kennedy's bid for the presidential nomination, with many people certain that this challenge to Carter would weaken the party. And although Kennedy was winning primaries in a number of states, he needed California if he was to have a chance at the nomination. Carl Wagner sent Dad to run the California campaign during the late winter/early spring of 1980. Having watched Dad getting along with everyone at campaign headquarters, Carl believed my father would be able to bring harmony to the various groups and factions in California. Dad was resistant when Carl sent campaign staffer Oren Teicher along to be Dad's director of organization; he thought he could handle California on his own. But within days, Dad grew to love Oren and admitted how much he was needed to handle the day-to-day details. As Carl explained, "You can't spend your day handling Walter Shorenstein and Willie Brown and Cesar Chavez and worry about the structure of your campaign. [Ron] didn't like that kind of stuff anyway. He got bored by the routine of organizational work. . . . I wouldn't hire Ron Brown to be chief of staff at the State Department, but I would hire him to be the secretary of state."

Finally, the California campaign ran out of money. But my father would not admit defeat and devised a creative method to get free publicity for Kennedy. The campaign could not afford to produce ads and buy expensive airtime, so Dad had the ads produced inexpensively, then aired them in low-cost markets. He followed this with a series of press conferences in major cities during which he'd screen the ads for the press and deliver an enthusiastic speech about the campaign. As a result, the ads got free play because they were aired on local news broadcasts in conjunction with coverage of the press conferences. My father shared the tapes with Kennedy campaign managers in other states, including John Sasso in New Jersey, who would become Dukakis's campaign manager in '88, and Paul Tully in Ohio, who would later become Dad's partner in leading the national Democratic party. Dad's creativity and ingenuity in California were so successful that he became known nationally. Because so many people saw Dad on television, all over California, some asked Carl Wagner if my father was seeking political office himself. "For weeks after . . . I would get calls from people asking whether he was running for governor. But that's the way [Ron] was all his life, a leader in the most fundamental sense. He could define goals, build a team of people to [carry out] the goals, and then lead that team."

Shortly before the 1980 Democratic convention, Teddy Kennedy turned his campaign around with a dynamic speech at Washington's American University and won a number of primaries, including California. But at the huge, contentious convention in Madison Square Garden, in August, there was such dissension within the party that no one was certain whether Kennedy would even come up on the stage. Some Democrats were so disgusted, they walked out of the Garden.

Alexis Herman, who would later work closely with Dad for more than a decade, recalled the divisiveness in the black community during this campaign. Alexis had been on the Carter side in the primary campaign while Dad believed he could best serve the Democrats, and African-Americans, by working for Kennedy. He viewed Kennedy as more progressive, since the senator worked much more closely than did Carter with the progressive wing of the party and with labor unions, women, Hispanics, and African-Americans. The black community was divided between Carter and Kennedy and there were strong, negative feelings between the two camps. "It was the typical 'field Negroes' and 'house Negroes,' " said Alexis. "We [Carter supporters] were in the system, we were status quo, so we were house Negroes. The other side [Kennedy supporters] were into 'we got to have change. We got to have movement.' "

The convention was unusually dramatic, with the two factions locked in battle and Jesse Jackson "running all around trying to mediate," Alexis recalled. Finally, representatives of the two groups held a "healing meeting" at which they discussed their differences and agreed that no matter who won, they would not lose sight of the goals of the Democratic party and of African-Americans. Alexis recalled that she and Dad were in total agreement that there could be no split in the black community. They agreed to work together with both the presidential nominee and the losing candidate to avoid bitterness and personal attacks.

This was the first time Alexis and Dad worked closely and it was a sign of their future relationship that plans worked out, negotiations went smoothly, and the two of them succeeded at what they set their minds to. Eventually, all the tensions in the factions dissolved as the Democrats joined to support their nominee, Jimmy Carter. After the convention, although Dad liked Carter, he had little relationship with the Carter campaign, most likely because of his close association with Senator Kennedy.

~

Right in the midst of difficult negotiations at the 1980 convention, my father was additionally troubled by his teenage daughter. That summer, I was twelve, going on thirteen, and about to enter eighth grade. I was at Camp Atwater, in Massachusetts, where both my mother and Nan had been campers when they were young. Just before the convention, Mom, Mere, and Bop drove to camp to pick me up and take me to New York for the event. Earlier, I had exchanged good-byes with my boyfriend, who was just so cute that we kissed for a while. When Mom saw me she sucked her teeth and shook her head, embarrassed in front of the camp administrators, whom she'd known all her life, that her daughter's neck was covered in hickeys. Mere and Bop didn't say anything, so I was hoping they didn't know what the little red marks were.

When we arrived in New York and went up to our hotel

room, Dad looked at me in horror. "What is that crap on your neck!?" he shouted. "Who was sucking on your neck!?" Here I was, the young woman he'd planned to introduce with pride to Senator Kennedy and his campaign coworkers. Instead he sent me out to buy shirts with stand-up collars and banished me to spend the rest of the summer in Sag Harbor; it was viewed as a safe haven to my parents since they knew so many families there and had visited so often. Dad didn't want me back in camp, and because he was mired in convention duties, we couldn't really have a long talk about the hickeys.

Dad appeared shocked that I was already involved with boys. Only a year earlier, I had been a sweet little girl of eleven, graduating from sixth grade at Shepherd Elementary School. I remember being upset about a graduation dance planned for the sixth graders because I didn't know how to slow dance. Dad showed me how, putting his arms around me and imparting crucial advice: "When you slow dance with a boy, you have to stick your butt way out so there's no contact in this area." Following Dad's advice, I went to the dance and did all my slow dancing with my butt stuck way out—as Michael, who was at the dance as an eighth-grade chaperon, laughingly told the family afterward.

Only a year after my father had taught me how to avoid bodily contact, I was out getting hickeys. After the convention, I left for Sag Harbor and, of course, met another boy. He was much older and this marked the beginning of my "boy problem." I always dated older guys, Dad was always angry about it, so I consistently lied to him through my teenage years and even into my early twenties.

~

Although Kennedy had not received his party's nomination for president, he was still chair of the powerful Senate Judiciary Committee. On September 16, 1980, he appointed Dad to the Judiciary Committee's top position, chief counsel, effective at the end of the year; until then, Dad would be a consultant to the committee. As chief counsel, my father was to succeed Stephen Breyer, formerly a Harvard Law professor and currently a U.S. Supreme Court justice. It was a prestigious appointment

Dad's graduation
picture from
Middlebury College,
1962

Mom and Dad,
August 11, 1962

Dad in ROTC at Middlebury with Nan and GD, 1962

Dad and Michael in Germany, 1965

Mom, Dad, Michael, and me, Christmas, 1967

Dad holding "his favorite girl," 1968

Mom and Dad, Barbados, 1971

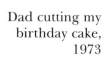
Dad cutting my
birthday cake,
1973

Dad and me at a
costume party,
circa 1984

Dad, GD, and Chip, Bressler, Pennsylvania, 1987

The three of us in Utah, January 1989

My law school graduation—Dad "hooded" me, 1992

Michael and Tami's wedding, October 5, 1991. *From left:* Mere, me,
Tami, Michael, Mom, Dad, and Nan

Dad in his "Ultimate Chill"
mode—the last family vacation,
California, 1995

My parents at a friend's wedding

Dad at the hospital with Morgan and Ryan

The headstone

and a wonderful opportunity. The Senate Judiciary Committee dealt with civil and criminal justice, the operation of courts and appointment of federal judges, constitutional protections, and other legal matters as well as certain economic issues.

During the period that Dad was a consultant to the committee, Teddy Kennedy recommended him to become a Fellow at the Institute of Politics, part of Harvard's JFK School of Government. My father was interviewed by Jonathan Moore, director of the Institute of Politics, and Charles Greenleaf, director of the Fellows Program, and several students. He had a good rapport with the students and educators, who noted that he preferred not to focus his teaching on black or minority politics but instead to cover the broader arena of electoral politics.

Dad was selected to be one of the six Fellows for the fall 1980 semester. As a Fellow, he was required to be on campus several times a week, so he needed permanent housing for the semester. At first, he stayed in the Kennedy suite, temporary guest quarters that had been John F. Kennedy's rooms when he was a Harvard undergraduate, but my father needed something more permanent. He looked at a few off-campus apartments, but he wanted to live on campus in order to have greater contact with his students and found a vacancy at Leverett House, an undergraduate dormitory. Each time he came to Harvard, Dad stayed in the large, top-floor suite with its views of the Charles River.

Dad taught a seminar composed of law, business, and education graduate students, and some undergraduate students. They met every Wednesday for lectures and guest speakers on "Decision '80," the name Dad had given to his course. With his students, my father traced the presidential selection process from the primaries through the conventions, and analyzed general election races as they developed. He arranged guest speakers such as Peter Edelman and Paul Kirk of the Kennedy '80 campaign, journalist Tom Oliphant, and syndicated columnist Jules Witcover. He also researched and wrote a paper, "Reform of the Primary System," which was published by Harvard University in a compendium containing papers written by Fellows. In addition to leading his Wednesday group, my father attended and organized panel discussions for the Institute's weekly suppers and lunches, including one on the media and another on campaign managers.

When his fellowship was over, in December of 1980, my father maintained his ties to the Institute. Theresa Donovan, then a staff person, now director of the Fellows Program at the Institute, recalled that Dad continued to be involved. In 1985, he was named as a new member of the Institute's Senior Advisory Committee and, along with other board members, including Jacqueline Onassis and Teddy Kennedy, attended regular meetings. One year later, my father was elected chairman of the board and remained in that position for a decade, until his death.

Even when Dad became chair of the Democratic National Committee and then U.S. secretary of commerce, he made certain to attend the board's twice-yearly meetings with staff, faculty (Fellows), and students. He read the briefing materials before board meetings, he knew the students' names, asked questions, and gave encouragement and praise to the students. Senator Kennedy recalled that when Dad was in Cambridge for these board meetings, he would often stay overnight in the dorms and eat in the student dining hall. "He never missed a meeting. Here is a Cabinet official, and no matter how busy or what his travels were he always made every one of those meetings."

~

When Ronald Reagan took office in January 1981, Kennedy, as expected, lost his chairmanship of the Senate Judiciary Committee. Dad worked as minority counsel to the committee for about a month, then became a staff member for Kennedy from February through April 1981. He worked on budget strategies with Kennedy, who was one of twelve senators who opposed Reagan's economic policy. At staff meetings, Kennedy recalled that after going around the room to get everyone's input, Dad, in the fewest words, could "cut to the bone" and state what had to be done.

In April 1981, my father's involvement with Democratic party politics, begun two years earlier in the Kennedy campaign, solidified as he was named general counsel to the Democratic National Committee. It would be years until the next presidential election but the party was putting its cast of characters in place. Dad was also contemplating going into private practice, since the Democrats had lost both the White House and the Senate. Socially, he spent a lot of time with Teddy Kennedy and played tennis often at the senator's house in McLean, Virginia. Dad was not a gracious loser, recalled Kennedy. He would throw tantrums and hurl his racket when he lost.

Dad also had tantrums when he played golf. Rick Greenfield, Michael's best friend, recalled his golf games with Dad, Michael, and Michael's college roommate, David Miller, and the many times Dad would become so frustrated with himself that he would whip his club over his head and throw it. Then he'd walk off, never looking back to see if the club was broken. If it wasn't, Michael would pick it up and put it back in Dad's golf bag. Rick recalled an incident at the Rock Creek Park golf course in D.C., years later. After a series of satisfying strokes, and a wonderful drive, Dad was relaxed and calm. But something went wrong and he ended up missing and missing, getting angrier and angrier. Said Rick, "Mike and I looked at each other because we knew what was gonna happen. There were tons of golfers around, waiting for him to finish so they could play the hole. He was so mad he swung his club as hard as possible, trying to hit the ball like a drive. He missed. Then he picked it up, tried to hit it like a baseball and missed again. He had swung so hard that his spikes dug into the green and ripped it up. Mike and I just walked quietly on to the next hole."

UDC

During the seventies, Dad got to know Marion Barry, the popular but beleaguered mayor of Washington. They first met at a 1974 Leadership Conference on Civil Rights. During his first campaign for mayor, Barry sought out Dad's approval as head of the Urban League Washington bureau because he wanted the support of the more traditional African-American organizations.

Said Barry, "When I was with SNCC [Student Nonviolent

Coordinating Committee], I thought the Urban League and NAACP were a bunch of fuddy-duddies." Barry soon discovered that Dad was more progressive than the average Urban Leaguer. Later, during Barry's legal troubles, my father was sympathetic and supportive, rather than judgmental; he never bad-mouthed Barry, even after he was convicted and jailed. After Barry was released, he ran for and won a seat on the D.C. city council. When Barry decided to run again for mayor, my parents hosted a "meet and greet" for him.

Earlier in their friendship Barry had appointed my father to chair the board of trustees of the University of the District of Columbia (UDC). The university had been involved in turmoil and controversy for years and needed someone with diplomacy and negotiating skills to help it out of its difficulties. Dad knew the job would be challenging, perhaps impossible, but he agreed to do it even though, in his own words, the university was "a thicket." Vinnie Cohen urged him on. He thought Dad should be UDC chair because "he could soothe [all] those egos. Because if you could soothe Jesse Jackson, you could soothe anybody."

UDC was comprised of three colleges merged into one university: Federal City College, D.C. Teachers College, and Washington Technical Institute. When Dad became chairman of the board, the three entities each had factions, and their infighting had weakened the newly forged university. Washington Technical, a junior college, felt it was a stepchild to the university. The teachers college was traditionally where members of Washington's African-American community were educated to become teachers. And Federal City had open enrollment, so many from the other schools looked down at the students who were admitted here.

The university's board had not stabilized the factions at the university. Neither had they promoted it properly or succeeded in fund-raising efforts. Dad's mandate was to create unity between the three institutions and secure more credibility for the fledgling university. No easy task. He worked to dismantle the three separate administrations and create a new, unified one; he focused on streamlining the new university, making it more productive. Most important, he tried to give students a sense of hope and security, to insist that theirs was not a second-class university but a first-rate academic institution. Eventually, by bringing all of his business and political contacts to bear on UDC, Dad managed to turn it around.

Dad's work with UDC led to his first experience with bad press (and my letter-writing escapade). Bob Greene, the newly appointed university president, had a budget that incorrectly included budgets from other departments, so that when a university department ordered carpeting, it appeared as if he had ordered the carpeting. Greene was an experienced educator with some good ideas who, according to Marion Barry, "got caught up in flowers and office expenses and stuff that was personal." The president was accused of lavish and unnecessary spending on personal items.

My father had tried damage control to little effect as UDC continued to make headlines. In 1985 when Dad resigned as chair of the UDC board, he told Marion Barry, "Thank God, my prison term, my sentence, is over."

Just ahead were the most productive years of Dad's life, a time when he would revitalize the Democratic party and help shape the history of our country.

I can picture Dad at his happiest. He is floating on a raft in a pool, eyes closed as he drifts to sleep with the warm sun shining on his sun-browned skin. A Pacific Ocean breeze caresses him as sweet soul music plays in the background.

It was August 1995, and we were in Coronado, California, on what would be our last family vacation. U.S. Ambassador to Switzerland M. Larry Lawrence and his wife, Shelia Davis Lawrence, had loaned us their beautiful home.

Mom was on a lounge chair reading, as Michael, his wife, Tami, and I slid silently into the pool, water guns in hand. As we moved toward Dad, we debated whether we should ruin what he always called his "ultimate chill." Our decision made, with a thumbs up and smiles all around, we took aim and blasted him. Three streams of cold water hit him and he awoke abruptly, cursed us, and rolled off the raft, diving below the water's surface. Seconds later, I felt him near me, trying to pull me under. Then he surfaced, splashing wildly, completely drenching us as we screamed with laughter.

Our family vacations were mandatory; we all had to partake no matter where we were or what we were doing; and even during the last decade or so, when Dad's career demanded so much of him, he still set aside time for these vacations. Although some of my friends found it strange that we vacationed together even after Michael and I were grown, our family always had so much fun together that, to us, it was a natural. Over the years, our home had become increasingly open to friends and colleagues, but we rarely let outsiders into the cocoon that was our family vacation. One time, when I was a student at Boston College, I told my parents and brother that I wanted to bring a girl-friend with us on a planned family vacation in the Caribbean. Mom, Dad, and Michael turned and stared at me. Was I daring to challenge our entrenched routine? "If you really want to bring her you can," Dad said. "But what if she doesn't play tennis? Does she like to just read? Will she want to go into town and shop when we just want to chill?"

Realizing I didn't know the answers and fearing she might not fit in, I decided not to invite my friend.

Only people Michael or I were seriously involved with were allowed to pierce our vacation cocoon. On that last vacation in Coronado, we had a huge family debate about whether I could invite my boyfriend. Since he and I weren't that serious but my family liked him, we compromised and he was allowed to come along—for one day only.

Six years ago, after Michael and Tami were married, we planned a family vacation in the Dominican Republic. We had to prepare Tami because it would be her first Brown family vacation. We all sat down and told Tami the routines we always followed. In the mornings, Mom took an aerobics class while Michael, Dad, and I played tennis. During the afternoon, Mom and I chilled in the pool or on the beach while Dad and Michael played golf. On certain days, we would visit Altos de Chavon, a nearby artists' village. Most evenings, we had a leisurely dinner in the gazebo by the ocean, then chilled on the porch, tropical drinks in hand. During dinner, only casual discussions about politics were permitted. Once in a while, we'd break our nighttime routine and take in the cabaret show at the resort. Since Tami was well acquainted with our family's idiosyncrasies and, as she understood the rules, Dad pronounced her one of us; thereafter our family vacations were enjoyed by five Browns, rather than four.

~ *EIGHT* ~

Rainmaker

DURING the eighties, my father came into his own and spent the years between 1981 and 1989 developing into an influential and prominent legal and political strategist inside the Beltway. In July 1981, Dad joined the Washington law firm of Patton, Boggs and Blow as a partner. (George Blow has since retired and the firm is now Patton Boggs.) Dad first met Tommy Boggs at a reception. They liked each other so much immediately that even during that first conversation they discussed the possibility of Dad's going to work at the firm. Patton, Boggs and Blow had deep roots in Washington: Tommy's father had been Louisiana congressman Hale Boggs. After Hale Boggs's death in a plane crash, Tommy's mother, Lindy, won her husband's seat in Congress. Tommy's sister is Cokie Roberts, the well-known radio and television reporter.

Dad was attracted by the idea of joining this powerhouse firm; many of its partners and associates had formerly been members of Congress or held other public offices. When he returned home from the reception, he told Mom he had a feeling that he might end up joining Patton Boggs. And it would be another first on his list. Said Dad, "I will be the first *bluck*."

He was joking around but he was pleased. At the time, black partners were rare at top Washington law firms. Dad was enthusiastic that he would finally get a chance to use his legal training more fully than he had as general counsel of the National Urban League. Also, he would be a corporate lawyer, which meant a larger income.

As Vinnie Cohen remembered of Dad's decision to join the firm, "We were all poor kids, out of New York, so we never really had a taste of any big money. Ron was smart enough to know that you . . . have to come to the real world, to the private sector . . . for big money." Vinnie suggested Dad avoid another public service position: Public service had too many rules, "too many fools," Vinnie said.

Shortly before he joined Patton, Boggs and Blow my father also became involved in national Democratic politics, a result of his work with the Kennedy campaign a year earlier. His work on Senator Kennedy's behalf made him well known in Democratic circles; some of his campaign ideas had been imitated by other Democratic strategists, and this led to his being invited to work for the Democratic National Committee. In 1981, he was appointed both deputy chairman and general counsel of the DNC by Chuck Manatt, who was then party chair. At that time, Dad and Yolanda Caraway, then administrative assistant to the DNC political director, Ann Lewis, were the only black DNC staff members. A short time later, however, after he began working at the law firm, he had to cut back and so resigned as general counsel. But he continued as deputy chair through 1985.

As deputy chair, Dad was charged with overseeing the Commission on Presidential Nominations. The commission, gearing up for the convention in 1984, looked for ways to improve the selection of delegates and the procedures for nominating presidential candidates. Lynn Cutler, a DNC official, said Dad was the one person she could count on to ensure that women would be represented at the party's policy-making level. When she worked on an intergovernmental issues commission the following year, Lynn asked Dad to intervene after a reluctant DNC official refused to appoint key Democratic women to the panel. Dad succeeded in convincing party leaders to appoint such high-profile women as Madeline Kunin and Ann Richards to the commission.

Meanwhile, at Patton, Boggs and Blow, Dad had to go through a difficult interview process during which he met and talked with every partner. Tommy worked behind the scenes to convince some of the skeptics that a Democrat such as Dad, with connections on the Hill, would be helpful, even though the White House and Senate were both Republican controlled.

After he was hired, the first thing Dad learned was the formula, called the attribution system, that determined his income. He discovered that income depended on bringing in new clients and that each partner received a proportionate share of the firm's profits determined by the amount billed to "their" clients. Since winning clients took time, including evenings and weekends, Dad worked longer hours than ever before. He worked twelve to fourteen hours a day, either in his office or at outside meetings with clients and potential clients. And he traveled so often that Tommy Boggs nicknamed him "out-of-town Brown." Said Boggs, "He loved to travel. And he loved to laugh. You know, he was a guy you could pick up the phone and call and have a good time with or talk seriously with. I used to call him and tell him jokes about Clinton. And then he'd tell them to Clinton."

During his years at the law firm, Dad earned in the high six figures, but while he enjoyed the lifestyle, money was never his prime motivator. In later years, he would give up his lucrative practice and, against the advice of many, return to public service. What drove Dad was his inner need to excel, to rise to the top, to add to his List of Firsts. He was also motivated by a desire to contribute to society, to justify his existence.

At Patton, Boggs and Blow, Dad at first shared a secretary with Joe Reeder, who was a partner at the firm and then went on to become undersecretary of the army, because office policy mandated that secretaries be shared if possible. But it didn't work out because that particular secretary showed more allegiance toward Reeder and did Dad's work only unwillingly. The firm's management committee approved Dad's request for his own secretary and on March 15, 1982, he hired Barbara Schmitz. It was a good choice. Barbara was highly competent and loyal and remained my father's secretary from that day on, accompanying Dad to the Department of Commerce. He trusted her completely.

My father's function as a lobbyist was to convince corporations and other entities that he could serve them better than any other public interest lawyer. He called on his wide network of friends and associates to make contacts, then did research on potential clients. He followed up with calls and meetings until a client was signed. Then his job was to gain access for the client to the appropriate government agencies and elected officials. He helped clients draft legislative strategies, outlining which members of Congress were potential allies or opponents, and how to gain access to the allies. While no lobbyist can guarantee that a client's objective will be achieved, a successful lobbyist promises that a client will at least be heard by the decision makers.

Dad was innately suited for this work; his charm and wit attracted clients, while his determination and diligence got them results. Over the years, he was successful both at bringing in new business and at being an effective lobbyist. Because of the attribution system of payment, Dad's income increased each year that he worked at Patton, Boggs and Blow and he continued to earn money even when he became an inactive partner during his years as chairman of the Democratic National Committee.

Unicorn Lane

Shortly after Dad went to work as a lobbyist, my parents decided they needed more space, both for entertaining clients and for their two feuding and fussing teenagers. Since Dad had not earned a regular salary since he left the Urban League, Mom and Dad first thought that enlarging the Orchid Street house where we'd lived since 1973 would be more practical for them than buying a new house. Then, one day in late 1981, Mom was driving to her office at the National Council of Negro Women when she saw a development on Unicorn Lane, in northwest D.C., called Chatsworth. She went inside the model house, and fell in love. Part of what attracted her was that the houses were brand-new and didn't need any renovations or fixing up. "You can move in, sit down, and eat your dinner," said Mom. She called Dad immediately and he liked the house, also, so they decided to buy it.

Unfortunately, we couldn't sell our old house immediately, so my parents had to pay two mortgages until it sold, a year later. But we were all excited in February of 1982 when we moved into our brand-new five-story brownstone. I loved it despite the fact that, for some time, it contained nothing more than curtains, carpeting, and beds. Mom and Dad bought themselves a king-sized bed and put their old double bed in the guest room; our old living-room furniture went into the library. Michael and I had our bedroom furniture but, basically, the house was empty. The living room, dining room, and my parents' bedroom remained unfurnished. Dad was grumpy about this; he was working long, hard hours to pay two mortgages and live in a house with very little furniture. But a couple of days after we moved in, he cheered up as he realized what a beautiful, comfortable house it was and how well it suited our family.

Unicorn Lane was perfect for entertaining clients. For about a year, my parents entertained in the family room and the library, or had cookouts on the back patio. Occasionally, the empty rooms worked in our favor. Mom was president of the Washington, D.C., Jack and Jill chapter then and held a meeting in our empty living room, with all 120 members present; they sat on folding chairs, lined up in rows. A party we gave in 1983 to celebrate my brother's high school graduation was wonderful because there was so much room for dancing.

My parents were often invited to dinner parties to meet clients of other partners of the law firm. Mom recalled the first formal dinner she and Dad went to, given by partner Jim Patton, and his wife, Mary, at their home in Great Falls, Virginia. My parents were the only people of color at the dinner. The Pattons' house was beautiful, filled with large, abstract canvases by a black painter, Sam Gilliam.

In 1984, Mom and Dad hosted their first formal dinner party for a guest of honor, the Haitian ambassador to the United States, and his wife. Also there were Tommy and Barbara

Boggs, Jim and Mary Patton, Bill and Sondra Raspberry (Bill writes an op-ed column for *The Washington Post*), Congressman Charles Rangel and his wife, Alma, and Dorothy Ford, wife of then-Congressman Harold Ford. My mother tried to keep it simple and did all the cooking herself, except for dessert. By this time, she enjoyed cooking and cooked the meals for the formal dinners she and Dad gave during his law firm years.

That first dinner began with a clear soup, served in delicate porcelain bowls that my parents had brought back from Hong Kong. The main course was Rock Cornish hens, wild rice, and vegetables, and for dessert Mom had bought fruit tarts from a gourmet bakery. Two people helped out, one in the kitchen and a man serving drinks.

The day of the dinner, Mom was so nervous that she told Dad to come home early.

"Since the guests are not due until seven," asked Dad, "why do I have to be home so early?"

"I want you home because I want to make sure everything is right," she said, adding that she needed him with her, she was that nervous. Dad came home at five, and Mom kept him busy getting ice, setting out the liquor, doing the place cards. He placed the ambassador's wife next to him and the ambassador next to Mom. This first dinner went well, and after a short time Mom, no longer nervous, hosted elaborate dinners and parties with style and élan. She always rose to the occasion, with delicious food, good wines, and beautiful table settings.

Teenagers

Michael and I were teenagers while Dad was at the law firm and, as always, a considerable amount of his time and energy was devoted to us. He encouraged us to get involved in sports and was most supportive of girls playing sports. We talked often about how boys and girls, men and women, are socialized, with Dad deploring that boys are brought up playing only with trucks, being active, and doing sports, while girls are taught to play house. My father told me it was important in life to learn how to be competitive, something one learns playing sports, rather than in school. "When you're in the workforce, having that competitive edge will make a difference," he said.

As a result of my parents' encouragement, I joined my high school's swim team; I attended a private school in the center of Washington, National Cathedral. We had evening meets and, although he was super busy, Dad managed to see most of them. He'd come straight from work, usually arriving after the meet had begun. He would look for me and I would look for him. I couldn't relax until I found him in the stands, making a thumbs-up signal, which meant, "Go, girl!" Afterward, he would drive me home and we'd analyze the meet and how I and my teammates had performed.

Dad also attended most of Michael's basketball games when my brother was on the team at his school, Mackin Catholic. Michael said he couldn't play until he saw Dad in the stands, so he'd wait and watch until Dad walked in, usually only moments before the game started. Then everyone would say, "Mike, your father's here, your father's here." Dad would give Michael a wink as if to say, "Okay, I'm here. Let's go." Only after he got that wink did Michael feel ready to play.

∽

When my father started at Patton, Boggs and Blow, Tommy shared some of his clients, including Burlington Industries, so Dad had work immediately. But the first client he got on his own was Lamont Godwin, the contracting officer at the Department of Labor during the Carter administration. At the end of 1980, when President Reagan was elected and the Democrats lost their majority in the Senate, Godwin was among those accused of "contract irregularities" by Republicans. They claimed that some Democrats were rushing to award Labor Department contracts to certain organizations before the administration changed parties. Dad's client acknowledged that he had given contracts to minority and civil rights groups while he still had the power to do so; he believed that such contracts would not be awarded by the Republicans then coming into power. Ultimately, no formal charges were filed against Godwin.

Dad's first foreign client was the Electronics Industry of Japan, a consortium of eleven companies whose concern was copyright legislation. Tommy Boggs believed that because of Dad's experience on Capitol Hill and with the Senate Judiciary Committee, his help would be invaluable. Dad was to accompany Tommy to Japan to meet with representatives of the consortium, but shortly before they were to leave Tommy remembered, as he told Dad, that "some Japanese are still very prejudiced against blacks." Dad was unconcerned and he went to Japan with Tommy as planned, with successful results. The client loved Dad and he represented the Electronics Industry of Japan for more than a decade.

The Japanese electronics companies were suffering from a terrible image in this country. During the eighties, Japan had been accused of dumping its products on U.S. markets without allowing a reciprocal relationship; we imported their cars and televisions, but they wouldn't accept our products. As a result, many Americans perceived Japanese companies as the bad guys. The electronics consortium wanted to get out the message that trade relations between the two countries were as much the responsibility of the U.S. government as Japan's, since both countries had signed the trade agreements.

Dad, aware that the Japanese electronics firms had corporate offices as well as manufacturing plants within the United States, thus providing jobs for U.S. workers, used that information to improve the image of his clients. As a lobbyist, he also took a unique approach and actually tried to negotiate a better trade agreement between the United States and Japan. Usually, lobbyists advocate for their clients, but years before he became secretary of commerce, my father tried to negotiate arrangements that would also help American interests. "If there's a way we can also work it out for the betterment of the American worker and American business," he said, "that's what I want to do."

The Japanese consortium also had a problem with the entertainment industry's efforts to have Capitol Hill pass a tax on blank audiocassettes, videotapes, and compact discs; this was an effort to prevent illegal taping of films and music. Dad tried to find a constituency in the United States willing to listen to foreign manufacturers who didn't want to pass a taping tax on to consumers. He organized the VCR Companies Coalition, comprising dealers who sold tapes, owners of record stores and bookstores, and consumer groups who opposed the tax. Under Dad's direction, the coalition lobbied the Hill, making the point that the tax would interfere with individuals' rights to tape materials. He was successful. Instead of a tax, a compromise was negotiated with regard to videotapes: Chips were inserted in prerecorded tapes to prevent large-scale copying.

During that time, Dad's main adversary was Jack Valenti, president of the Motion Pictures Association of America, who believed that videocassette recorders would undermine Hollywood, whose films were a major U.S. export. But Dad argued that VCRs would make people buy more movies and that a new technology often doesn't get rid of an old technology but rather provides more ways to market it. Jack Valenti has since admitted that he was wrong and Dad was right. (Dad loved being right.) VCRs have tripled the revenues of the movie industry, generating billions of dollars for U.S. businesses.

~

In 1983, Dad signed a major client, the government of Haiti. Although Haiti was ruled by a dictator, Baby Doc Duvalier, Dad didn't think the Haitian people should be punished because of their leadership. He also felt this way about Cuba and other third world countries that are denied aid because the U.S. government disapproves of their government. Most Haitians live in poverty. By turning our backs on them, we were allowing millions of men, women, and children to suffer, according to my father.

Some of those most adamantly anti-Haiti were members of the Congressional Black Caucus who had human rights objections to that country's government. Dad met with these members of Congress to explain "commercial diplomacy," a new concept of his. If we were not commercially engaged with a country, he said, then we could not bring about change in that country. Almost a decade before he became commerce secretary, he organized a "trade mission" to Haiti, to introduce black-owned American businesses to the Haitian marketplace.

Through this period, however, Dad was somewhat ambivalent about Haiti. He had been hired to help the government of Haiti secure aid from the United States. At the time, the Duvalier government received no foreign aid from the United States because of its human rights violations. My father's first step was to advise Haitian representatives that their country had to change its human rights policies so that the United States would perceive it differently and be more inclined to grant aid. Barbara Schmitz recalled him saying that he felt responsible for making the Haitian government understand it must make concrete changes in order to have Haiti perceived differently.

As a client, Haiti took up much of Dad's time as well as that of other lawyers at Patton, Boggs and Blow. The firm, therefore, billed a considerable number of hours and was paid an ample fee; the government of Haiti kept money for retainer fees in banks outside of Haiti and the law firm was paid from those funds. Dad earned quite a bit for this work and that increased his ambivalence. He encountered considerable resistance when he tried to arrange meetings between Haiti's foreign minister or its U.S. ambassador and legislators in both houses on the Hill. Often, Congressman Charles Rangel, a good friend, would be the only legislator willing to see the Haitian representatives. As usual, Dad focused on the positive: "At least Charlie [Rangel] is seeing us. That's a big step," Dad would tell us. Prior to this, Haiti and its representatives were persona non grata anywhere on Capitol Hill.

During my holiday breaks in high school, Dad sometimes took me with him to Haiti. While Dad was busy meeting with his clients, I would pal around with the children of some of the businesspeople he knew there. Once, after I'd spent a day with my new friends, I rushed back to our hotel room in Port-au-Prince to tell Dad what I'd seen that day. I had been swimming over at a friend's home in a neighborhood called Petionville. When I noticed some movement nearby, I saw, not more than ten feet away, a family of about eight in a tiny shack that appeared to be without water and electricity. Outside the shack, I saw a woman bathing in a tin pan with a small boy. They were both really skinny. I stood there staring at them until they noticed me. Then I went inside and pointed out the people to the girl I was visiting. She said, "They've been there for years. Don't be scared. They won't bother you." Then she dove back into the pool. I stood there with my mouth hanging open.

"Didn't she care that people lived like that?" I asked my dad. Dad thought over his response, then told me to sit down.

"Tra, I know this is hard, but unfortunately it's not that much different at home. I don't think that your friends didn't care, but they've grown used to their own comfort level. There will always be haves and have-nots. Not everyone is wealthy, or even middle class. Most people struggle. Most people are poor. It's not fair and it's not right. That's why it's so important to share and give back to the community you come from. So that everyone has a chance at a better life."

In 1986, Dad ended his representation of the Haitian government when Duvalier was exiled for his human rights violations; after that, he maintained only a few Haitian business clients. In terms of his career, snaring Haiti as a client was both an achievement and an albatross. There is no doubt that my father was affected by the criticism he received for his work with Haiti. And his representation of Haiti would haunt him when he was nominated for secretary of commerce.

～

Dad had many other clients, including the city and county of Denver; MCI; Wayne County, Michigan; the government of Zaire; Household Finance; and American Express. Dad shared his workload on Denver, which had major environmental concerns, with Elliot Laws, a young associate whom he mentored. Elliot was an environmental lawyer. Denver mayor Federico Peña, currently U.S. secretary of energy, and my father were credited with a new, high-tech airport that was built in Denver.

Elliot recalled the day he received a call from Penny Farthing, of counsel at Patton Boggs. "We're pitching Denver and Ron needs to talk to you," she said. Elliot walked into Dad's office and Dad said, "Tell me what's going on with the Clean Air Act." Elliot did his best to explain this very complicated subject to my father. Then he remained in the office as Dad talked on the phone with Mayor Peña, discussing in detail environmental issues, the Clean Air Act, and the benefits the city of Denver would gain if it hired Patton, Boggs and Blow.

Said Elliot, "I sat there with my mouth open. There was no

way that what he talked about was based on what I had told him. This man obviously knew environmental law."

Wrong. Dad had taken what Elliot had told him and made it sound different, even better. His ability to digest material and then restate it eloquently always surprised people at first.

Peña was proactive about the environment and had traveled to Washington numerous times to testify on the Hill about clean air bills. During the course of Dad's work with Denver, a crisis erupted when representatives of other cities charged that Denver's clean air policies were excessive, even stronger than those set by the U.S. Conference of Mayors and the National League of Cities. The other cities did not want to be perceived as less concerned about the environment than Peña and were afraid that his enthusiasm would show them up. My father agreed to negotiate between Peña and the representatives of the other cities.

On their way to this meeting, Dad asked Elliot Laws, "What's happening?" Denver needed its stringent ozone regulations, Elliot told him, because of its carbon-monoxide "brown cloud" problem and its unique location in the Rockies. At the meeting, Dad defused the tension by explaining that Peña's goal was not inconsistent with goals of the other cities. He had mastered what Elliot told him in the car and presented it so that everyone emerged, if not in total agreement, then at least agreeable to further discussion.

The 1984 Presidential Campaign

In 1984, Jesse Jackson was recruiting people to serve on the Advisory Committee for his presidential campaign. Since Dad was active in both Democratic party politics and civil rights, he was approached.

After thinking it over, he declined. To many Democrats, Jackson's run for the nomination was threatening, "just too hot," as Marion Barry recalled. Very few establishment black politicians supported Jackson; most of the big-city mayors did not support him. Although Dad chose not to be Jackson's campaign manager, he never tolerated or allowed anyone to denigrate Jackson's rights. Although he was not in the majority position, Dad viewed the reverend as an essential member of the Democratic party, not only because of racial factors but also because of his views on policy issues.

At the '84 convention, Walter Mondale was chosen as the party's candidate. At the request of Paul Kirk, newly elected DNC chair, Dad agreed to attend Democratic policy meetings. He also attended midyear policy-setting Democratic conventions and meetings of the Business Council, which raised funds for the party.

~

When the convention ended, our family went to Sag Harbor for a short vacation. Dad drove Mom, me, and my two best friends, Wren Mosee and Karla Fitzgerald, in his black Jaguar, which he loved. I was sixteen at the time. Mom and Dad were in the front and I was in the back with my friends; we all fell asleep except Wren, who was stuck in the middle between me and Karla. She stayed up, looking in the rearview mirror, watching Dad's eyes; he was exhausted from the convention and his lids were heavy. She told me that at one point, he was just about falling asleep. Wren tapped Dad on the shoulder and said, "Excuse me, Mr. Brown, your eyes were closed for a second there. Do you want me to drive?"

He dismissed her, saying, "Do you think I'm gonna let you drive my car, Wren Mosee? You've only been driving for about two minutes." She stayed awake, watching Dad for the entire trip until we finally got onto the Long Island Expressway and everyone awakened. Somehow, with a lot of luck, Dad finally got us to Sag Harbor.

My junior and senior years in high school tested my relationship with Mom and Dad. Although we were close and got along well, I consistently lied to them about boys. I justified my lying by blaming my parents for never liking anyone I dated. Dad especially disliked the older ones. During my teenage years and early twenties, if I dated someone he approved of, he would say, "Why play the field? He's a good guy and there's no reason for you to be dating five hundred people." If he didn't approve of the boy, which was usually the case, he'd advise the opposite:

"You ought to be playing the field and enjoying your youth." It was easier for me to lie. I would meet my boyfriends outside the house, at a party or a Jack and Jill function, keeping my love life a secret from Mom and Dad.

The one time I recall dating a guy that my parents actually liked was during my junior year of high school. Even then, I had to test Dad's limits. Since my boyfriend, who was a senior at my school, was from Chicago, he boarded on campus. As a result, he spent a lot of time with my family instead of in his lonely dorm room. One night, my father came home after a long business trip abroad. Normally, when he returned from a trip, I would be there, excited, to greet him at the door. This time, I was out with my boyfriend and Dad was disappointed I wasn't home. When we got back, Dad heard us pull up and went running outside to see me. But at the curb, he saw us kissing furiously on the front seat; Dad retreated in embarrassment and went into the house so we wouldn't see him. When I finally went in, Dad told me he'd seen this boy slobbering all over me. We were both uncomfortable. I also felt bad that Dad, all eager for our reunion, had seen me that way. Of course, Dad later made it into a joke and teased me about it. "I came up to the car and saw that Negro slobbering all over you," he'd say. ("Negro" is often used like a term of endearment within the black community.) While Dad saw him slobbering on me, he didn't seem to recognize that I was slobbering back. He obviously had difficulty accepting that I was becoming a woman.

Also, whenever I got into any trouble, whether it was a school prank or related to boys, Dad blamed the other person. Even though he considered me to be strong-willed and a leader, as opposed to a follower, when it came to trouble, he could never blame me. He placed responsibility on either bad influences or older guys. I was Daddy's little girl and could do no wrong. I was his sweet angel.

But Dad's little angel kept getting into trouble. That same year, I was suspended from school when I cut classes one day to watch videos with my boyfriend in his dorm room. When a friend warned me that one of the deans had discovered I wasn't in class and was looking for me, I drove home immediately.

When Mom and Dad were called up to school, Dad's refrain was, "Not my child." Asked Dad, "Did you see Tracey in the dorm? Did you see her leaving the dorm?"

When the dean answered no to both questions, Dad saw that as proof that I had done nothing wrong. He was particularly offended when Dean Goodrich attempted to tell him how I should be punished at home. "Don't tell me how to raise my child," Dad said. Dad was most angry that I had lied—I had told my parents that girls were allowed in the boys' dorms—which put him in a situation where he didn't know what he was talking about. When the dean said I was off campus, he told her it was okay to be in the dorms. It wasn't until he understood the truth and that I had lied that he became furious. In the end, the school suspended my boyfriend for skipping classes and me for that and for being off campus. At home, I was grounded for weeks.

Later in life, Dad would tease me about how I could just sit and lie to his face without blinking. And I would respond, "I'm sorry, Daddy, but I was a teenager."

During senior year, I participated through my high school for the third time in Model United Nations. Of course, since the regional conference always takes place in a Washington hotel, my friends and I saw it as an opportunity to have fun. For three years in a row, the conference was held at the Sheraton, where Dad would reserve a suite for ten of us. This year was different. We threw a party that got extremely out of control and noisy. People were drunk and eventually some boys started fighting, so hotel security came up to our suite to break it up. Since many of us were minors and none of us were actually registered in the hotel, the security guards called the police.

The police let all the white kids go but held the black kids. We black kids who were being held were angry the authorities had let the white kids go. But we were more frightened than anything. What would happen to us? Would we be arrested? Finally, the hotel decided to throw us out but, as we tried to pack, we were informed that we couldn't take anything from the room until the person to whom the room was registered—my father—arrived. At two in the morning, I wasn't about to call him, so we all left and slept in a friend's room at George Washington University.

In the morning, I called Dad, told him I was in trouble, and asked him to come to the hotel. As I saw his black Jaguar pull up, I was so terrified I felt like throwing up. Dad talked with the hotel security people and convinced them not to file an official report. Everyone went home, and Dad never said a word to any of their parents. They were so grateful to him that each one wrote him a letter, thanking him for his help and, most of all, for not being a snitch. Not one of my friends ever forgot what he did.

After I graduated from high school, just before I was to leave for Boston College, Dad and I went shopping at the Giant supermarket, in Silver Spring, Maryland. We found ourselves in the aisle with birth control products. Dad pointed to the contraceptive gels and said, "Are you sure you don't need anything in this area because I don't want to hear nothing about nothing." Speak now if you need birth control, he was saying. I said, "No, I'm fine." On the drive home, we discussed birth control pills and whether he thought I should go on them. He suggested I call our family doctor and, if he thought it was okay, to start on the pills. I followed his advice and it worked out. So, unlike most girls, I had the birth control conversation with my father, rather than with my mother.

∼

Between 1984 and '86, Dad played less of a role at the DNC as his law practice took up more and more of his time. But his heart was still in politics. He told me he thought the values and positions of the Democratic party were superior to those of the Republicans. The Democratic platform could make life better for people; it gave working men and women more of an opportunity to get ahead. The Republican party, he said, focused on the rich and powerful. Working for the Democrats was one way for Dad to affect the world. And since he knew firsthand the power of the executive branch from his interactions with various administrations during his years at the Urban League, it was essential for the Democrats to control the White House. Sometime in 1985 or '86, he had a conversation about politics and his goals with Yolanda Caraway, who had left the DNC to work for Jackson's Rainbow Coalition, and told her, "The one thing I really want to do is be chairman."

In 1986, Dad was appointed by Paul Kirk to chair the DNC Task Force on Voting Rights. Dad emphasized voter registration and was given a mandate to maximize voter participation in the next presidential election. A scandal erupted at this time when Democrats discovered that Republicans had suppressed minority registration and minority voting in several key races. There was even a smoking gun: a memo from a Republican field director to the Republican political director stating that if they kept sending out their message on postcards, they could keep the minority registration and vote down, and win the election. These illegal postcards, sent to targeted groups, told recipients that it was against the law for them to vote without registering if they had moved. These intimidation tactics frightened people and stopped them from registering and voting. My father, along with Christine Varney, a lawyer who helped found the National Lawyers Council, and others, succeeded in getting a court order against the Republican party in the state of New Jersey; the decree forbid them from mailing any more of the postcards. Dad then joined the National Lawyers Council, which would act as a law firm for the Democratic party.

The '88 Convention

In conversations with friends such as Ken Chenault, now president of American Express, Dad admitted that he was somewhat restless at the law firm. As Dad and Ken grew to be good friends, they often discussed options, the future, and, specifically, Dad's political future. Said Ken, "I got the feeling that Ron was saying, 'If they take these chains off, I can do an unbelievable amount.' If he didn't have to do his law practice, he could do great things."

When Jesse Jackson was organizing his campaign for another try for the Democratic presidential nomination, he asked Dad to be his campaign manager. Alexis Herman, then an adviser to Jackson's campaign, recalled, "I remember a fund-raiser . . .

me, Percy Sutton [President of Inner City Broadcasting and Chair of Jackson '88], and Jackson. We decided we were going to corner him and sit him down, tell him why he had to do this. We went upstairs to a bedroom, and Percy was very persuasive, and Jesse was very eloquent. . . . I could see your daddy's eyes light up: 'Well, maybe this isn't such a crazy idea here,' but at the same time trying to be practical about it. He obviously caught the enthusiasm of the meeting. I can remember him saying he would want to pull together the right team if he did this. And he said he wanted to think about it." Dad ended up turning it down, unwilling to give up his practice at Patton, Boggs and Blow, which he would have had to do to run the campaign.

Dad didn't think Jackson could win but agreed with his platform. As he said, "I believe in his message and in helping people. And Jesse is the only one who is really out there speaking for black folks."

Dad recruited others to work for Jackson and took many middle-of-the-night calls, for which Jackson is famous. If the phone rang at 3 A.M., you knew it was Jackson on the other end. The reverend didn't mind waking up the folks he was calling—or their spouses. Dad would say, "Hey, Jesse, what's happening, man? Oh, is that where you are? You just landed in L.A.? Oh great." Or if Mom answered and said my father was in the shower, Jesse would say he'd wait. You couldn't escape him if he wanted you, Dad said. After one such call, he told Mom, "God, it was Jesse. He wanted me to call someone and ask him such and such." Then they went back to sleep, accepting nocturnal calls as part of the demanding Jackson personality.

Then, in May, Jackson asked Dad to be his convention manager. Dad was at a meeting at a private club in Washington—Pisces—with several of Jesse's advisers, including San Francisco mayor Willie Brown, then speaker of the California assembly; Congresswoman Maxine Waters, then a California state representative; and Howard University historian Dr. Ron Walters. Jackson walked around the table and put his hands on my father's shoulder. "It's now time for the first team to be on the field. Ron, I need you to run the convention for me." Dad said he needed time to think.

After discussion with Mom—there was always discussion with Mom—and with Tommy Boggs and a couple of other partners, Dad told Jesse yes. It would help Jackson and also get Dad back into the action at the DNC. At Patton, Boggs and Blow, my father made the necessary adjustments to his schedule. Tommy thought that working with Jackson would help Dad's party credentials and help the firm's pull on the Hill. Recalled Boggs, "Ron asked what he could do for me and I said I only wanted one thing: Jesse's parking space at the convention."

By taking the job of convention manager, Dad would be center stage at the convention, working to protect Jackson's interests, ensuring that he retained leverage with the other Democratic candidates. Dad discussed his feelings with Ken Chenault, telling him, "I want to have an impact and an influence both in being supportive of the Jackson candidacy but also making sure there's something after this convention for blacks in politics. We can't be [a] totally fractured [party]." He told me and Michael that he had to get involved because he saw "a train wreck about to happen."

Dad's role caused some dissension in the Jackson ranks; his campaign workers had toiled for months and then, near the end, Dad strolled in, as some viewed it, and took charge. My father was aware that some people thought him not radical enough to represent Jackson, while others viewed his alliance with the reverend as proof that he was radical. When Dad agreed to be Jesse's convention manager, his ultimate goal was to prevent a fracture in the Democratic party that might arise from a divisive convention; he also tried to avert a split in the African-American community.

Jesse Jackson always had a price at which his goodwill could be purchased by the Democratic party: He forced the party to treat African-Americans with complete and total dignity. And Dad went along with that 100 percent and wanted Jackson's message to reach the American people.

Finally, being Jesse's convention manager would give my father an opening; he would be able to demonstrate his qualifications and would gain recognition and prominence, thus putting him in place should he decide to run for party chair. Dad could also have achieved this by working for the Dukakis team. But it was important for him to identify with the progressive African-American candidate, and in keeping with the way he'd handled his career so far he chose the less conventional path: Jesse Jackson.

Dad spent most of his time between May and July working in Jackson's Washington office or the Atlanta headquarters. The toughest moment occurred after Jackson had submitted the required papers so that he could be considered for the position of vice president and then Dukakis chose his running mate without informing Jackson. Members of the Dukakis campaign later claimed they had tried to contact Jesse but were unsuccessful. Jackson received the news from Yolanda Caraway, Rainbow Coalition chief of staff, who called him after she heard it on the news. Jackson was furious and the stage was set for a tense confrontation at the convention.

Dad truly came into his own at the 1988 Democratic convention. He rose to a whole new level, negotiating and brokering deals between the Jackson and Dukakis camps. At this point, Michael was working for Dad on the Jackson campaign and was in Atlanta with him. I had a summer job working at the convention for the DNC's finance committee. So Michael and I were in Atlanta, with Dad, for four weeks before the actual convention.

My father's job at the convention was to make certain that Jackson's issues were considered by the Democratic party; Jackson's issues included increasing voter registration, controlling defense spending, funding education programs, using education as a way out of the poverty cycle, increasing the minimum wage, and bringing about statehood for the District of Columbia. The seven million votes the reverend brought with him would only go to the party's nominee if the concerns of those voters were included in the party platform. The tension between Dukakis and Jackson was enormous, and Dad's role was to negotiate a deal that would satisfy both candidates and their campaign staffs.

It ended up with four people in a hotel room: Dad, Jackson,

Dukakis, and Dukakis's campaign manager, Paul Brountas. Jackson wanted his demands satisfied before he would publicly support Dukakis as the presidential nominee. Dad told us that he imagined Dukakis thinking, "Why do I have to even listen to this guy?"

Said Marion Barry, "It had to do with power, who was going to do what, who was going to control what, who was going to say what when. . . . After it was clear that Dukakis was going to win the nomination, his people started playing hardball. . . . They were arrogant."

Finally, Dad negotiated an agreement. Jackson got Wednesday and Dukakis got Thursday. On Wednesday, the reverend could deliver his speech in prime time and have as many floor passes as he wanted. His delegates could take every seat in the Omni Convention Center; they could hold signs and have their slogans on the scoreboard. But on Thursday, when Dukakis was nominated, there could not be a single Jackson sign; it had to be all Dukakis. And the two men would hold a press conference earlier in the week, on Tuesday, to announce that Jackson was endorsing Dukakis.

The '88 convention was a high point in my father's life. Our whole family was there. "I've decided to take Pops to the convention," Dad told us and brought GD to Atlanta even though he was ill. He sat him in the Jackson box next to Rosa Parks. GD had heart problems and he moved slowly, but he wanted to be there, to see Dad in action. He was so joyful and so proud of Dad. Recalled Charles Rangel, "I saw Bill Brown standing in the lobby stopping people, saying, 'My name's Bill Brown and that's my son in there!' I couldn't believe it! I mean this wasn't any yokel from the South coming up to see his big-shot son; this *was* a big shot. In black society, Bill Brown was a big shot, and here he was so proud of his boy."

Mom was in Atlanta for the convention also, but her experience was not so positive. Our family had a three-bedroom suite at the Atlanta Marriott Marquis, which Jackson's staff quickly took over. They turned one bedroom into an office, removing all the furniture and replacing it with computers, desks, and phones. Michael and I shared a room with two double beds next to Mom and Dad's room. Since my brother and I were working, we were happily involved and busy, but Mom was not. She arrived in our suite to find none of us there and a dozen people she didn't know running around. Fortunately, our good friends Kent and Carmen Amos were there also; Kent was working at the convention, but Carmen was free, so she and Mom spent most of their time together.

One morning my father awakened very early to meet Jackson; one of the reverend's strategies was to be "the people's candidate," so he chose to arrive at the convention by bus rather than limo. Dad was going to meet him somewhere in the middle of Georgia and ride with him so they could talk. Mom woke up also when Dad did because he tended to involve others in his morning routine, asking questions such as, "Where is my blue shirt?" After he left, Mom wandered through the suite. Later, when Maxine Waters and Willie Brown came in, they ignored Mom and went about their business without acknowledging her. Said Mom, "To this day they probably don't even remember. . . . I felt totally brushed off. Totally useless."

Of course, she wasn't angry at Dad. She had missed the last two conventions and wanted to be in Atlanta. But she hadn't realized how isolated she would feel because Dad was either on the podium or backstage and wasn't available at all. However, Mom's sense of humor got her through, as always.

"Carmen and I turned it into a real joke," she said. "We used to talk about it all the time, how we were treated like ninetieth-class citizens, how we went to all the free corporate cocktails parties to entertain ourselves. . . . Later, Ronnie used to laugh about it, too. He said, 'Really I didn't know that. I didn't know you guys did that.' "

Michael

After my brother worked at the convention with Dad, Dad got him an interview with the Dukakis campaign and he was hired to work from August through Election Day as one of seventy young men and women on the advance team. They would travel around the country, building crowds for Dukakis's appearances. At the same time, Michael was accepted into the spring class of Delaware Law School and would begin classes in January 1989.

One of Dad's proudest moments came at UCLA's Pauly Pavilion, where Dukakis was scheduled to deliver a prime-time speech. Michael and others on the advance team had packed the pavilion with a crowd of twenty thousand. When the candidate was late, Michael took action. He went onstage and got the audience going, doing "the wave." He wanted to fire them up so no one left before the candidate arrived.

After Michael had spent fifteen minutes on the mike, which felt like hours to him, Dukakis arrived. Unknown to Michael, Dad was standing on the side of the stage, watching. When Michael finally got off the stage, he saw Dad.

As Michael explained, "He's got his hand on his face in disbelief that his son was up on the podium rallying the roof off this crowd. [It was] Election Eve and we thought Dukakis had a chance and everyone was excited. I walk off the stage and he hugs me and kisses me. He said he pointed me out to Dukakis and the campaign people and said, 'That's my son over there. That's my son. You know, that's Michael.' He was just that proud. And he hugged me again."

Leaving the Ladder Down

At the end of a decade at Patton, Boggs and Blow, Dad had become one of the firm's leading rainmakers, constantly bringing in new business. For most of his years at the firm, he was happy, although he particularly disliked disputes involving money. Inevitably, in a partnership, such arguments arise. According to Tommy, when that happened, Dad would rock up and down on his toes as if he couldn't wait to get away. But he would argue on his own behalf if he felt something unfair was going on.

Although Dad was the first black partner at Patton, Boggs and Blow, the firm did hire other black attorneys. Elliot Laws, the second black lawyer hired, said that as my father became the firm's number three rainmaker, after Tommy Boggs and Jim Patton, you could just see the wonder on the faces of many of the white attorneys: "Who's this black guy who has the third or fourth highest billings in the firm?"

Dad's success was a factor in the hiring of black attorneys by Patton, Boggs and Blow, and other Washington law firms. If Dad could do it, the thinking went, then other bright attorneys who happened to be black should not be held back by race. Dad spent time at the law firm mentoring Elliot Laws, Florence Prioleau, Clyde Robinson, and some other young associates. Dad included Elliot in much of his work and, when he began spending most of his time at the DNC, left Elliot in charge of many of his clients.

Changing Direction

Dad liked being a lobbyist but "was more interested in public policy and politics than making money, or practicing law for that matter," recalled Tim May, a lawyer at Patton, Boggs and Blow. In 1988, after seven years at the firm, having successfully navigated both the '84 and '88 conventions, Dad decided it was time for a change. He chose to return to public service, his real love, and, being Dad, he picked a most difficult arena. But again, being Dad, he succeeded.

After the convention and election and Dad's impressive work as political negotiator, a number of the party faithful questioned him: Had he considered running for chair of the Democratic National Committee? It had been almost a decade since my father first went to work for Senator Kennedy's campaign, his first real involvement with national Democratic politics. He had spent the eighties working for the DNC in various capacities; he understood how the party mechanisms worked and he believed he could make a difference. When he was asked about running for chair, that was all the encouragement he needed. The answer was yes. He had finally decided to say out loud what he really wanted to do. It was 1988, and Dad's greatest challenges and accomplishments were just ahead.

When I was younger, I would sometimes set goals that I didn't always meet. Dad was not happy with what he called my lack of stick-to-it-iveness and would talk to me about it often. In the fourth grade, when I was eight, I decided to learn to play the string bass. Many of my friends were studying instruments and my music teacher at Shepherd Elementary encouraged me to try the bass. I asked Dad to buy me one so that I could begin practicing.

"Tra," he said, "if I were to buy you a string bass, you would play it for five seconds and then forget all about it. Besides, a string bass is bigger than you are."

"I'm strong, Daddy," I countered. "I know I can handle it. And I will stick to it."

He would not budge on this issue but finally compromised, suggesting that I pick a more reasonable instrument for my size, one that I'd be more likely to follow through on. When I chose the clarinet, Dad got excited about it. "Maybe you have musical talent, after all," he said. He went to a music store and, with great care, selected a clarinet. He brought it home to me in a beautiful, velvet-lined box. I was thrilled and started blowing into it right away.

I began weekly lessons. I polished my clarinet daily and, for three weeks, practiced like my life depended on it. Then, one day, Dad noticed that my clarinet box had been sitting in the same place for a while. "What happened?" he asked me. "Daddy, the clarinet is boring. And besides, my dance recital is coming up and I have to rehearse."

He shook his head and said, "Tra, you have no stick-to-it-iveness. I bought you that beautiful clarinet and you quit already. You'll never be the best at the clarinet or dancing or anything else if you give up after only a few weeks. You have to stick to the goals that you set for yourself."

I listened carefully to this important lesson. I nodded and smiled, then said, "Okay, Daddy, but will you get me some new leotards for my dance class?"

~ NINE ~

DNC Chair

ALMOST everyone Dad was close to is certain that he or she was absolutely first to hear about Dad's plan to run for chair of the Democratic National Committee. Tommy Boggs said Dad talked to him about it during the 1988 convention, on the night that then-governor Clinton gave his famously lengthy speech nominating Michael Dukakis as that year's Democratic presidential candidate.

Tommy said he broached the subject with Dad, saying, "You ought to run for chairman."

"Why would I want to be chairman if there's a Democratic president?" asked Dad, certain that Dukakis would win. With a Democratic president, who would be the party's spokesman, the party chairman would have little real power; plus, the president appoints the chair so there would be no election for that position. Tommy told my father that Dukakis didn't have a chance, but Dad, always optimistic, believed the Democrats would take the White House.

Mom recalled that Dad first brought up running for chair some time in late 1988. "What do you think if I ran for chairman of the party?" he asked her. She dismissed the idea because she didn't believe he was serious. But Dad was more interested in politics than ever. He'd been involved in the DNC since the early eighties in a range of capacities. During the '88 convention, he negotiated issues between Dukakis and Jesse Jackson. Then, during the campaign, he became involved in Dukakis strategy sessions through Susan Estrich, the candidate's deputy campaign manager, who had known my father from the 1980 Kennedy campaign. When Dad attended Dukakis policy meetings in Boston, he found an excitement in behind-the-scenes politics. At this point, he had been at the firm for about seven years and had worked for the DNC for the same number of years. He realized how much more he loved politics than lawyering.

His heart and soul was elsewhere in September of 1988, however, because GD, who had been ill for some time with congestive heart disease, went into the hospital for what would be the last time. GD entered Howard University Hospital in Washington, suffering from heart failure. While in the hospital, he had a heart attack and died on September 23, 1988. Dad, who had spent much of that week at GD's side, left the hospital after his father died. He was with his half brother, Chip, then twenty-four; GD and Peggy had divorced some years earlier. Dad and Chip drove to GD's apartment in Silver Spring, Maryland, and Dad called Nan. Even though his parents had been divorced for almost twenty years, they had remained close. "He's gone. Dad's gone," my father cried into the phone. Chip said that he'd never seen Dad sob before, never seen him totally lose control. Later, they looked through some of GD's photo albums and saw that he had collected every single clipping and picture of my father. He had saved that funny photograph from *Jet* that showed my father with his seventies-style sideburns, as well as articles and pictures of my father throughout his career.

GD was taken home to Bressler, Pennsylvania. A few days later, at a funeral home in Bressler that was owned by the Brown family, GD was memorialized and laid to rest. My father gave the eulogy and was both funny and emotional as he remembered his father: "Dad was a very opinionated man, and he swore he knew everything about everything. You couldn't tell him anything because he knew everything. And what you had to say couldn't hold a candle to what he had to say."

Chip recalled how, after GD's death, Dad took over as "father." "He was very sensitive to the fact that I was twenty-four years old when my father died, and I had nobody," Chip said, adding that his male role model was gone. Dad spent the next few months coming to terms with the fact that his father was gone, that he could never talk with him again, never see him again, never ask for his opinion again.

∾

Two months after his father's death, Dad, thinking hard, spoke to Mom just after the November elections: "Honey, you know, I'm really thinking I'd like to run for chairman of the party. That would be something, wouldn't it?" She still didn't take him seriously. Then, at a meeting of Democratic state chairs in Phoenix that my parents and Michael attended, Mom saw people wearing huge buttons that said "Keep Kirk," and that reinforced her opinion that Dad shouldn't run. Paul Kirk, then DNC chair, was a friend of Dad's, and Mom didn't think Dad should or would run against a friend. My father agreed with her but said that because the party had not elected a president in years, it appeared to need a new direction and different strategies. "This is ridiculous," he told Mom. "There's got to be a reason why we're losing. We've got to start winning. I want to be chairman and turn this around." At that time, 1988, the Democratic party controlled both houses of Congress and most big-city mayors and governors were Democrats, but the party had lost the White House three elections in a row.

Dad held a meeting at his office at Patton Boggs with a dozen friends and potential advisers. They discussed the possibilities: Should he run? He had already decided that if Paul Kirk chose to run, he would stay out of the race. If Dad did run, who would handle his campaign? Could he win? Everyone gave Dad input and there were several differing viewpoints; no one, however, disagreed with Dad's running for party chair. Tommy Boggs said he did have a dilemma because if Dad ran, one of his opponents would be former Oklahoma congressman Jim

Jones, a close friend from Tommy's law school days. Jones, the Democratic Leadership Council candidate, had a more conservative image; he represented the ideology of the white South. In the end, Tommy chose to support my father, believing that he could best lead the party to victory.

After the meeting, Dad set Thanksgiving as the date by which he would make up his mind about running. He missed his own deadline and, in December, was still equivocating. At former DNC chair Chuck Manatt's annual black-tie Christmas party, party finance chair Don Sweitzer whispered to Mom that Paul Kirk would definitely run again. Mom repeated this to Dad on their way home but Dad didn't believe it. He told Mom that he just knew Paul wouldn't run and began discussing with her how his campaign should be handled, how much it would cost, how to raise funds for it, and who to hire for his campaign staff. Mom was resistant. Paul Kirk, a friend since the Kennedy campaign, was the incumbent; she believed he was going to run and told Dad his was a lost cause.

Dad turned out to be right, though. In December, Paul Kirk shocked the political world, which fully expected him to run again for chair, by announcing that he was stepping down. When a half dozen candidates popped up—Rick Weiner, Jim Jones, Jim Stanton, Mike Barnes, Richard Celeste—Dad asked me, Michael, and Mom, "If they can run, why can't I?" We had no answer that would dissuade him, so he considered it a done deal and made his announcement. Carl Wagner, Dad's old buddy from Kennedy '80, agreed to run the campaign for Dad after some arm-twisting. "I couldn't imagine why anybody would want the job of chairman of the Democratic National Committee," said Carl. But once Carl agreed, he delivered; Dad trusted him totally and Carl did a great job.

That was step one. Step two was getting office space. Dad, along with his tiny staff—Carl, Yolanda Caraway from the Rainbow Coalition (Jesse Jackson's organization that was created as a result of the '88 Jackson campaign), and Christine Varney from the National Lawyers Council of the DNC—rented rooms in the basement of the Patton Boggs building at 2550 M Street, and "Friends of Ron Brown" was in business. Michael and I were on holiday break from school—I was a senior at Boston

College and Michael was in law school—so we worked with Dad for the duration of his eight-week campaign.

In the South, Dad's decision to run almost precipitated a second Civil War. Louisiana state chair James J. Grady said that "moderate, everyday voters [whom] we have to depend on to win elections don't feel comfortable with Ron Brown." He told my father that if he succeeded in being elected chair, the South would secede from the party. Christine Varney, who was there, recalled Dad's response. With a gracious smile, he told Grady, "Well, you attribute far too much power to me."

"Brown's election will say that Ted Kennedy, Mario Cuomo, and the other Northeast liberals are back in control," said John Baker, state chair of Alabama. "It's a giant step backward for the Democratic party." This was in late 1988, when Reagan and Bush were in their conservative heyday and many Democrats believed they could win only by becoming more moderate. Dad was not perceived as a moderate but as more toward the liberal end of the Democratic spectrum.

And, to many, he was the wrong color.

The New York Times, The Wall Street Journal, The Washington Post, and the *Los Angeles Times* all ran articles stating that Dad was the wrong person with the wrong politics, a Jesse Jackson–type liberal whose election would destroy the party. "It was as negative a press as I've ever seen in twenty-five years of politics," recalled Carl Wagner.

The blatant racism of many southern leaders was a wake-up call for my father. Not since that day in 1963 when he and Mom were turned away from the Shoney's drive-in had Dad had his color thrown in his face. His life had been free from the kind of racism he was now experiencing. It seemed as if white people, who had previously supported him, were now saying, "Okay, it's time to stop. You go no further." This hurt and surprised Dad, but it certainly didn't slow him down. At lunch one day, Dad asked Yolanda, "You really think we can win this thing?" Self-doubt was not Dad's usual mode, so as soon as Yolanda answered "Of course we can" his eyes sparkled and he sat straighter. "Yes. I can win. I know I can."

"When I said I wanted to do this," Dad told me, Mom, and Michael, "they came back and said they had three raps on me.

One, you're black. Two, you're liberal. And three, you can't raise any money and the southern guys ain't gonna like you."

The worst experience he had was at a meeting in Atlanta of the southern regional chairs and southern governors, one of whom was Bill Clinton. Despite the closeness that would later develop between them, Clinton did not issue his public statement of support for my father until January 1989, quite late in the process, after only a few candidates remained and when Dad already had gained considerable support and momentum.

Said President Clinton, "I thought it was a little bit of a gamble . . . but I thought it was one well worth taking. . . . He called and asked me to support him. I told him that I would think about it. And I checked around and asked some other people what they thought. I decided that I thought that, number one, he was the best person . . . [and] number two, I thought it would be a good thing for the party to have its first African-American chairman, especially since he was the ablest person interested in the job. And thirdly, I thought that he was, more than anything else, a very shrewd politician, so that he would try to broaden the base of the party, not shrink it. . . . And so I endorsed him."

That day in Atlanta, all the candidates other than Dad were received with standing ovations. For Dad, they didn't even applaud. He was shocked that he had been snubbed; only months earlier, during the summer of '88, the same people "were grinning in my face at the convention," he told Mom.

"Honey," Dad told her, "you wouldn't believe it. They just sat on their hands when I walked in, and when it was time for me to speak they just sat there. I spoke to them and I got no reaction. No matter what I said, they just gave blank stares back. I told them what I was going to do. How I could put a president in the White House. How we could win. How I was going to depend on all the state chairmen to help. They gave nothing. No response. They just looked at me like I was a blank wall. I felt like a penny waiting for change."

The few who did speak told Dad that, based on some of his experiences and associations, they didn't believe him to be the best man to lead the party. John Breaux, the Democratic senator from Louisiana, believed it would send the wrong message to have an African-American as chair of the party. "You're the wrong man at the wrong time for the job," he told Dad. A woman from Georgia stood up and blasted him: "When you talk about loyalty, when Jimmy Carter, my President, was running and Ted Kennedy challenged him, you were with Ted Kennedy," she said. "What kind of a loyalist are you?"

"I am proud of my service with the senator," Dad responded.

Another man said, "I can't vote for you and go home."

The message was clear: We don't want a black man as chairman of this party.

My father was distressed by what happened in Atlanta. He had been taught: You go to school, get an education, get a vocation, do the right thing—and the world will open up to you. He had done all that, and more, and now he was faced with opposition because of his race. "What do we tell our African-American kids?" he asked Lynn Cutler, candidate for vice chair of the DNC, almost in despair.

In the end, Dad's optimism and fighting spirit won over any negative feelings he may have had. He viewed the southerners' attitudes as a challenge and chose to do battle, rather than retreat. "I'm going to crack 'em," he said to us, and in the weeks that followed he called everyone who had rejected him in Atlanta, repeatedly asking for their support and reiterating his plans for the party. He never gave up, never stopped trying to change their minds. He refused to allow his campaign to be sidetracked by race.

"My chairmanship won't be about race," he said. "It will be about the races we win!"

He viewed his relationship with Jesse Jackson as an asset rather than a liability, and challenged those who used "the Jesse thing" as a way of attacking his ability to be an effective DNC chair: "People who criticize me for working with Jesse Jackson act as if I was born in May of 1988. In fact, I've worked in Democratic politics for a long time and am close to many Democrats across this country, both at the national and state level."

Rick Weiner, state chair from Michigan and head of the Association of State Chairs, was Dad's main opponent. The DNC establishment who ran DNC headquarters at 430 South Capitol Street wanted Weiner to be chair. Weiner was a nice man whom

Dad liked; as did Dad, Weiner campaigned with his children, who were about the same age as me and Michael. We'd run into them and chat together on the campaign trail. To balance the votes Weiner would likely receive from the Association of State Chairs, Dad sought endorsements from the most powerful Democrats in key states: Cuomo in New York, Bradley in New Jersey, Kennedy in Massachusetts, Casey in Pennsylvania, and others. These politicians could override their state chairs and deliver the votes of their entire state delegations.

Before Dad had a chance to contact Bill Bradley, the former New Jersey senator contacted him. Bradley had been in a cloak-room when he overheard some senators making racist comments about my father. Bradley walked out of the room, went to a phone, and called Dad, saying he wanted to endorse him. Not too long after that, the other key Democrats agreed to support Dad and each delivered their delegation's votes.

After he had these important endorsements, Dad turned his attention to raising money. He knew that funding his campaign was essential to winning; he needed money to get out his message and to be able to travel around the country to meet party leaders. Around that time, *The New York Times* ran a front-page, above-the-fold article stating that Dad was unable to raise money, especially from Jewish contributors, because of his liberal background and his relationship with Jesse Jackson. Rob Stein, who had worked with Dad on a DNC voter registration task force in 1987, was so angered by the *Times* piece, he immediately volunteered for Dad's campaign and helped with fund-raising. Rob and other members of Dad's campaign staff raised between $300,000 and $350,000, more money than had ever been raised for a chairman's race. The campaign funds came from friends, from other attorneys at Patton Boggs, and from members of the black community.

The money allowed Dad to lease a plane, expediting his travel from state to state in order to meet with Democratic committees. He was so persuasive when articulating his vision for the next election and his plans for uniting the party in order to retake the White House that he blew his competition out of the water. By mid-January, a month into the campaign, Rick Weiner and Jim Jones were the last remaining opponents. "The only person who could possibly give me a run for my money at this point is Rick Weiner, but I don't see him staying in," Dad told us.

Dad made personal appearances everywhere because, according to Rob Stein, "he was his own best advocate." During his campaign, all of Dad's speeches were about his certainty that the Democrats could elect a Democratic president if they were organized. Since 1976, the party had lost the White House because there was no real national party apparatus. Every four years, the DNC would self-destruct after its convention, then have to rebuild itself as the next convention approached. After a convention, the party chair became a lame duck because the presidential candidate would appoint a new party chair. Dad wanted to change the rules, remaining on as chairman through the primaries, the election, and the inaugural. It was a simple but radical idea and, when the time came, Dad carried out his proposal and it was successful.

Dad told me and Michael, with him on the campaign, to meet DNC members and "chat 'em up," introduce ourselves and talk about our family and Dad. Both Michael and I always included a bit about Dad's driving us crazy at home going on about his commitment to elect a Democratic president.

If Dad made calls from home to DNC members around the country, Michael would set them up. He would dial a party leader in a state somewhere and say, "My father will be calling you in fifteen minutes to discuss his campaign for chair. Are there any issues you want to bring up so he can be prepared?" Dad would get a chance to think about the issues and check his policy sheets before he made the call. Sometimes my brother would stay on the phone during Dad's conversation; Dad would of course inform the other person that his son was listening in. Dad was surprised at how unwilling some people were to commit their votes; many of them hedged their bets and talked in generalities when Dad asked for their support.

One call that we always remembered was to Roland Burris, who later became Illinois attorney general. A black man, he was a member of the DNC in large part because of my father's sponsorship. With Michael listening in, Dad said to Burris, "Hey, buddy, I want you to know the campaign is going wonderfully.

I hope I can count on your vote." To Dad's shock, Burris would not make a commitment and said, "Well, Ron, I have to assess the situation."

Michael recalled that Dad kept cool and said, "I hope I can earn your support. I know you have some other issues. . . . Whatever you need me to do, I'll do. Talk to you soon." But when he hung up, he was boiling and actually cursed, a rarity for him. Burris was afraid to support him, Dad explained to Michael, because if Dad lost the election Burris would lose stature with the new chair. Of course, when my father won, Burris was right by his side during photo ops. That line of Burris's was a running joke in our family and we laughed about it for years; one of us would answer a direct question, a request to do this or that, with "I have to assess the situation."

Michael was with Dad at a campaign rally in the Dakotas when a white man walked up to them. He looked about sixty-five and, living in the Dakotas, had probably not met many black folks during his life. The man looked Dad in the eye and announced, "I just want you to know that if you ran for president, you'd be the first colored person I'd vote for." Dad shook his hand and said, "Thank you." The man was completely sincere, so my father probably meant his "thank you," while some part of him recoiled at the man's insensitivity.

As the campaign went on, Dad gained more support from party leaders who saw him as able to lead a party that would be truly inclusive because he wasn't wedded to either liberal or conservative dogma. They recognized that he was pragmatic, that he would work hard to get the job done. Even the press began to turn around, becoming more objective than negative.

Critical to winning was gaining the AFL-CIO's votes because labor held 25 percent of the DNC seats. The union's chief, Lane Kirkland, supported my father and that helped enormously when the members voted. After the vote, Rochelle Horowitz, legislative director for the teachers' union that is part of the AFL-CIO, ran out of the meeting, called Dad's campaign office, and screamed into the phone, "We've got the AFL-CIO votes!" Carl Wagner turned to Dad and said, "Congratulations, Mr. Chairman!" because it was over.

Both Jim Jones and Rick Weiner dropped out of the race

shortly after this. Two weeks before the election, Dad was at a state party meeting when he found out that Weiner was out. He still devoted his allotted two hours to convincing the delegates to vote for him. A scheduled fund-raiser after the meeting turned into a celebration because, at that point, Dad was certain he would be the next chairman of the DNC. Back at "Friends of Ron Brown," my father's campaign staff began assessing and analyzing the national party to determine what his first acts should be when he took over.

On February 10, 1989, as we drove to the DNC meeting at the Washington Hilton, Dad was more excited than I had ever seen him. Our whole family was there: me, Michael, Mom, Mere, Nan, and Dad's cousin Nick Jones. The mini-convention was divided into states, each state in its own section, with a total of 404 state representatives holding aloft their slogans and signs. These representatives vote on party platform and bylaws and elect chairs, as with state and national political conventions. After roll calls and a few brief speeches, I heard: "I move that Ron Brown be made the chairman of the Democratic party unanimously!" The motion was seconded and Dad was elected by unanimous voice vote. At that moment, Dad became (and remains) the only African-American ever elected to a national political office. There was screaming and cheering, and outgoing chair Paul Kirk handed the gavel to my father. Dad pounded it on the lectern and said, "Will this meeting of the Democratic party come to order!" Then he gave his acceptance speech, an amalgam of drafts submitted to him by several staff people, which he had rewritten and rehearsed in front of me, Michael, and Mom at least five times:

"The Democrats have always been in the vanguard for change. Democrats elected the first woman chair, the first Catholic chair, the first Jewish chair, and now I'm the first chair of African descent. . . . When I came up here to accept, I felt a certain feeling run through me that made me understand the history of the moment and how important it was. Not only to me, but to a lot of people around this country. . . . I am proud of who I am and I am proud of this party. For we are truly America's last best hope to bridge the divisions of race and region and religion and ethnicity."

The vote, the speech, the triumph—this was Dad's big night and he was thrilled, as we all were. Afterward, there was a party at the hotel with music by the band from *Saturday Night Live*. My father was ebullient, sheer happiness and joy radiating from him. Mom recalled that, even in the midst of the hoopla, he quietly reassured her that their life wouldn't change; they would still be able to take their family vacations and see their old friends: "This was a big triumph for him—that he had won over a lot of skeptics. He also thought that he was going to have to prove himself. As a black person in America, you always feel that you have to prove yourself, and he knew that."

Even though my father had finally convinced even the recalcitrant southern delegation, he told me that its members watched every move he made to ensure that he didn't get too cozy with Teddy Kennedy or Jesse Jackson.

Dad's first big test came on April 4, 1989, in a special election to complete the unexpired term of Mayor Harold Washington, who died in office on November 23, 1987. Richard M. Daley, son of former Chicago mayor Richard J. Daley, won in the Democratic mayoral primary. In the general election, Daley was opposed by another black man, Chicago alderman Timothy C. Evans. Evans, endorsed by Jesse Jackson, was running on the newly created Harold Washington party. Dad, as DNC chair, ignored race and supported Daley, the Democratic candidate.

When Michael and Dad arrived in Chicago the day before the election, picketers organized by Illinois congressman Gus Savage greeted them at the airport. One demonstrator carried a sign that read, "Welcome to Chicago, Ron Beige." Another wore an Oreo cookie costume and danced around singing, "Daley lackey, Daley lackey."

The mostly black crowd was angry at Dad for supporting Daley over the black candidate. But my father, tipped in advance about the protest, displayed no anger at the demonstration. Even though he was annoyed at Gus Savage, inside he was laughing because "Ron Beige" was funny, as was the Oreo cookie costume. This was the only time in his life he had been picketed by his own people. Dad was disappointed that the other candidate and his supporters didn't understand that his function as DNC chair was to support Democratic candidates independent of race.

After the demonstration, when Dad appeared at a press conference, Michael recalled that he became fiercer than he had ever been as he addressed the crowd and the press. In a loud, emotional tone, while pounding for emphasis on the podium, he said: "I'm the chairman of the Democratic party. Richard Daley is the Democratic nominee for mayor of the city of Chicago, and as chairman of the Democratic party, I'm endorsing him to be mayor of this great city!" Michael joined the crowd, which went crazy, cheering and yelling. He told Dad that he had never been more proud of him than at that moment. Dad also spoke to Jesse Jackson to remind him that he, Dad, as DNC chair, had to support the Democratic nominee and he hoped Jesse would not attribute more to his endorsement of Daley than that.

Dad passed the litmus test of the Chicago mayoral contest and began remaking the Democrats into a winning party. Much of what he did was outreach, which he loved. In February, he began what would be four years of television appearances, pumping up the party and preparing the public for the Democratic campaign to come in '92. Mark Steitz recalled that the reason Dad did so well on the small screen was that he truly enjoyed doing television. But Mark also recalled that he had to curb Dad's naturally high energy and enthusiasm so as to make him more television-ready. The first time Dad went on the *Today* show, he and Mark were sitting around the set at 5:45 in the morning, Mark still half asleep although he was drinking coffee. Dad, who drank orange juice rather than coffee or tea in the morning, was bouncing with anticipation, all ready to go on.

Remembered Mark, "He's read all the papers and is ready to take on the world. I had to find a way of explaining to him that you don't go into this full tilt. I see Willard doing the weather with a funny hat on. I said, 'Stop, Ron. Look out there.' I point to Willard and say, 'He's a superstar this early in the morning because he wears funny hats and he smiles and he's not too hard on people. Morning show. Be nice. People have just woken up. They don't want to hear rat-a-tat-tat. They don't want to hear debate.' And he says, 'Oh, yeah.' "

So Dad went on at 70 percent speed, had fun, and was an excellent guest.

Whenever he appeared on interviews or debate shows, my father loved trashing the Republicans. At the National Press Club he said, "The Republican party keeps sending relief pitchers that I have to go up against. Obviously, I started with Lee Atwater, who was an extraordinarily formidable opponent. After Lee's tragic illness, they sent Ed Rollins, then Charlie Black, then Newt Gingrich. Then, they sent Bill Bennett and then Clayton Yuetter and now Rich Bond. Rich, don't unpack your bags."

The buzz after Dad's election was about the direction in which he would lead the party. Some insiders at the DNC believed that Mondale and Dukakis had lost in '84 and '88 because of the traditional liberal policies they represented. The more conservative faction of the party, the Democratic Leadership Council (DLC), wanted the party to abandon its liberal ideology for a moderate stance and had supported Jim Jones for chairman. But my father believed in liberalism and chose to align the party with its liberal tradition; on the other hand, he also understood that the party had to change just enough to win back the votes of the so-called Reagan Democrats who had deserted the party during the eighties. Dad compromised and, during his years as DNC chair, maintained the party's liberal traditions even as he embraced some more moderate ideas.

Immediately after his election, the transition period began, that time during which the reins of power changed hands from former chair Paul Kirk to Dad in a smooth and easy manner. While Dad scrambled to get the committee running under a new chair and a new staff, his friends voiced shock that he had actually won.

"I just couldn't believe it," said Alexis Herman. "I was in shock this boy had won. I asked him two questions, 'What's your vision of the DNC? What kind of team do you see helping you implement the vision?' "

Dad planned to run the DNC like a campaign and not a

bureaucracy. He wanted the party to have the energy and excitement of an electoral race, which meant relating to voters, not to state party structures. Not getting bogged down in rules and regulations, but figuring out which were the critical races and how to get involved in them.

"What's our role?" Dad asked Alexis the day after he was elected. "How do we practice now to elect a president in 1992? I want to elect a president in 1992, but I don't want to wait until 1992. I want to start today doing that. That's the kind of energy I want [my staff] to have. I want people who are campaign-oriented, who can relate to voters and real people."

Dad wanted to hire a staff immediately, but Carl Wagner, who'd worked on his campaign, suggested he wait and define his goals before hiring a team. Recognizing good advice when he heard it, Dad and Carl created four units: finance, politics, communications, and management. These teams would be asked to submit policy, goals, and budget suggestions. Dad chose a staff that would reflect the diversity of the DNC: Paul Tully for politics, Mark Steitz from the Jackson campaign for research, Christine Varney as general counsel, Melissa Moss from the DLC as finance director, and Bill Morton from the Jackson campaign, for advance work for Dad. Dad kept Mike McCurry from the Kirk administration to do communications.

The party had always had an executive director but Dad changed that to a chief of staff who would serve as a coordinator. In May, he offered the position to Alexis Herman because he felt she was the best qualified person. That she was black and a woman would mean a lot to many people. But Alexis was reluctant.

"I told him, 'Ron, with all due respect, I think you need a white chief of staff. You've already taken a lot of hits.' But he said, 'I need my person at the top. That's more important to me than whether you're black, white, or whatever color. You're qualified to do it. I know you can do it, and I need you there. . . . Think about it. Out of everybody that's on the team, you're the only one who's actually worked for a president of the United States. You're the only one who's been there, who can remind us that it's possible.' Then he went on and on about this moment in history. Finally, he said, 'I'm going to give it everything I have because I believe if we don't do it now, we never will.' Of course he was right."

Dad's only staff problem was with Robert Farmer, who had run for party treasurer at the same time Dad ran for party chair. Farmer told Rob Stein that he wanted to name the finance director and the finance chair, he wanted to fly first class, and, according to Rob, "he wanted this and he wanted that." Rob recalled that when Farmer and Dad finally talked about Farmer's demands, Dad said, "Well, I think you ran for the wrong office, Bob; you should have run for chair. Only one person can be in charge—one person. I'll value your input, and we'll work together . . . and we'll talk about these other things as we go along." After that, Dad and the new treasurer managed to work together with a minimum of tension.

Dad's hiring policies revitalized the party and it was seen as the party of inclusion as he brought in young people, people of color, and women. Young men and women were hired for prominent positions. They wrote position papers and they traveled around the country representing the DNC so people could see them. By asking for the ideas and contributions of young Democrats, Democrats of color, and women Democrats, the DNC resonated and became a new, vibrant party.

Maria Cardona, Dad's deputy press secretary at the DNC, recalled how Dad reached out and solicited minority press outlets; he wanted to be interviewed by minority publications and TV and radio stations. One day in 1990, Dad was being interviewed by a Latino reporter; the Latino media had previously been ignored. That day, the reporter became adversarial; he believed the Democrats had abandoned the Hispanic community and were taking the Latino vote for granted. Maria recalled that Dad answered each question head-on, eventually disarming the reporter. By the end of the interview, he had become a cover story whose headline would read: A NEW DEMOCRATIC PARTY COMMITMENT TO LATINO VOTE!

Ginny Terzano, now press secretary for Vice President Gore, was hired to be Dad's press secretary in the spring of 1989; she set up interviews and responses to the press while Mike McCurry, the communications director, did overall planning. Dad's hiring was based not just on inclusion but on ability and loyalty. He hired people he had worked with before either at the Urban League, at Patton Boggs, or on the Kennedy campaign. Their loyalty to Dad was tremendous. One staffer at the DNC recalled, "If he asked you to come with him, you would and you would do it blindly because you know you wouldn't be taken advantage of." Dad attracted brilliant people, and with brilliance came individuality, even eccentricity. Said Barbara Schmitz, "I know [he] hired these people, I know they're good at what they do, I know they're the best in the country, maybe the best in the world. But this is the biggest bunch of Easter bunnies I have ever seen in my life. When you take them out of their element, they're all crazy."

Ginny Terzano recalled that reporter Paul Taylor of *The Washington Post* said to her, "I'm just sitting here, and I was counting up the staff that Ron Brown hired. Isn't it amazing? He's brought in the best of the Democratic party."

During his years as DNC chair, Dad developed and refined his management skills, demonstrating his usual strengths and weaknesses. For example, if you were not loyal, you became an outcast, no longer intimately involved in the party's work, or with Dad. If he disagreed with you, or was angry with you, he might castigate you privately but would present a united front to the public. He never berated a staff member in public. Mark Steitz recalled how he would make errors, only to have Dad "chew me out privately and defend me publicly." He would tell Mark that he had made a serious mistake, that the situation had blown up in his, Dad's, face and that he should think about what he was doing next time. Then, my father would pick up the phone and say to, for example, Speaker Tom Foley, "You're absolutely out of line on this. What Mark did was utterly appropriate."

This reminded me of how Dad was with me and Michael. He'd yell at us if we had done something wrong; but to the world out there, he stood up for us and acted as if we were his two angels.

He hated firing people and preferred to give staff members space, rather than fire them. If something really bothered him, he would turn to Alexis and say, "This has got to stop!" When he couldn't control something he wanted to, or thought he should be able to, his frustration showed in his body language. He paced or shook his leg or rolled his eyes. When he was in a bad mood, a rare occurrence, he would avoid people altogether.

~

For four years, 1989 through 1992, while Dad ran the DNC, he remained a full, although nonworking, partner at Patton, Boggs and Blow. He stopped by occasionally at the firm to sign papers or consult with attorneys who had taken on his clients. Most of his time was spent at DNC headquarters.

During this period, his work at the DNC engaged him spiritually and intellectually. As the leader of a national political party, he could achieve a lifelong goal: He had always wanted to have an effect on the world. By being the force behind the '92 election, in which the Democrats would take back the White House, Dad believed he would help make the world a better place.

When Dad became DNC chair, Mom finally understood why this job had been so important to him and why he had to do it at this time. His acceptance speech had explained it: His goal, from which he never deviated, was to win the White House. Every state or local race, no matter how small, was important to him. There were always issues. For example, an elected official had died or resigned, so the party had to help choose a replacement to fill out the elected term. Each race was part of his master plan to rebuild the party.

Dad came home each night from his office at Democratic headquarters exuberant and excited about his work. He saw himself as the support person who helped get Democrats elected at all levels—governors, mayors, senators, congressmen and -women. He had promised the party in his acceptance speech that he would visit all fifty states. And he did. "Out-of-town Brown" flew from state to state, race to race, never reflecting on what he was doing with his life. He just did it. As Mom said, "He lived his diary. Didn't write one." Dad believed that life and the future would take care of itself.

In February of 1989, shortly after he was elected, Dad called a meeting of trustees—individuals who had raised more than one hundred thousand dollars for the Democrats—at the Waldorf Astoria in New York City, with Mario Cuomo as the evening's keynote speaker. Dad gave a speech, then took comments and questions from the trustees. This was his first appearance in the transition from the old Dukakis-dominated DNC (as the presidential candidate, he was the party's real leader) to the new Ron Brown DNC. Many trustees present that evening were either friends of Dukakis or Massachusetts developers. They didn't appear to be interested in contributing money or raising funds for this "new" Democratic party. Other trustees that evening, longtime members and supporters of the party, were dissatisfied with the past lack of professionalism and organization within the national party.

Nineteen eighty-eight was the first year the Democrats had raised so much money, the first time there were such large individual donors, and many of these contributors were very disappointed, according to Melissa Moss. Some trustees were furious. As Shelia Davis Lawrence said, "We felt like the DNC was being run by a bunch of kids who every four years would try to reinvent the wheel. . . . We felt like we had basically flushed our checks right down the toilet."

Since the Democrats did not control the White House, the trustees blamed the party's failures on the chairman. In this case, Dad was the chair, even though he had only been in office one month. People were so angry, that didn't matter. That night, at the Waldorf, Lawrence stood up and let him have it.

"You keep asking for money, taking it, running away, never listening to anything that we have to say. . . . It won't fly. We're fed up; we're tired of this party not being run like a business. . . . We're not stupid and we're tired of losing." The other trustees applauded her outburst and Dad's face reflected his discomfort, Lawrence recalled, but he stood there and took it and came back at her. "I believe I can change things around," Dad told the disgruntled donors. Then he asked for a leap of faith, a chance to rebuild the party with their help. He pledged to meet with Lawrence at her home in California to hear her suggestions for how to make the party better.

Then, Mario Cuomo rose to address the relatively small audience of about one hundred. "I had a speech prepared but

I'm going to take your questions instead," said Cuomo. Using the audience's questions, he managed to segue into his message for the evening: Both Christian philanthropy and Jewish *tzedakah* are based on the concept that charity is the basis of democracy and freedom. Therefore, democracy and freedom depend upon the largesse of those individuals, such as his audience, who are so spiritually grounded that they are compelled to become part of something bigger than themselves. By the time he was finished, the trustees felt as if they had been beatified and walked out of the meeting elevated, feeling good about themselves and about supporting the party.

Six weeks later, true to his promise, Dad met with Lawrence. They hashed it out; he listened while she talked, and by the meeting's end they had "bonded," according to Lawrence. "He showed me that he was really serious about being successful." (Mom and Dad later became close friends with the Lawrences; their San Diego home, across from their famous hotel, the Hotel del Coronado, was the site of our last family vacation. When Larry, Shelia's husband, ambassador to Switzerland during President Clinton's first term, died in January of 1996, Dad gave the eulogy.)

A major part of my father's work was to raise funds, and as he helped finance Democratic races around the country he looked beyond the traditional political donors—unions, corporations, wealthy individuals. Dad suggested expanding donor bases to include young people and people of color.

Dad also sought funds from Jewish groups. He had to work to develop an affiliation with them because of uncertainty arising from Dad's relationship with Jesse Jackson, whose notorious anti-Semitic remark years earlier had alienated the Jewish community. During his first year as chair, Dad met in New York City with the heads of about fifty major Jewish organizations; the meeting was arranged by Hyman Bookbinder of the American Jewish Committee, with whom Dad had worked on civil rights issues. The group grilled him on Israel and other issues of concern to their community and, in the end, he won them over. Except for a handful of holdouts, these Jewish leaders seemed to love my father and were among his most loyal supporters.

Gary Barron, deputy treasurer of the DNC, recalled that some of these holdouts were in Hollywood. But a meeting at Howard Sterling's Beverly Hills house turned it around for Dad. Sterling, a Jewish businessman, also distrusted Dad because of his connection to Jackson. In addition to his own refusal to contribute to the party, Sterling was also convincing other former donors not to contribute. Barron said the meeting was standing room only, the room jammed with the Jewish elite of Hollywood. Dad was bombarded for two hours about his views on Israel, Palestinians, and the peace process; he was also asked about Jackson's role in the party. Recalled Gary Barron, "He was like a wet sponge and people were throwing their hardest and biggest rocks, and he withstood the blows."

Dad kept going until there were no more questions. At meeting's end, he stood and, beaming, received an ovation. He was thrilled because he knew that he had hit it out of the park and the Jewish community would no longer be reluctant to donate to the DNC.

~

Donors, both high and low end, would gather for what were called finance council weekends, usually held at resorts in warm climates so the donors could play golf and tennis and socialize. The party sponsored weekends for the Democratic Finance Council donors, who gave up to five thousand dollars; the Democratic Business Council, corporate donors who contributed twenty-five thousand dollars; and the Managing Trustees Council, those who gave or raised one hundred thousand dollars. The weekend retreats usually had business meetings the first day, golf and tennis the second day, and a brunch on the last day. And there were featured speakers, usually members of the House and the Senate. Under Dad, these weekends changed a bit to include taking contributors' ideas in addition to their checks. My father told donors that their suggestions would be acted upon to improve the party.

Under Dad's chairmanship, the Democratic party became a more professional organization. For example, trustees would conference via phone to discuss who was raising funds where, what methods were successful, and how much was being raised.

My father made sure that research and studies were initiated to assist political strategists and help party fund-raisers get maximum results. He and finance director Melissa Moss would sit down together weekly and cold-call potential donors. "He would stay on the phone until they understood what we were doing and why it was important," Melissa recalled. His belief in what he said was communicated to the people on the other end of the line, because most of those phone calls got results.

Paul Tully

All DNC meetings, all Finance Council weekends, had a single focus: to win the White House in 1992. Major presentations were given by Dad and by Paul Tully, Dad's partner in leading the party. If my father was the voice and spirit of the national Democratic party, Paul was its nuts and bolts. Before Dad hired him as the party's political director, Paul had worked for individual candidates. He knew how to do electoral politics on a daily basis: the ins and outs, the details. My father thought Paul was the brightest person he had ever met; for years, Paul had nursed creative ideas on how to win a presidential campaign but was unable to communicate them successfully. Dad, who met Paul on the Kennedy '80 campaign, understood the man and his ideas, and wanted to put him to work helping to run the party.

Dad and Paul were such opposites: Paul smoked, was overweight, and always had his shirt collar open, tie loosened, and jacket off. He often looked rumpled, as if he'd put on any old thing that had been lying on the floor. My father was immaculate, never a hair out of place, never a wrinkle in his clothing. Some folks had trouble talking to Paul because if the subject wasn't politics, well, then—what else was there? He wouldn't discuss the game or the weather or the latest movie. But ask him about the most remote election in the smallest district, and he had the data in his head. Opposites, but with the same goal, Dad and Paul worked closely. They liked each other, respected each other's abilities, and were a perfect pair to revitalize the party.

They traveled together around the country with a dog and pony show to raise funds and gain support for the party. Paul would speak first, backed up with charts, maps and an overhead. Then Dad would take over. The two of them took turns explaining the party's objectives, discussing which sections of the country needed which types of outreach, and getting out their message about running the coordinated campaign.

The '89 elections were a testing ground for the concept of the coordinated campaign; if it worked now, Dad and Paul Tully thought, it would work in '92 and put a Democrat in the White House. The concept was to have the national party contribute money to state elections, which would be matched by funds from the state parties. And all Democrats, local, state, and national, would pool their energy in efforts such as get-out-the-vote drives, phone banks, and voter registration. With a coordinated campaign, Democrats in state races, and in the national race to come, would save money and use their resources more wisely. Dad also believed the benefits of people working together were both psychologically and practically significant. If the coordinated campaign worked in '89, it would build a coordinated base in each state from which to launch the '92 presidential campaign. Of this experience Melissa Moss recalled, "Ron, Paul Tully, Mark Steitz, Ginny Terzano, and I worked together [to create] the coordinated campaign, which was Paul's and Ron's brainchild. We had a real turning point in 1989."

The three big contests in '89 were the races for governor in New Jersey and in Virginia, and the mayoral race in New York City. The Democratic candidates were Jim Florio in New Jersey, Doug Wilder in Virginia, and David Dinkins in New York City. Under Dad, the DNC succeeded in getting Democrats to work together, pooling resources and efforts in these races. And all three Democratic candidates won.

Election night, 1989, Mom and Dad were in a Washington hotel waiting for election returns at the DNC reception. Staring at the big board with the numbers, Dad grinned as Democratic winners came in, one after the other. When Dinkins was elected, it was a particularly sweet victory to my father because Dinkins and GD had been old friends from the Hotel Theresa days.

Having Doug Wilder win in Virginia meant a lot to my father. He very much wanted to win the South, for both personal as well as political reasons.

Between 1989 and 1991, using the coordinated campaign, the Democrats consistently won races: state, local, and municipal. Anytime a local or state chapter called national headquarters seeking help, Dad would send staff or whatever else was needed. He never turned down a request; he wanted Democrats around the country to feel that the national party would supply whatever resources they needed.

In 1990, he and Mom again watched the board as the numbers came in. Dad said, grinning, "Looks like Ann did it." Ann Richards, the newly elected governor of Texas, had run a tough race against a right-wing good ole boy, William Perry Clements. Maria Cardona recalled a trip Dad and some DNC staffers made to Houston during Richards's campaign. One evening, Maria was waiting for Dad, who was running late and was overdue for an interview. As my father emerged from the elevator and began to head toward her, a man walked up to him and began speaking. Maria recalled that Dad stopped and listened as the man told about his troubles: He had been fired and wasn't certain he would get his last paycheck. "Ron looked him in the eye and nodded," said Maria. "No indication that he was in a hurry, just listening with a concerned look. When the man finished, Ron said, 'I completely understand. This is why I am working so hard to get Ann Richards elected.' And then he went into his message. . . . The man listened closely and, as he did, the concern in his face faded a little bit."

Before 1989, Dad had spent much of his time convincing people that the national party would help them out, despite its poor track record. Now, he felt these wins had proven he could lead the party to victory. "Yeah," he said to us, "this puts us on the map. Now we can get ready for '92." Under Dad, the DNC's winning streak continued. In seven special congressional elections between '89 and '92, Democratic candidates took all seven. During President Clinton's first term, when Dad was no longer DNC chair, there were four special congressional elections. The Democratic party lost every one.

Trips

Mom was involved in Dad's work at the DNC and accompanied him on many of his campaign trips. In January 1990, she and I went with Dad to the Middle East on a trip sponsored by the American-Israel Public Affairs Committee (AIPAC). Mom and I were in the conference room when my father met with Israeli prime minister Yitzhak Shamir and were seated right next to Dad. While we didn't say very much, we listened with fascination to the discussion that went on. For me, it was more educational than any college or law school course, and Mom had a sense of being included in Dad's work.

We also went with Dad to see former prime minister Menachem Begin's son, Benny, who spoke with us on behalf of his father, who was ill. In Egypt, Mom was at Dad's side when he met with President Muhammad Hosni Mubarak. Since Dad and these heads of state were exchanging political ideas, rather than government secrets, there were no restrictions against us being there. This was actually the only job Dad had where our family's closeness was taken into consideration; politics allowed me, Michael, and Mom in, rather than excluding us.

We shared many laughs on these trips. In Egypt, a carpet maker's assistant in a shop kept addressing Dad as "Your Excellency." Bill Morton—who became a close family friend while he worked for Dad at the DNC and at Commerce, and who died with him in Croatia—was with my parents in Egypt that day. Bill and Mom loved to tease Dad and would call out, "Your Excellency," laughing as he turned around.

Amazingly, Dad was able to maintain good relations with the Jewish groups as well as Arab groups. Jim Zogby, president of the Arab-American Institute, received a call from Dad the morning after he became chair, inviting him over. "I want to send the message that this party is going to be open to your community," Dad said. During Dad's years as chair, he spoke at Arab-American Institute conventions about inclusion and the Arab community's right to participate in the Democratic party. When Zogby, a friend, warned Dad that he risked losing Jewish contributors, Dad insisted that the Democratic party was a friend to both communities. "I'm pro-Israel," he said. "But I am also pro–your community being active, and I respect your leadership."

In June 1991, Dad and Mom went to several African countries, accompanied by several DNC staffers, including DNC vice chair, Lynn Cutler, and Lauri Fitz-Pegado, an international public relations executive and a consultant to the DNC. They first went to Senegal, and Gorée Island, a most emotional journey. Gorée Island is where African families, kidnapped into slavery, were torn apart, with husbands and fathers going one way, mothers and wives another way, and children a third way. There is a long passageway into the sea, down which the old and infirm were sent to their death. Mom and Dad told me how moved everyone was at Gorée Island. When a film crew from Black Entertainment Television asked Dad to walk down the passageway, he did and said, "As I walk this passage where my ancestors walked, I'm struck by the inhumanity that people are capable of."

Dad, Mom, and DNC staffers next traveled to South Africa. In Soweto they met with Nelson Mandela. The meeting took place in Mandela's home. Dad spoke with him about his plans and hopes, and Mandela said that he hoped that those Americans who supported him in the past would remain supportive. Mom recalled that Mandela was pleased to meet with Dad and viewed his visit as a positive statement by the Democratic party and by the United States.

Dad was shaken and disturbed by Soweto, a city of raw, open sewers, covered by a never-ending fog of coal smoke, whose residents lived in tin shacks. "Can you imagine," he asked Lynn Cutler, "people getting up in the morning and putting on a shirt and suit and tie and going to work—under these conditions?" Mom, Dad, and the others, with a group of Sowetans, toured a rough soccer field, a day-care center, and several houses. Then a man said, "He's a great leader of his party and he supported our school"—Dad had helped raise money for the school—"and he's here to visit us." The Sowetans stood in a circle around Dad, raised their arms, and sang the South African national anthem. It was, he told me later, an amazing moment. He felt a foot taller, and connected forever to the Sowetans.

Mom had to leave Africa then to return home to her job at WKYS radio, while Dad continued on to visit six more countries in two weeks. In Angola, Dad and Lynn Cutler and other DNC staff members arrived while a cease-fire was being negotiated in the guerrilla war, so there was still considerable shooting in the streets. They landed in Luanda, the capital, at 5 A.M. and were taken to the only hotel with running water. They got into a tiny, ancient elevator that, after a minute or two, came to a halt and stalled between floors. Lynn took deep breaths and reminded herself not to panic. Dad said, "They'll be here any minute. Everything will be okay." Lynn was so traumatized that the only thing that kept her from panicking, she said, was Dad's relaxed demeanor.

Dad's ability to calm people helped in politics, of course. The purpose of the African trip was to promote the economic development of several African nations and to exchange with them political ideas and goals. In Angola as a result of Dad's intercession, representatives of the warring factions shared a dinner table and spoke to each other for the first time in years. He had listened to each group, then asked questions and gave advice on methods for working out certain problems. He talked to each person in turn and asked for their reaction. Dad was aware that he had taken a risk by bringing the different sides to the table, but was jubilant at the successful outcome.

As he had done in each African country he visited, Dad met with representatives of every political party. Meetings were often long and tedious but, as Lynn Cutler recalled, before Zambia, Dad had never even loosened his tie. In Zambia, however, my father gave in and took off his tie and wore a bush jacket. Of course, everyone teased him about this. When Dad returned from Africa, he told us many dramatic stories. In Zambia, there was a rally at the airport as Dad was leaving. Steel drums playing in the background while Dad talked about the value of free and open elections. In Nigeria, Lauri, who always traveled with bug spray and disinfectant, had to run from room to room in their hotel, spraying, to get rid of the bedbugs. The next morning Dad rode in a motorcade in which the lead man, riding a motorcycle, beat traffic back with a stick. Finally, as they left Nigeria, a government official ripped Lynn's camera out of her hand; and Bill Morton had to pay another official in order to get gasoline for their plane.

Back Home

As DNC chair, Dad was in control. He was the man. If you wanted to run for office, you called Ron Brown and said, "You know, Ron, I'm thinking about running." In the early days of his tenure, he welcomed all candidates. He was looking ahead to '92 and wanted to see which individuals could raise money, appeal to the audience, and sustain a campaign. And which candidates he could work with. Dad believed in the Democratic party's values and platform. Early on, he began to think about the candidate who would sit in the White House in four years: "We need to find a candidate that the American people feel comfortable with, that they trust and respect." He had strong views on voter participation and registration and in speeches throughout the country and on television talked about his goal of adding at least five million new voters to the rolls.

"Voter registration is crucial," he explained at the 1992 National Urban League conference. "And we've got to remove the barriers that still exist in America so that everyone can participate in the political process. We're about the only democratic society that makes this hard. People ought to be able to go to a polling booth on the same day as the election and register. . . . It's also turnout. We need to get registered voters to the polls."

Between 1989 and 1992, only one person consistently went out to the American people and talked up the greatness of the Democratic party. And that was Dad. No one else was willing to go on television shows and talk about George Bush and his 90 percent rating. No one else repeated the same message, day in and day out: "The Democratic party is on the right side of all the issues. We want to build a coalition. We want your trust and we want your vote."

These were wonderful years for Dad, and for our family. He loved what he was doing; Mom, Michael, and I were involved and often traveled with him. He remained an optimist at all times and, according to Rob Stein, brought a "core strength" to his work that was based on his spirituality and his energy. During these years, my father was focused on getting a Democratic president elected in 1992. He helped reinstate pride and good feelings in the Democratic party. His optimism was taking hold among party members as, over and over, he repeated his message: "We're going to win in '92." Eventually people began to believe him.

When I handled my first case as a prosecutor in September 1992, I had been out of law school only for a few months and at the Los Angeles District Attorney's Office for a few weeks. It was a preliminary hearing, where I called witnesses and asked them questions under oath so the judge could determine if there was enough evidence to make the defendant stand trial. I was both anxious and excited and spent a lot of time preparing. It was an assault case that was complicated because the defendant and the victim were friends. I had spoken to Dad the night before and he promised to call me the next day to see how it had turned out.

When I walked in the door to my apartment that evening, I wanted to talk to Dad right away, but I knew I wouldn't be able to reach him because he was traveling with the Clinton/Gore campaign. Thankfully, as soon as I put down my briefcase, the phone was ringing. It was Dad calling from the campaign bus. I can't remember where he was, but it was a small town in the Midwest. I excitedly told him about the case and how different it was in a real courtroom with real people versus on paper. I described every detail, including the victim's shark-skin leisure suit, and how he tried to tell a completely different story in court than he told on the day of the incident.

Through the static of the cellular phone he was using, Dad asked, "Was the judge nice to you?" I told him that the judge was a bit brusque, but very respectful. "Boli, I'm so proud of you. I can't believe my baby girl is in court trying cases."

He then began to repeat the story of my day in court to people on the campaign bus with him. Then he said, "Hold on, Tra. Someone wants to talk to you." The next voice I heard had a slight southern accent. "Tracey, it's Bill Clinton. Your Daddy said you knocked 'em dead in court today."

"Hi, Governor. I was so nervous, but it was so much fun," I said.

"Well, we're all proud of you. Your Dad has been driving us crazy talking about you being in court today. He misses you out there in California."

Dad got back on the phone and told me that the next time he was in L.A., he wanted to be able to see me in court.

"Okay, but you'll have to sit in the back, so people don't recognize you and lose their focus, and also so I don't get nervous and distracted."

"Are you kidding? I'm gonna sit in the front row and point at you and tell everyone that you are my daughter."

We both laughed, said our "I love yous," and hung up.

TEN

Kingmaker

W HEN Dad became DNC chair in 1989, there was nothing he relished as much as going head to head with the formidable chair of the Republican National Committee (RNC), Lee Atwater. They were both well suited for their positions and, in many ways, brought out the best in each other. For the first two years of Dad's tenure, Atwater was there, in his face on every television debate, on every split-screen interview. During 1989 and 1990, you couldn't turn on a morning show without seeing Ron Brown and Lee Atwater sparring.

Dad told us he thought Atwater was smart and tough and deserved his reputation as a Republican warrior. Jousting with Atwater kept Dad on his toes and also reminded my father how much he loved what he was doing, how right his decision had been to seek the chairmanship of the Democratic National Committee.

My father's relationship with Atwater also had a private, less contentious, more lighthearted side. When Atwater's daughter, Sally Theodosia, was born in 1990, Dad sent a gift of a stuffed animal: a donkey. His note read: "I just wanted to make sure that little Sally has a well-balanced upbringing. Please make sure that this donkey stays by her side at all times (smile)."

When Atwater discovered that he was suffering from a brain tumor, Dad was shocked and upset and felt as if he were losing a friend in the ring. Atwater and Dad had been professional peers; the contest between them always got Dad's political juices flowing. When he first heard the bad news, he wanted to call Atwater but also didn't want to seem intrusive. He said to Mom, "I wonder if he'll take my call." Dad also didn't want a call to be seen as a media gimmick; he really wanted to reach out to Atwater. He did call and eventually visited his old adversary in the hospital. There, he sat and read to Atwater. When he returned home from the hospital, he kept saying, "You never know, you just never know." When Lee Atwater died at age forty on March 29, 1991, Dad ordered the flag at DNC headquarters to be flown at half-mast. Dad attended the funeral and was deeply affected and saddened by Atwater's death.

The New DNC

During all his media appearances, Dad focused on the '92 election, talking about the campaign strategy that he and his DNC team had developed in 1990. At home, he told us the right candidate would have to be vibrant and vital to counter George Bush's image as a benign older man. The candidate would have to look and sound and carry himself like a leader. To regain the votes the Democratic party lost during the Reagan eighties, the party had to appeal to the American worker, the average Joes and Janes. Every word Dad uttered on television, every plan he and his staff devised, had a single purpose: to recapture the confidence and votes of the men and women who had lost faith in the Democratic party.

Dad came home at night from the DNC all excited about his vision for the party and its aggressive programs to regain these voters. He told us the party had always been about inclusion and participation and it was time to remind Americans about the basic difference between Us and Them. In his speeches, he said that the party would work toward expanding the economy and creating jobs; Democrats would look out for workers here at home.

Dad worked to get southerners and moderate and conservative Democrats involved in the party. He also maintained the base of the party, those individuals who always voted Democratic. He was consistent about his goals: rebuilding the party and winning the White House. He never changed, never backed down, and never altered his message from the day he took office as DNC chair in 1989 until Election Day 1992.

My father was a one-man pep rally for the Democrats and, in that capacity, he had to be critical of George Bush. Bush was not a leader but a follower, Dad said, and had been elected president on the coattails of the popular Ronald Reagan. Dad never missed a chance to attack Bush on his administration's lack of domestic agenda, inadequate economic solutions, and poor civil rights record. He always linked Bush to Reagan and the greed of the eighties.

"George Bush has economic solutions for every nation in the world, except ours," he'd say.

George Bush's greatest vulnerability is that his administration has no domestic agenda. And the saddest part is that they almost gloat about it. . . . They're evidently . . . bored with the kind of issues that affect the American people—health care, housing, employment, the state of the economy, the environment.

People talk about President Bush and his travels around the world [and] it's almost like he's running for Secretary General of the United Nations. We need a President who can take care of home. . . . George Bush and Ronald Reagan want us to believe that the 1980s were a glory period for America. . . . I think the 1980s were a disaster for America. They were a time of cynicism and greed and self-centeredness. The rich got richer, the poor got poorer, and the middle class got the blood squeezed out of them. . . .

The President's performance with respect to the Civil Rights Bill has been an absolute disgrace; it's been disgusting. It is clearly not a quota bill. It bars quotas. . . . The fact that the President chose two very interesting forums to announce his opposition to the Civil Rights Bill is significant. The first was his speech at the FBI academy. The second was his speech at the United States Military Academy at West Point.

In addition to criticizing the Bush administration, the other key element in Dad's strategy was to reiterate his certainty that the Democrats would win the White House in 1992. On every morning show, and at every public appearance, he told the nation why it should and would elect a Democratic president in the next election. After each appearance, Dad would call to ask, "How'd I do?" The first call was always to Mom. Often, he would call me and Michael and some of his friends: "How did I do?" My father seemed so confident but even he needed affirmation from those closest to him. And we were honest with him. If he was strong and on point we'd say so, but on the rare occasions when he fumbled, we would let him know.

During 1990 and 1991, the DNC reestablished itself as a professional organization led by my father and competent professionals from the political and business world. Because each staff member was so bright, and so different, the DNC offices at 430 South Capitol Street were often tension-filled. Dad rallied his troops whenever they had doubts, anxieties, or internal disagreements. Dad's spirit was essential to the campaign effort. His glass-is-half-full attitude helped many DNC staffers maintain their own optimism whenever there was a negative incident or poll or article. Said Maria Cardona, "Obviously as a spokesperson for the party, he had to give a certain message. I would look during interviews to see if I could read [optimism] in his eyes or in his voice. It was always there. And it was real."

There was friction between the DNC and the Democratic Leadership Council during these years and Dad was often the conciliator between various members of the groups. Some Democrats, including Jesse Jackson, according to President Clinton, fanned the flames: "Jesse didn't help anything because Jesse called [the DLC] a southern white boys' club." Dad had resolved in the beginning of his tenure as chairman of the party that he would negotiate and mediate to avoid or limit the internal conflicts that had often hurt the party. "We Democrats are always really good at beating each other up," he said. "I hope this time is going to be different and we save our energy to . . . really fight the Republicans and put a Democrat in the White House."

My father devoted time and effort to this. Eventually, internal squabbling was minimized and Dad received credit for running the smoothest and least contentious Democratic election process in decades.

Dad and Paul Tully's plan for Victory '92—the presidential campaign—was based on three C's: the coordinated campaign, the campaign for the cities, and the campaign for California. They also stressed the importance of fund-raising to pay for research, communications, and political strategy. This was the Democratic party's basic message for the duration of the campaign. Bush's ratings soared, Democrats were terrified, and the only steady voice was Dad's.

Convention Site 1990

One of Dad's first tasks was to determine the site of the '92 Democratic National Convention. Planning the convention was a huge job and Dad enlisted his DNC chief of staff, Alexis Herman, to oversee the event. The result was one of the best conventions the Democratic party ever had. Despite the many problems that inevitably developed, everyone, looking back, recalled it as the smoothest-run convention in years.

Fifteen of the largest cities in the country competed to host the convention. After the cities submitted bids to the DNC, the field was narrowed down to four possibilities: New York, New Orleans, Cleveland, and Houston. The site-selection committee visited each city. Cleveland did not have the hotel space and Houston was the planned site of the Republican convention so, finally, the choice came down to New York City or New Orleans. David Dinkins, then NYC mayor and an old friend of GD's from the Hotel Theresa, lobbied hard for New York. When that city was selected, Dad was accused in the press of favoring his hometown unfairly. More disturbing, he was falsely accused of telling New York that he'd choose the city for the convention site if it awarded a contract to a sludge-treatment company in which he had a small interest. In reality, the company never received the contract and Dad didn't even know that they had applied for it until he heard it on the news. Dad and the site-selection committee chose New York because its mayor had committed to help the Democrats raise money and also because of its status as the hotel and communications center of America. The site of the convention was announced on July 11, 1990.

Finding a Candidate

Two years before the election, Dad's challenge was to find a candidate and then make sure that candidate had a clear field, that the primaries weren't marred by serious internecine wrangling. Several possible candidates emerged in 1990 and 1991, though no one was clearly The One. Mario Cuomo, whom Dad respected and admired, went through some public soul-searching that led to an awkward display of ambivalence. Other possibilities included Congressman Dick Gephardt and Senators Al Gore and Sam Nunn. Each time a potential candidate declined to run, Dad issued a statement about how much the DNC respected that individual and looked forward to his continued work for the party. By the spring of '91, only two men had thrown their hats into the ring: Senator Paul Tsongas of Massachusetts and John Silber, president of Boston University. Tsongas, who had an academic approach to government and was usually armed with studies, data, and statistics, battled cancer during this period. Silber was a conservative Democrat whose pro-life position and opinions on several other controversial issues alienated the party as well as voters; he later lost the Massachusetts gubernatorial race to Republican William Weld.

During this early period, while the stars of the Democratic party—Bill Bradley, Cuomo, Gore, Bob Kerrey—seemed unwilling to make a commitment, Dad filled the vacuum, trumpeting the Democrats and challenging the Republicans; whenever I turned on the TV, there was Dad. He discussed the DNC's new professionalism, record fund-raising, and the party's general election strategy, already in place and operative.

The Gulf War

Dad's optimism was tested during hostilities between Iraq and the United States over Iraq's invasion of Kuwait on August 2,

1990. When Iraq ignored the U.S. government's order that it remove its troops from Kuwait, and this led to a swift buildup of American forces in Saudi Arabia, President Bush enjoyed an immediate and soaring rise in his approval ratings because of his leadership role in the U.S. response to Iraq's aggression. When the media called DNC headquarters for a reaction, Dad issued a statement in support of Bush. During an international conflict, he said, both Democrats and Republicans should back the president. The Gulf War, marked by an air war that began on January 16, 1991, and an invasion of U.S. troops on February 24, had nothing to do with politics, Dad said. He added that the '92 election would be about the U.S. economy and Bush's lackluster efforts on behalf of the American people's economic security.

The Gulf War ended with a cease-fire on midnight, February 28. The polls came out immediately afterward and "took the wind out of our sails," Alexis Herman recalled. When she and Dad saw that George Bush's approval rating was 90 percent, Alexis went out late at the end of the day and bought a bottle of vodka, an unprecedented act, and she and Dad had a drink in his office. She asked him if he *really* believed they would win in '92. Remembered Alexis, "He takes a little drink. He says, 'Well, I'll tell you this. It's going to be a lot harder.' I say, 'Harder? It's going to be damn near impossible. You don't really believe this, do you?' He says, 'I still think we can do it. This can't last. Bush won't be able to sustain this.' I say, 'Ron, you're talking to me. You don't really believe this, do you?' He says, 'It's going to be harder, but we still got a chance.' I say, 'Lord, you are the most incredible human being I have ever met. I never met anybody as Pollyanna in my whole life as you are. Harder? It's impossible.' He says 'No, it's just going to be harder.' "

Dad referred to history in talking to his staff as well as the American public: Historically, he said, the approval rating of most presidents falls after an astronomic rise such as Bush's following the Gulf War. He talked about how most Americans didn't really want to reelect Bush, even though they approved of him. Dad said that Bush didn't handle anything well, other than foreign policy, and had problems with the economy and with education. Within the DNC offices, Dad reminded everyone that before the last national convention the Republican party had spent two million dollars on research and polling while the Democratic party spent only sixteen thousand.

~

Meanwhile, my father and Alexis Herman were "having fits" because there were no real candidates yet, Alexis recalled. It was an inside joke: Everything was go at the DNC except for finding a candidate. Dad decided to do some recruiting, so he held meetings with Jay Rockefeller, Bob Kerrey, Mario Cuomo, and others, but no one stepped forward. Said Alexis, "It was an awful, awful period for us. We were ready. We set this infrastructure in place. Somebody's supposed to come in and just love us to death. He spent three years [planning] for this moment—and we had no taker."

Finally, Dad organized a weekend designed to invigorate the campaign. He invited a group of potential candidates to spend June 13 and 14 at Willow Oaks, Pamela Harriman's huge, beautiful estate in Middleburg, Virginia. Dad hoped a candidate would emerge as a result of this weekend so the campaign could get under way. Dad and his team at the DNC worked hard and cooperatively to organize Middleburg. Eleven potential candidates showed up: Congressman Dick Gephardt; Senators Al Gore, Jay Rockefeller, Paul Tsongas, Tom Harkin, Bob Kerrey, Bill Bradley, George Mitchell, and Lloyd Bentsen; and Governors Bill Clinton and Bruce Babbitt. Mario Cuomo and Jesse Jackson were invited but did not attend.

Also present that weekend were key Democratic contributors. My father and Tully knew the party would need an infusion of nearly ten million dollars during the next year in order to carry out the planned nationwide coordinated campaign. During this weekend, contributors would be asked to commit to raising or contributing one hundred thousand dollars each. At the first gathering, late Thursday afternoon, Dad went around the room, introducing everyone; sitting on chairs, or on the floor, members of the group talked about what they did, why they were there. Finally, Dad described the coordinated campaign's effectiveness in winning elections for the party during the last two years and how it would win the presidency.

The weekend brought together key Democrats, both political

figures and financial supporters; it also encouraged several of the politicians to enter the presidential primaries. Middleburg was a turning point and its greatest effect was on the party itself. As Shelia Davis Lawrence remembered, "There was an energy in the air. . . . You knew that something historic was taking place. . . . It was the heart and soul of the party coming to-gether. . . . [Ron] began the meeting by talking about what it meant to each of us to be a Democrat. . . . People just bared their souls, and you could see that it wasn't about power, and it wasn't about money. It was about . . . all the best of what we humans should be."

Another major goal of Dad's was to encourage candidates to run their primary campaigns in a civil manner. He asked poten-tial candidates to run positive campaigns so they wouldn't de-stroy each other during the primary process. If they followed his suggestions, the candidate who emerged victorious would have a better chance at winning the general election, Dad said. He in-tended for Victory '92 to be run to win, but with class and style. What not to do in a campaign, according to my father, was make vicious public attacks such as the Republican-generated Willie Horton ads for Bush in '88. Another example of vicious ads was the conservative onslaught against Senators Kennedy, Biden, and Cranston, three Democrats who had opposed the nomination of Clarence Thomas to the Supreme Court. Dad pledged that un-der his administration the DNC would not condone attack ads.

Many of those present at Middleburg recalled that, for the first time, they witnessed Governor Clinton's leadership abili-ties. When he spoke, Shelia Davis Lawrence felt "there was something special about him . . . a special spark. . . . He was a leader, the right person." It was evident to those who heard Clinton handle the press, and meet and greet other Democrats, that he would make an excellent presidential candidate. But the future president had attended the Middleburg weekend against his better judgment. "I didn't want to be at any kind of cattle call," he said. "I wanted to make my own decision and then run my own campaign. But I did want to do it in a way that would help [the] Democratic party if I didn't win."

Middleburg's success was not only in finding candidates; it also helped the party do what the Republicans had been doing for years—raise substantial sums of money to support the party's nominee.

~

Shortly after Middleburg, Dad took a break from the intensity of Victory '92 for our annual family vacation. As we had done for the past ten years, we stayed in a villa borrowed from a friend on the grounds of Casa de Campo, a resort in the Dominican Republic. My father and I were sunbathing one afternoon by the pool, with its view of the Caribbean, while Michael napped and Mom read. Suddenly, he leaned over and said, "What's on your leg? You have a mark on your leg. At the top, on your hip." Then he reached over to scrape it off. When the mark remained, he looked surprised. "Is that a tattoo?" When I replied that it was, he asked me if it was fake. I just looked at him.

"Oh, my God, why would you ruin your body that way? You're going to be stuck with that thing forever!"

After a few seconds, though, Dad became curious and asked about the process: Did it hurt? How was it done? I told him about the needle and how it was most painful when the outline was done. "Oh, my God, did you cry?" asked Dad, his disapproval overridden by his interest and concern. While he never approved of my tattoo, my father accepted it as quickly and easily, as he accepted most things that troubled him, and never mentioned it again—except, of course, to tease me.

Even with the intensity of the presidential campaign heating up, Dad took the time to help make arrangements for Michael's upcoming wedding. On Saturday, October 5, 1991, my brother was married to Tamera Smith Barnes. Tami and Michael had known each other since high school. The wedding at the National Presbyterian Church on Nebraska Avenue, with a reception at the City Club, a private club in downtown D.C., was beautiful. Mom and Dad couldn't stop beaming with joy and pride.

Clinton's the One

In November 1991, Governor Clinton, in an appearance at the party's Conference of State Chairs, again demonstrated his potential as a candidate. And in December Mario Cuomo finally made up his mind not to run. When Clinton made his commitment to run that month, he called my father to discuss his decision. Dad encouraged him and said he would be part of what would hopefully be a talented field of Democratic candidates. Clinton recalled that Dad seemed optimistic about his chances: "I think he always thought I had some chance to win, even though I had a very narrow base and a narrow shot to get through it."

For a while, Clinton and the other men who publicly announced that they would seek the nomination—Tsongas, Gephardt, Kerrey, Jerry Brown, Tom Harkin, Douglas Wilder— were called the Seven Dwarfs behind their backs, recalled Maria Cardona, because no one really believed any of them could win the presidency. Except my father, of course. During the primaries, January through June, Dad was crucial as a conciliator, minimizing the internal squabbling that had been so detrimental in the past. After Clinton began to show a strong lead, Dad encouraged the other candidates to get out of the primary race and back Clinton. He told them, "Hey, we've got to rally around our candidate so we can start pushing against Bush." Dad worked to coalesce the party as early as possible; he always said it was essential to have a short primary period so Democrats could concentrate on beating the Republicans, not each other.

That winter, the Gennifer Flowers accusation hit, which was quickly followed by the Vietnam draft story. Even when others, whom the President recalled as a "weak-kneed chorus," suggested he withdraw, my father remained loyal to Clinton. Dad believed the Republican party viewed Clinton as Bush's greatest threat and so had targeted the Arkansas governor in an attempt to knock him out of the running early.

Observed Clinton, "The press . . . always want[s] to take somebody out at presidential election time. And [Ron] understood that; he got it." Dad stayed committed to Clinton despite the pressure from other Democrats, some of whom wanted to be the candidate and others who were fearful about the party's ability to withstand the erupting scandals. Late one night in April Pamela Harriman called Dad at home to tell him that she didn't think Clinton could survive the scandal and that he, my father, should immediately look for another candidate. Dad ignored her suggestion.

Many Democrats wrongly believed that Dad and Clinton had a "preexisting" relationship because of Dad's loyal attitude toward the emerging front-runner; they had known each other only slightly before the campaign. On Super Bowl weekend in January 1992, Dad, Mom, and I went to the Mauna Kea resort on the Big Island in Hawaii with RNC chairman Clayton Yuetter and his late wife, Jeanne. Dad and Yuetter were to give major policy speeches on the presidential race. On that Sunday evening, we saw Governor and Mrs. Clinton on *60 Minutes* addressing the Gennifer Flowers allegations. Dad was so impressed with how "Bill and Hill," as he called them, handled themselves. He told us, "Clinton's the one. He is going to be our next president." But publicly my father remained neutral, encouraging all the primary candidates.

Clinton won major primaries, including New York, California, Ohio, Florida, Michigan, and Illinois. He had enough delegate votes to win the nomination but was running third in the polls, behind George Bush and third-party candidate Ross Perot. Despite Clinton's delegate lead, there was still pressure on Dad to find a more acceptable candidate, one who did not have scandal dogging him. Said President Clinton, "He wasn't just being loyal to me. He understood that the process had to have some integrity, that I had won this thing fair and square."

My father was optimistic that once the convention was over and Clinton had been nominated, the public would look differently at the candidates. He remained enthusiastic about Clinton.

"You know, Clinton," Dad told Michael, "he brings the right stuff, he's charismatic, he's young, he's tall. He has all the little cosmetic pieces, [including] a strong wife. And he's a successful governor. Arkansas is doing well economically."

Dad stuck to his original ideas: that George Bush had not given the American people a compelling reason to reelect him and that the Democrats would win the presidency. Clinton and my father spoke often, with Dad encouraging him and reminding him not to worry about the polls. "We have the right issues and the right message," Dad told Clinton.

My father was certain that if Clinton could survive the merciless beating he was getting in the press, he would win the election and succeed as president. It was a trial by fire for Clinton and, unknown to us then, a taste of my father's own future problems with fabricated charges and allegations blown out of proportion in the press.

The President has always credited my father for his role in the winning of the presidency. Since 1989, Dad had rebuilt the party into a well-run organization and had become a charismatic public figure and spokesman for the Democrats. But if he had wavered at all in his support for Clinton, none of that would have meant anything. Said President Clinton, "If he had ever given a signal that it was okay to vote [against] the person who had won the primaries and won the nomination fair and square the . . . press would have savaged me."

On November 5, 1996, in his televised acceptance speech on the night of his reelection to a second term as President, he again talked about Dad's role in his being President.

"I thank those who served this administration and our cause who are no longer here tonight. And one especially I must thank—my friend and brother Ron Brown. You're looking down on us and I know you're smiling, too."

Lynn Cutler, deputy chair of the DNC under Dad, saw Clinton on the south lawn of the White House the day after this speech. "Thanks for talking about Ron like that. It meant a lot to me," Lynn said. And President Clinton responded, "It meant a lot to me." Said Lynn, "I don't think he's got anyone around him now who can do what [Ron] did, which was deliver the truth, deliver bad news, but do it in a way that the other person could hear it."

At the last Business Council meeting before the '92 convention, in Pebble Beach, Florida, on August 1, Clinton was the keynote speaker and Dad was celebrating his fifty-first birthday. After dinner, Dad was presented with a birthday cake topped with a white-chocolate replica of the White House. Dad and Clinton sat side by side while Dad blew out the candles and, of course, everyone knew that what he had wished for was sitting right on top of that cake.

Convention '92

One of Dad's goals was to clarify during the '92 convention what the Democratic party was all about. He wanted to connect to ordinary citizens, regular men and women who lived all over the country. He also wanted to make clear that the DNC was the party of inclusion; he wanted the delegates at the convention to reflect that. Dad also intended that the new unity in the party forged over the past three years would be evident to all who participated in the convention and all who watched it. Finally, he wanted a new level of enthusiasm, a joy and happiness to be projected by the delegates, a sense that this was the Democrats' year. By the time of the convention, it was all happening: Ross Perot withdrew on July 16 and awkwardly reentered on October 1—and the Democrats were up in the polls. We were winning and we were happy. As President Clinton described it to me, "We were rocking."

The '92 convention was well planned and well executed, successful in terms of the handling of logistics and personalities and all the hundreds of details. "Bill Clinton happened to be very lucky that Ron Brown was chairman of the DNC," said Shelia Davis Lawrence. "Using the DNC, he pulled together the states, and made this country ready to elect a Democrat—which we weren't prepared to do before. And the fact that he did it in four years is amazing. The transformation was astonishing."

Of course, there were internal problems at the convention, which Dad handled. He refused to allow the appearance of the two speakers who would not endorse Clinton: would-be candidate Jerry Brown, former governor of California; and Bob Casey, the pro-life governor of Pennsylvania. Pro-lifers said the DNC was gagging them, preventing them from being heard. And Clinton himself was sympathetic to Casey, since Casey had survived a multiple-organ transplant; maybe he should be allowed to talk during the convention even if he refused to endorse, Clinton proposed. But Dad was adamant: No endorsement, no speech. "This is a party convention," Dad told Clinton. "We are open, we are inclusive, we are letting everybody in, we've been generous to everybody. But we cannot let this man speak unless he says he will endorse you. That's what this is about; we've got to win the White House with a unified party."

Since the Democrats were celebrating "The Year of the Woman," Dad wanted to put all the major women candidates onstage together. But former New York State attorney general Robert Abrams had a fit because he didn't want Geraldine Ferraro, his opponent in the Democratic primary for a New York senate seat, up there. Then some of the women candidates starting complaining about who they'd have to be onstage alongside. One woman said, "I can't go on with her because she's running against a guy on my committee. He's my friend." Dad insisted they do what they had to do for party unity, and everyone acquiesced. The image of all these women standing together was a dramatic announcement to the American people that the Democratic party was strongly behind its women candidates.

On a more prosaic level, the forty-first Democratic National Convention was about logistics. More than twenty thousand people convened in Madison Square Garden for four days to nominate the presidential candidate. Behind the scenes, Dad and the DNC staff worked day and night to ensure the convention would be run smoothly and without incident.

Dad's office was at the New York Hilton. Michael worked with Dad on credentials, or passes, for my parents' friends while DNC staffers handled credentials for members of Congress, state chairs, and other political officials. Mom hosted events for the spouses of elected officials, while I, having just graduated from law school, tried to balance filling in for my parents at events and studying for the California bar exam.

The first day of the convention, Dad was up on the podium with Mayor Dinkins and Alexis Herman during the opening ceremony. It was a moment that Dinkins will never forget, a proud moment for African-Americans. Recollected Dinkins, "We looked out at this vast expanse and I thought, 'We're in charge.' And we were. I was the mayor. Ron was chairman of the whole shooting match, and Alexis was CEO of the convention."

During convention week, Dad was accompanied by members of the NYPD wherever he went. The security and protection were necessary because he was high profile that week; his photograph appeared in *The New York Times* daily and was often featured in *USA Today*. At night, after Mom went to sleep and I went to my room to stay up all night studying, Dad and Michael would kick back and do their standard relaxation ritual: room service—lobster bisque, hamburger, duck, and salad with both Thousand Island and blue cheese dressings—and ESPN. Said Michael, "We'd split the duck, split a burger, split a salad, and watch sports. Then we'd go to sleep."

Dad made the decisions at the Democratic National Convention in 1992; it was his show. For example, when Clinton was nominated on Wednesday night, he made a dramatic entrance into the vast arena, beaming, shaking hands with hundreds of people in the cheering crowd as he made his way to the podium. This entrance had been Dad's brainchild. Usually, the candidate remains out of sight until he is nominated and only enters the convention the next day, when it's time to make his acceptance speech. Although Clinton would normally not have made an appearance until Thursday night, Dad thought it important that Clinton join the convention and say hi to the thousands of delegates. His point was that Democrats were the party of the people and this was the candidate of the people.

~

During convention week, the subject of My Future Husband came up; it was always fodder for my family's conversations. Plus, that week I was meeting many attractive, mature, and employed young men. Sometimes we'd talk about it seriously, but more often Dad would joke. His favorite running joke was that when I was ready to get married, he would convene a group of ten men he and Mom had selected as appropriate for their daughter. I would date each, pick the man I liked most, and Mom and Dad would tell us what time to be at the church. In this scenario, my father could be certain that I'd marry someone appropriate. He often questioned my judgment because I had dated so many "knuckleheads," as he put it. Of course, he assumed there was no man in the world who wouldn't want to compete to be my husband.

Dad often talked about my marrying someone who "would bring something to the table." He hoped that whomever I married would not be overwhelmed or intimidated by our gregarious family and would participate in our family life. Whenever I dated someone who was quiet or timid, Dad would say, "He's not ready for prime time." That meant my date was not ready to step up to the table; he was not a contender. Whenever I talked to Dad on the phone, from senior year in college on, he would say, "Let me know when you are ready for me to get the panel together."

The Campaign

In January 1992, Dad had sent a confidential memo to senior DNC leadership, outlining his strategies for bringing defeat to Bush and a win to Clinton. He first listed goals the party had already achieved:

> (1) Bush is way too concerned with foreign policy. . . . His foreign policy "strength" is being made into a weakness. Our success is measured by the amount of effort they are spending trying to counter this theme. . . . (2) The elitist George Bush favors the rich and powerful. . . . His inaction is a natural consequence of his just not "getting it." (3) Most of what Bush is saying and doing is *political,* designed to halt his support hemorrhage. . . .

Dad concluded with a policy statement about the party and how basic Democratic principles could win the election:

> We Democrats need to speak frankly and often about personal responsibility, knowing right from wrong, loving our country and the American ideal, hard work, and caring about those who need help (the safety net has been shredded). Policies that are important to our future which strain the Republican Presidential Coalition: pro-choice, environment, children and poverty, racism, fair trade and job exports. . . . If we keep our eyes on the prize and approach the major, basic issues with common sense, then we will, in 1992, elect a larger congressional majority—as well as a Democratic President.

Clinton's campaign had a strong start because each state in the nation already had a coordinated base in place. The coordinated campaign elected President Clinton. It required that the DNC contribute an amount of money to the state Democratic parties, which would then contribute a matching amount. Both the national party and the state party would then pool their efforts to elect the president: one master voter file, one get-out-the-vote drive, one phone bank, one voter registration drive. Training campaign workers to do scheduling, advance, and organizational work was done by teams from the DNC. These teams traveled to thirty targeted states and worked with those states' campaign staffs. Said Carl Wagner, "Every state we targeted was won by Bill Clinton in '92."

The coordinated campaign maximized individual and statewide efforts by utilizing them wisely and efficiently. Resources went further, Democrats saved money, and the party demonstrated the benefits of working together.

Dad gathered together the best and strongest team to work on the campaign, and he and the presidential campaign team put out only one message: Election '92 was about the economy. The message was repeated over and over and eventually everyone involved in the campaign began to focus on it. Dad based his message on what he'd heard from the American public. Their concerns were work and income and whether they'd have enough to feed and clothe and house their families. It was mainly the press and the Republicans who cared about the manufactured scandals concerning candidate Clinton. Real people had real concerns and that's what Dad focused on.

There was also a turnaround in the party's fund-raising results after fellow Democrats began to understand and accept Dad's methods, the coordinated campaign, and his unswerving optimism. And this was reflected in increased donations to the party. Dad's fund-raising message was the same as it had been since 1989: Democrats need to work together. It made a difference who was president because there was a real difference between Democrats and Republicans. By working together through the coordinated campaign, Dad said, Democrats could elect a president and take back the White House. The DNC's fund-raising team focused on federal money, called hard money, which can go directly to help individual candidates, and on funds to help the party generically, called soft money.

Clinton's campaign headquarters were in Little Rock, and some DNC staffers, including Paul Tully and Mark Steitz, moved there to work on the campaign. As would be expected, some tensions over division of labor and territory developed between the DNC staff and Clinton's campaign people. Dad was constantly on the phone with his staff members and with Clinton's campaign manager, James Carville, and most problems were worked out.

Dad went to Houston as part of a "DNC Truth Squad" when the Republican convention was held there August 17–20. He held press conferences daily at a Houston restaurant, Papadeaux's, giving the Democratic spin on the day's events at the GOP convention. DNC staffers in Houston with Dad recalled the morning he and two Republican senators greeted each other with big handshakes and warm embraces all around. Remembered staffer Jim Desler, "They greeted him as if he were an old friend: 'Oh, hey, yeah! I heard you were around here. How are you?' They had this wonderful camaraderie, friendship, and true respect for him."

One evening, a busload of Young Republicans, all in white shirts and ties, disrupted the daily DNC press conference by shouting and pounding on the restaurant's windows. Dad continued talking, unflappable, and said, "They're just doing what they have to do—create a diversion—because we're talking about the issues and we're telling the truth here."

Of course, the Democrats had their own high jinks during the campaign. Dan Carroll, head of the DNC's opposition research, ordered thousands of little plastic lips to remind the American public of Bush's infamous goof: "Read my lips: No new taxes." My father had the lips distributed everywhere and had Democratic campaign workers shout the broken promise at the Republican convention.

Dan Carroll also came up with T-shirts that mimicked those seen at rock concerts. Printed on the front was: "The George Bush Anywhere But America Tour." They were a huge success and became the official garb of Democratic campaign workers. I still wear mine. The back of the T-shirt had a list of the foreign countries Bush had visited during his term, pointing out how little time he'd devoted to a domestic agenda.

During the campaign, the Republicans constantly brought up issues such as race, abortion, and health care; these are wedge issues, which divide people, causing different groups to become angry at each other. Dad would become quite emotional about these issues, saying to me and Mom and Michael, "How can they do this? I don't understand it!" George Bush's approval rating was sky-high at this time and DNC staffers often felt as if they were "swimming in Jell-O," as one said. Dad, always optimistic, would double his efforts to speak out against Bush in television interviews and in public appearances. He did well in interviews because he was great at hitting a fastball. And Dad was one of the campaign's most valuable speakers, substituting often for the presidential and vice-presidential candidates at campaign stops around the country because he was familiar with the platform and was charismatic enough to attract and hold crowds.

When the crowds were tough, as they were sometimes in the South, he still held his own. Asked how he would deal with southern Democrats who didn't want to deal with a black man or see a black man as head of the party, he responded, "I have had to put up with this all my life." And then he told the anecdote about when he and Mom were not allowed to eat their lunch in the Shoney's parking lot. Dad's remarks about race were repeated often to us as well as to various audiences.

"All my life," he said, "I've had to deal with southern attitudes about blacks and about black men in positions of power and authority. I've been able to make it work. And I'm going to make it work."

He loved debate, loved being on the spot, loved television. On May 5, 1992, he debated Lynn Martin, Bush's secretary of labor, on *Larry King Live*. This was a few days after the L.A. uprising that had occurred after not-guilty verdicts were handed down for the police officers who beat Rodney King. In this instance, Dad directed his remarks both to working people and to the disaffected population who had participated in the devastation of Los Angeles neighborhoods: "Violence takes place all over America every day and nobody pays attention. Nobody seems to care . . . when you don't have a job and can't support your family.

"We need the courage and the moral leadership to deal with race," Dad said, referring to the Rodney King situation. Shocked and horrified as he was by the beating, the verdict, and the uprising, Dad never expressed anything but a "How do we fix it?" attitude. He was not bitter or angry. "What do we do now? How do we solve this?" he asked. The optimistic belief that we could fix what was broken was how he lived his life, how he dealt with all adversity, whether it was personal or political.

My father's core strength helped him survive the tragedy of Paul Tully's death. On September 24, 1992, shortly before the election on which he had worked so hard, Paul died of a heart attack alone in his room at the Excelsior Hotel in Little Rock, Arkansas. Dad had to overcome his own grief to help Paul's daughters, Jessica and Miranda, plan their father's funeral. Then he had to bolster DNC staff members who were crushed by Paul's loss. "You can't stop. You have to go on," Dad said to dispirited staffers who felt paralyzed without the man who ran their day-to-day operations. Although he too was crushed and felt very alone, not once did he let the others know. He prodded and pushed, cheered them up, motivated them to keep on with the work of the party. Always searching for the positive, he told the DNC staff that Paul had started the process and their responsibility was to finish it. No one was hired to replace Paul and the campaign went on without him.

The night of Paul Tully's funeral, my father and Mickey Kantor, chair of the Clinton-Gore campaign, were chosen by Bill Clinton and Al Gore to negotiate all aspects of the upcoming debates between them and George Bush and Dan Quayle. Areas under discussion included: when and where the debates would take place, their format, how many there would be, and who would moderate.

By the end of October, just before Election Day, Bush's poll numbers were down and Clinton's were up. Dad's strategy had worked and even skeptics believed the Democrats had a chance. No one scoffed now when they heard my father's optimistic chant: "We will win in '92." As the campaign wound down, Dad and Governor Clinton made appearances all over, with my father receiving ovations as long and as loud as Clinton's. People began to realize that this election might be won by a Democrat and they cheered the man they believed responsible.

The night before Election Day, Dad and President Clinton made eight campaign stops, flying from city to city; Michael was with them. At four in the morning, they landed in Brownsville, Texas, for an airport rally. It was cold but they were warmed by the cheers of the ten to fifteen thousand people there to greet them. Clinton made a wonderful speech and he and Dad received rousing applause. Michael recalled that Dad and Clinton were affectionate and keyed up. One could feel the momentum. Remembered Michael, "Dad and Clinton were touchy-feely, always holding each other and bonding, saying, 'We're really going to do this. This is really going to happen.'"

On Election Night, Dad, Mom, and Michael, along with DNC staff, watched returns at the Democratic base at the Omni Shoreham Hotel on Connecticut Avenue. I was in L.A. hosting my own election party and spending a lot of time on the phone with Mom and Dad, talking about the California returns. When it became clear that Clinton had won, Dad returned to the ballroom, doing a walk through the hotel, during which he gave spot interviews to the press who were staked out. The following morning, Dad did a round of morning interviews on the networks and then had a press conference at the DNC offices. He and Mom then flew down to Little Rock to personally congratulate the Clintons and the Gores, as well as the campaign staff that worked so hard.

There is no way to adequately describe my father's elation at the election of Bill Clinton. He had helped put a president in the White House. He had helped elect a Democratic president for the first time in sixteen years. For four years, my father had been a man with a mission. Now, he'd met his goals and carried out his mission. I spoke with Dad on the phone the day after the election and heard in his voice a deep joy and sense of fulfillment that I will never, ever forget.

"We're finally running things," Dad said as we stood, arm in arm, in the state dining room of the White House. "Let's paint the White House black," I said to Dad, referring to a popular seventies funk song. We kept bursting into giggles after that.

The racial makeup of the Cabinet was different than it had ever been before. And at the buffet reception hosted by the President and First Lady for new Cabinet members and their families, the difference was apparent. The room was dominated by people of color: Mike Espy, secretary of agriculture; Hazel O'Leary, secretary of energy; Jesse Brown, secretary of veterans affairs; Federico Peña, secretary of transportation; Henry Cisneros, secretary of housing and urban development; and Dad.

A few minutes earlier, Dad and the other new members of President Clinton's Cabinet had taken the oath of office in a ceremony held in the East Room. Our family was there seven strong—Mom, me, Michael, Tami, Chip, Mere, and Nan, all looking on proudly as Dad was sworn in.

Now, at the luncheon, Dad and I told each other that never in its history had the White House held so many black and Hispanic guests who were there as members of the Cabinet rather than visiting dignitaries. One of the black waiters, who approached us with a tray of drinks, said how great it was to see so many brothers and sisters in the White House.

Dad was so happy, he could not stop laughing. And I was no help. When he was across the room talking to the President, I mouthed to him, "Let's paint the White House black!" and he had to clear his throat and cover his mouth to keep from laughing out loud.

~ *ELEVEN* ~

The Commerce Years

Dᴀᴅ's career rarely left him much free time, but the period directly after the 1992 presidential election was unusually hectic. My father was still chair of the DNC and also a partner at Patton, Boggs and Blow when President-elect Clinton appointed him chairman of the Presidential Inaugural Committee. The Presidential Inaugural Committee organized the week of activities and events that made up the inaugural. The Congressional Inaugural Committee, on the other hand, handled the actual ceremony where the President was sworn into office. From November 1992 through January '93, Dad wrapped up his work at the DNC and, at the same time, plunged full speed ahead with inaugural planning.

Dad and the Inaugural Committee staff worked out of an office at the Navy Yard in southwest D.C. He oversaw committees for each aspect of the inaugural: parades, children's events, entertainment, and events at the Mall, the expanse between the White House and the Washington Monument. An example of Inaugural Day hoopla were the dozens of colorful, enthusiastic high school marching bands brought to D.C. from all over the country.

During the inaugural preparations, Dad was thinking hard about his future. He was certain that President-elect Clinton would offer him a Cabinet post. Mom was also certain of this, but she was dismayed, rather than elated, as Dad was. She didn't want Dad in government; she didn't think it was the best place for him and urged him to return to Patton Boggs. But my optimistic father had no doubts. Mom and Dad endlessly discussed the issue, a discussion that, for them, contained only loving exchanges and no real dissension.

Mom: "Do you really want to do it, honey?"

Dad: "Baby, I really, really want to do it."

Dad's friend Courtland Cox told me that Dad "could have made a lot more money [practicing law], but I think he felt it was his duty [to join the administration]." In part, to carry out his goal to improve life for all Americans, my father had long ago decided it was better to operate from a position of power, rather than a position of protest. He wanted to be able to set the agenda. And even though most of his friends and relatives believed he should remain outside the government, there was no question in his mind: He wanted a seat at that Cabinet table.

Shortly after the election, Dad told the President-elect that he wanted to be secretary of state because the position contained all the elements that excited him, especially international relations. He even talked to Lauri Fitz-Pegado about assisting him in composing a letter to the President-elect that would list his qualifications for this top-level job. But before he could draft such a document, Clinton told Dad he planned to appoint an experienced, mature secretary of state in order to balance Clinton's own relative inexperience in foreign affairs. He would nominate Warren Christopher, who had been deputy secretary of state under President Carter, Clinton told Dad, adding that Dad's chance for this post might well come during a second term.

Said Mom, "Ronnie said he would really like to be secretary of state. I said, Who wouldn't? But from what I could see, with Jim Baker and George Shultz and the rest of them, all they ever did was fly somewhere on a plane. They were never home. So I didn't think that was so hot. Secretary of state didn't impress me."

Mom wanted a private life with Dad and a family life, and that was her priority. Mom felt that Dad could help Clinton and the Democratic party more as an outsider because government employees frequently had to temper their views and positions in order to work within the system. Everywhere they went, people would say, "So, Ron, now that Clinton has won, are you going into the Cabinet?" Mom would respond, "No, he's going right back to 2550 M Street"—his law firm address. Dad would just laugh.

Many of Dad's friends agreed with my mother, seeing public service as synonymous with smaller income, lack of privacy, and compromise of one's personal values and beliefs. Dad felt he had to explain to his doubting friends why he wanted to go into the administration and spoke with Ken Chenault, Earl Graves, publisher of *Black Enterprise* magazine, and others who believed Dad should remain in the private sector. Even some of Dad's friends in government couldn't understand his view. Mom remembers Congressman Julian Dixon saying, "Why, Ron? You don't need the grief." Dad tried to persuade his skeptical friends that he was doing the right thing, but like Mom, they remained unconvinced. However, they told him they would support him in any choice he made.

As soon as it was clear to everyone that Dad was determined to take a position in the Clinton administration, my mother had to accept it. And while Mom and Tommy Boggs cried on each other's shoulders because Tommy wanted Dad back at the firm, my father was busy negotiating with the President-elect over which Cabinet nomination he would receive. Vinnie Cohen, Dad's lawyer and close friend, continued trying to convince him not to take a government post.

"Look," Vinnie said to Dad, "you brought this man [Clinton] to the promised land. Now, you've got access to the President. You go to the private sector. You make your money. If he has a good term, you can come in on the second term."

Truth is, my father had dreams larger than law firms and fees. Our family knew he wanted to return to public service. But Vinnie said what I had always suspected and had heard from a couple of other people: My father wanted to be the first African-American president of the United States. Vinnie thought that after working closely with the Democrats and the President-elect, Dad had decided that the highest office in the land was not beyond him and was something he might very well one day attain. "You start to lose your awe of these people when you see them up close and personal," said Vinnie. "You see there isn't anything special there. 'I speak better than they do. I'm brighter.' So I think, in the back of Ron's mind was, 'Hey, you know, why not?' "

Jim Desler, who worked with Dad at both the DNC and Commerce, told me the same thing. "I think he was going to be vice president or president of the United States at some point." Two days after my father's death, his friend Bill Raspberry wrote that Dad had spent the last twenty years moving "toward the goal he really had in mind: the Presidency." Jim Desler said that Dad was motivated more by his desire for social justice than by a desire for power. Jim was with my father in 1993 when Dad criticized the CEO of a California business he was visiting for not having a single woman or person of color in a position of authority. While Dad enjoyed the good life, money was never a driving force. And if his goal was to someday be elected president, he had to take a Cabinet post in 1993 to position himself for the future.

∼

Mom told me that some DNC staffers encouraged Dad to take a position in the Clinton administration. She believed much of this was self-interest; they wanted jobs. While Dad didn't necessarily disagree with her, he also felt responsible for his loyal DNC staff. But what most drove my father was his always present desire to be part of something important. Dad wanted to work alongside President Clinton and the others in his administration to shape the country for the next four years. Imagining how he would have felt about not joining the Clinton team, Dad told Mom, "The first time I see the Cabinet together, I am going to be angry that I'm not at the table."

He told me that he would feel out of the loop watching the new Clinton administration take shape without him. "I never want to look back and say I should have gone into the Cabinet. I don't want any regrets." Dad was also clear that only the "real

Cabinet," the fourteen positions legislated by Congress, would do. The other high-level posts, called the Sub-Cabinet, are seated at the pleasure of the president and include U.N. ambassador and U.S. trade representative. It is up to the president instead of Congress, to determine their role and funding. That would not have done for Dad. He said, "If I'm going to do it, then I'm going to be at the table." And in succession. The fourteen legislated Cabinet posts are in line to succeed the president should anything happen to him.

The order of succession is important to protocol, determining the order in which Cabinet members sit in the Cabinet Room at the White House and at the State of the Union address, even how they enter certain rooms on state occasions. Each Cabinet member's succession is based on when that department was established. Dad was tenth in line to succeed the president, after the vice president, speaker of the house, president pro tempore of the Senate, and six other Cabinet members. On Dad's List, being an African-American in line to succeed the president of the United States was no small achievement.

Later, after Dad became secretary of commerce, he described the Cabinet Room to us, as almost completely filled with a huge dark wood conference table around which were placed leather chairs embossed with Cabinet members' names. The president sits in the middle, with the vice president across from him. Dad sat one seat away from the President, next to the secretary of defense. I guess you could call that A Seat at the Table. (During the summer of 1996, we finally saw the chamber for ourselves when our family was invited by President Clinton to the first Cabinet meeting since Dad's death for a ceremony where he and Vice President Gore presented Dad's Cabinet chair to us. The chair is now on display at the Ronald H. Brown Foundation in Washington.)

My father made it clear to the President-elect that he didn't want a position that had been held before by an African-American and that he didn't want to deal with "traditional minority issues" like labor, welfare, and housing. Dad wanted to add to his List of Firsts. There were several possibilities, including attorney general, chief of staff, U.S. trade representative, or U.S. ambassador to the United Nations.

Dad told us that some of the options were not even in the running: He had no desire to be the nation's top prosecutor, the attorney general, and chief of staff was a shaky position because it generally changed yearly. Although my father was attracted to the negotiating and international aspects of U.S. trade representative, in the end, he did not believe the position had enough clout. Dad gave much thought to the job of U.N. ambassador, which would have given him foreign policy experience that might have helped him in his goal of becoming secretary of state. Also, since U.N. headquarters are in New York City, he could have established residency there, which would have set him up for another possible career move that he'd thought about—running for U.S. senator from New York. In the end, Dad decided he wanted to remain in Washington, inside the Beltway, helping set government policy. One night, President-elect Clinton called Dad at home and formally offered him the U.N. position; Dad was disappointed, since he'd already thought about and rejected that post. He told Clinton that he would think about it and they planned to meet to discuss it further.

Several days later, they met at the Hay-Adams Hotel, and President-elect Clinton offered my father the post of U.S. secretary of commerce. On the way home, Dad called Mom, who was next door at the Amoses. "The President has offered me Commerce. I have to let him know in the morning, so let's talk about it as soon as I get home." Kent and Carmen Amos were thrilled, but Mom still couldn't get excited. "I just knew I didn't want him to go into the administration," remembered Mom. "It had nothing to do with my love and respect for the President, or my belief in his views for the country. I just wanted Ronnie back at the law firm." Nan agreed with my mother and kept asking Dad, "Ronnie, why do you want to do it?"

When Dad returned to the Inaugural Committee office after his meeting with Clinton, Christine Varney, the committee's general counsel, burst into his office and shut the door and asked, "What'd you get?" They talked back and forth, with Dad excited about the international and diplomacy aspects of Commerce. Recollected Christine, "It was the right job for him and

I think he felt that way. . . . My guess is that Clinton wanted Ron very close to him, and I think he could have had virtually any Cabinet job he wanted."

That night, he showed Mom a book about the department, with its thirty-six thousand employees all over the world. He was so thrilled, she recalled, because Clinton had told him that Commerce would be in the forefront of the new administration's aggressive agenda to perk up the lagging economy. Dad was certain that he could make a real contribution as commerce secretary.

"We can really do something for the American people," said Dad. "[Commerce] is not mapped and the Republicans have used it as a dumping ground. But the President has a real interest in it and a whole economic agenda can come out of it."

Mom finally had to accept the inevitable; there was no holding Dad back.

Tommy Boggs warned Dad that he thought it would be difficult, running a large, amorphous department with no constituency, no outside advocates who cared about it as an entity. In contrast, Tommy pointed out, the Defense Department had relationships with hundreds of defense contractors who would fight to see that department get its funding.

But Commerce appeared to be a good fit for my father. With the end of the Cold War, global economics was increasingly important, perhaps the major issue in the international arena. Dad saw Commerce as a way for him to take on a leadership role internationally, and also to help "grow" the U.S. economy, as Clinton had promised to do during his campaign.

Dad called the President-elect the next morning to accept the post of commerce secretary. The next day, December 12, Mom, Dad, Michael, and Tami traveled to Little Rock to attend a press conference that Clinton had called for the purpose of announcing Dad's nomination. I was stuck in L.A., prosecuting a case. On his way to Little Rock, Dad spoke to Jim Desler at DNC headquarters. Jim congratulated Dad, then said, "I'm really embarrassed about asking you this, but what does a commerce secretary do?" Dad answered, "I don't know. I'm about to find out." When Clinton made his announcement, he said, "I want the Commerce Department to become the powerhouse of the government. And the one person that can do that is Ronald Brown."

After the press conference, Dad told Mom he had a real problem. Clinton had scheduled an economic summit in Little Rock for the next morning. He wanted Dad to attend. The problem: Dad didn't have any spare contact lenses with him. He wore soft lenses and was fanatical about keeping them immaculate, cleaning them constantly. He debated whether he could survive the meeting without glasses or contacts. He decided to fly back to Washington, get his contacts and a change of clothing, and then fly right back to Little Rock.

∽

In order to accept a high-level government post, Dad would have to end his twelve-year partnership at Patton, Boggs and Blow. Severing this relationship was difficult because, as managing partner Tim May recalled, the law firm had to change the way it did its bookkeeping in order for Dad to resign. To satisfy the President-elect's staff and the Senate Republicans, the firm had to immediately pay Dad all monies due him so that relations between my father and Patton, Boggs and Blow would officially be over by the time he joined the Clinton administration in January.

Under the firm's normal partnership agreement, my father would collect profits earned on clients he had brought into the firm even if he were no longer with the firm. But because of the sensitive nature of a Cabinet post, and the potential for conflicts of interest with the firm or its clients, this was unacceptable. His share of accounts receivable and work in process as of the date he was to resign would normally have taken the firm about two years to collect. Again, that was unacceptable. "So we had to change the whole system," said Tim May, "forcing us to guess how much we were going to collect on . . . stuff we hadn't billed for yet."

After considerable discussion, the firm paid Dad a sum calculated to be his share of what the firm expected it would ultimately collect. Later, when other partners had to go through the same process as they too joined government service, Tim

May recalled there was a bit of wrangling about the sums being paid. Not Dad. When he saw the check, Dad said, "Fine. Where do I sign?" He was ready to move on.

∿

After the news broke about Dad's nomination as secretary of commerce, Mom said, "everything just like took off, with dozens of people coming and going at our house." During this period, in addition to wrapping up his work at the DNC and the law firm, and in addition to running the Inaugural Committee, my father began preparing for transition—the period of time when one administration hands over the reins of government to the next administration—and confirmation, the process by which the Senate Commerce Committee would question Dad to determine if he was qualified to be commerce secretary. He was briefed by dozens of people on the myriad aspects of the department so he could be confirmed and then take over the department with competence.

I will never forget Christmas that year. Even with all that was happening, Dad and Mom managed to have their annual Christmas party at the house. There was a lot to celebrate and the regulars came out in full force. More than three hundred guests attended, including friends, DNC staffers, Mom's colleagues from the radio station, journalists, and Dad's law-firm buddies. Mom also managed to have our family's traditional Christmas dinner. I came home from L.A. and joined Mom and Dad, Michael and Tami, Mere, Nan, the Amoses, and other family members for our holiday dinner, having taken a short leave of absence from my job to attend Dad's confirmation hearing, the inaugural, and Dad's swearing-in. Then Michael and Tami announced that they were expecting. (At that time none of us knew there would be twins.) Dad was laughing with sheer joy as we pored over the sonogram picture. Dad and Mom were exuberant, Michael was proud, and Tami was horribly sick. Dad gave a toast to his future grandchild at that Christmas dinner: "If the baby is lucky, he or she will look just like me!" We all laughed at his silliness.

During that holiday season, Mom and Dad had so many social obligations, they sent me or Michael or both of us in their place to events they couldn't attend. At home, the phone and doorbell never stopped ringing as dozens of people dropped off résumés, hoping for jobs at the Commerce Department; other people called Dad in hopes of setting up job interviews. We even had a mystery visitor who would drop off letters concerning many wild conspiracies, all of which had Dad as their target.

~

Since my father was the first of Clinton's Cabinet appointees to go before the Senate, he had a relatively short time to prepare for his confirmation hearing on January 6, 1993. For three weeks, night and day, aides briefed him on the Commerce Department. He learned about such disparate areas of the department as international trade, export promotion, technology, small business, fisheries, the Census Bureau, and the Weather Service. Although Dad didn't know much about Commerce when he was nominated, his ability to absorb and understand data came to his aid, and by the time of the hearing he was prepared.

We began to hear rumors that Dad would be "crucified" by the Senate Commerce Committee. The rumor was fueled by some Republicans who felt that if it were not for Ron Brown, Bill Clinton would not be in the White House, so getting at Dad would also be a way to get at the President-elect. As a result, some White House insiders were running scared, afraid that Dad had something in the closet that might pop out and hurt not only himself but, by association, Clinton. We even heard rumors that Clinton, advised by his inner circle, was wavering in his nomination of Dad for commerce secretary. Said his friend Courtland Cox, "It was touch and go for a little while as to whether Clinton would stand up for his nomination . . . [Then] it became clear that Clinton was not going to back down."

Given the contentious nature of politics, it might be payback time for the Republicans; four years earlier, the Democratic party stopped cold two of President Bush's important nominees, Robert Bork for the Supreme Court and Texas Senator John Tower for defense secretary. In 1993, when Dad was up for confirmation, Senator Trent Lott of Mississippi was the designated Republican pit bull who was expected to lead the Republican attacks on Clinton's appointees. Shortly before his hearing, Dad scheduled visits to all the senators on the committee. Dad was at ease with them because he had spent twenty years pressing issues on Capitol Hill. When he visited Trent Lott, as soon as the senator opened the door, Dad grinned and said, "Hey, how you doing?" No matter how formal he had intended the meeting to be, Lott broke down and he and my father gave each other a half-handshake, half-hug; the meeting turned out to be constructive, friendly, and positive. There was no Lott-led attack against Dad during the confirmation hearing, and they ended up having a good working relationship.

As the date of the hearing approached, one could see him growing restless and impatient for it to begin. Mom, Michael, and I were at the hearing, as were several of Dad's closest staff people from the DNC. I remember how nervous I was in the Senate committee room, which is set up to be intimidating: The committee sat in a semicircle several feet higher than my father's table. Dad answered every question clearly and directly. He laughed off some questions, then hit others out of the ballpark with strong and substantive responses. The hearing was one of Dad's shining hours. He deflected negativity and criticism, answered tough questions, and did it all with a smile and a twinkle that I can still see so clearly.

The hearing lasted half a day and Dad sat through it, calmly. He was not concerned that he wouldn't be confirmed by the Senate; historically, only a handful of Cabinet appointments in U.S. history have been defeated. But he was eager to get it over with so he could begin his work as secretary of commerce. Dad was never good at anticipation; he always wanted to get on with it.

Committee chair Senator Ernest Hollings, a Democrat from South Carolina, introduced the individuals who would introduce Dad. Senator Daniel Moynihan of New York talked about Dad's commitment to small business, followed by the Republican senator from New York, Alfonse D'Amato, who had battled with Dad on every partisan issue for years but supported him for commerce secretary, and Charles Rangel, the congressman from New York. Senator Ted Kennedy, a boss turned friend, said that Dad was a whiz at negotiating as well as an inspiration to many of the students he taught at Harvard's Institute of Politics within the JFK School of Government. Congresswoman Eleanor Holmes Norton focused on Dad as a civil rights worker, and Senator Lloyd Bentsen talked about Dad's paying for his own college education by waiting on tables and receiving an ROTC stipend.

After the introductions, Senator Hollings said that he was satisfied with Dad's written answers to all his questions, even on "controversial issues," and suggested the committee move ahead. When Missouri senator John Danforth, ranking minority committee member, asked my father if he'd be willing to advocate for labor as well as for management, for business as well as for environmental interests, Dad answered that as commerce secretary he would become a bridge between these normally opposing interests, a middle ground where all could have their concerns addressed.

Dad was asked about his expertise in science and technology, in foreign trade, even in the area of weather prognostication. Did he have the right stuff to head a department that included the U.S. Weather Service, the National Marine Fishery Service, the Office of Travel and Tourism, the Patent and Trademark Office, the National Telecommunications Information Service, and was also a lead agency in developing U.S. foreign trade policy. Could he oversee thousands of employees? Sitting behind Dad in the Senate chamber with Mom and Michael, Commerce sounded to me as if it were diverse, complicated—and overwhelming. But Dad didn't seem to have any doubts about his ability to take on the job and do it well. He never doubted himself. Can-do. That was Dad, all the time, every issue, each stumbling block. Can-do Brown.

The Democrats on the committee asked the difficult questions of Dad before the Republicans could; this allowed my father to answer fully, diffusing the Republicans' questions' potency. Senator John Breaux, a Louisiana Democrat, began by referring to the racially tinged remarks he'd made during Dad's campaign for DNC chair.

"I happen to think he is the right person, at the right time for the right job," said Senator Breaux; "there's a little history to that." Breaux then asked questions about Chem-Fixx, the New York City–based sludge-treatment company.

Said Dad, "I had nothing to do with efforts of Chem-Fixx to get a New York contract. . . . They also didn't get the contract." He reminded everyone that the location of the '92 convention, while certainly influenced by him as party chair, was decided by a fifty-member site-selection committee.

In another question, Breaux asked my father if there would be a potential conflict, should he be confirmed, by his past representation of Japanese electronics companies. Since Dad would resign from Patton, Boggs and Blow on January 20, the day before he would be sworn in as commerce secretary, he saw no conflict of interest, since he'd no longer be working for the firm.

Finally, Breaux brought up another potentially troubling issue for my father, his representation of the government of Haiti. Dad explained that Haiti was a poor black Caribbean country whose best interests required competent representation in the international economic arena. He felt he had helped the people of that country by advocating for them and saw no problem with his work for Haiti. Dad saw this as his most vulnerable area, aware that many people did not understand how he could have represented a country led by a dictator. Said Dad, "I'm not going to be defensive about this. We did a lot of good stuff down there. If we hadn't been involved, it would have been much worse. I will never say that representing Haiti was a bad idea." He noted that while he was Haiti's advocate, the Peace Corps sent representatives for the first time, and Haiti's leaders were forced to reexamine their policies on human rights and the treatment of prisoners.

Breaux brought up all of these potentially controversial issues to give Dad a chance to clear the air. Or so I thought then. None of us, even my politically savvy Dad, could have imagined that controversy and false allegations would haunt my father from the day he was first nominated as commerce secretary until . . . well, until the day he died.

When the Republican members of the committee began, Senator Lott, Dad's sort-of-friend, sort-of-foe, asked whether my father would recuse himself from matters involving former clients. Dad said he would. The remaining questions asked by the Republican members were difficult, but since the Democrats had already asked the hard questions, my father had no problem answering.

~

When the confirmation questioning ended, Dad was jubilant: "Let's go to lunch!" First, we all went to the offices of the Senate Commerce Committee and socialized and chatted with the senators and their staff members. Then Dad, Mom, Michael, chief counsel to the committee Ralph Everett, and I had lunch at the City Club. We talked about the hearing and I congratulated Dad for "smacking" the tough questions and questioners. We talked about Trent Lott's civil, pleasant persona. Then, after a few minutes, my family got down to discussing what was really important: A cute, young lawyer had been particularly attentive to me at the hearing. To my father, the confirmation hearing paled in importance as compared to my love life. Dad was enthusiastic about my dating this lawyer and couldn't wait to tell me how pleased he'd be to see me date someone in a suit and tie with a real job. We laughed a lot but Dad was serious about the suit, the tie, and the job.

In the full Senate, only Republican senator Paul Coverdell of Georgia voted against my father's confirmation. Coverdell was a one-note adversary who, on the day of the vote, and afterward, continued to bring up the nonissue of Dad's prior representation of foreign countries and foreign governments.

As Dad was chair of the Inaugural Committee, my parents were invited to attend a breakfast at the White House on the morning of Inauguration Day, January 20, 1993. The outgoing President, George Bush, and his wife, Barbara, entertained the President-elect and his wife, plus other guests, including Senator Wendell Ford of Kentucky, chair of the Congressional Inaugural Committee; the outgoing Vice President; the Vice President–elect; and their wives.

Mom said President Bush was extremely charming, and said to Dad, "Hi, Ron, come right in," but Barbara Bush gave Dad a chilly look, barely acknowledging him. When Dad introduced Mom to President Bush, Mrs. Bush, standing right next to her husband, turned her head away so she wouldn't have to look at either of my parents. Mrs. Bush couldn't rise above her disappointment at losing the White House, and her lack of graciousness shocked my parents. Dan and Marilyn Quayle, on the other hand, were friendly, Mom told me. They were, of course, the only people of color in the room that morning. Afterward, my parents received dozens of notes and calls from acquaintances and friends, even some strangers, all of them proud and thrilled to see, for the first time, black people entering the White House through the front door as if they belonged there.

After the chitchat and coffee, everyone was driven to the swearing-in at the Capitol. This was Mom's introduction to protocol: One did not just walk out of the White House and drive off. There was an order to who went first, second, and so on. The President and President-elect left in one car, followed by a car carrying Hillary Rodham Clinton and Barbara Bush, then the Quayles and the Gores. Dad and Mom rode in their own car in the motorcade to the Capitol, where they were seated on the stage to watch the President take the oath of office. In addition to those who'd just come from the White House, the stage held other Clinton Cabinet appointees and members of Congress. Mom and Dad had great seats, sixth row back, three in, and were both thrilled to watch Bill Clinton become the forty-second President of the United States. Dad told us later how proud he was of the part he'd played in this historic moment.

Afterward, Mom and Dad joined members of the Cabinet and the leadership of Congress for a private lunch at the Capitol with the new President. My parents stopped to pick up their place cards, then entered the room, Statuary Hall, holding hands because they always held hands. They were not happy to discover that Dad was at one table while Mom was seated at another one. At the DNC, they always sat together at formal dinners and other functions so they could chat; because of Dad's hectic schedule, sometimes these were the only moments they had to talk together. At first, my mother conversed with the folks on either side of her; but they left after they ate lunch and she found herself on her own. The folks across the table from her didn't seem very chatty, and as she looked over at

Dad Mom felt abandoned. "Here was Ronnie chatting at his table, which was all full. My table was nearly empty and I thought, 'Oh, is this how it's going to be?' "

After lunch, they had fun riding in the motorcade, waving to the crowds, and then sitting in the front of the reviewing stands for the inaugural parade. That night, my entire family, including both my grandmothers, went to all ten inaugural balls. Mom looked elegant in a black velvet and tulle gown, her hair in a French twist, and, of course, Dad was debonair in his tux. I wore a black lace gown with décolletage, which Dad didn't like at all; he insisted on walking close to me in hopes of covering up what he believed was too exposed.

The inaugural festivities were exciting and we had so much fun as we raced from one to the other. My favorite was the MTV ball, which was jammed with celebrities. I spent most of my time whispering their names in Dad's ear as they came up, eager to meet him. He was treated like royalty; everyone congratulated him and tried to shake his hand through the crowd: Jack Nicholson, Evander Holyfield, Ron Silver, Magic Johnson, Dr. Ruth Westheimer. Dad always recognized athletes and major film stars but was unfamiliar with most television actors; he didn't know Jerry Seinfeld from Martin Lawrence. We also had a great time at the D.C. ball because we knew everyone there, so it was like a giant house party. I had the time of my life, in part because I had two dates: my original date, a young doctor, plus a magazine executive whom Dad had met, liked, and invited along. It seemed to be okay with both men, since this was basically a group date.

Two days later, January 22, was Dad's swearing-in ceremony, but we were upset, in the midst of our excitement, by news that Mere's mother, my great-grandmother, was in the hospital. Mere didn't want to miss Dad's big moment but she also wanted to be with her mother. In a family photo from that day, one can see Mere, holding her little purse, wearing her traveling pantsuit, looking so sad. She decided she couldn't miss the moment Dad would be sworn in as secretary of commerce, but immediately after the ceremony she headed for the airport.

Morris Reid had just begun working as an aide to my father. His first assignment was to get Mere safely to the airport and make certain that when she landed in New York her cousin, Roy, would be waiting for her. Dad gave Morris detailed instructions, including Roy's telephone number, so he could be notified about Mere's arrival time. Emphasizing that this was an important job, my father warned Morris not to make any errors.

The swearing-in ceremony was held in the White House, with a buffet reception afterward. Since it was my first time in the White House since I was there at age seven on a tour with my Jack and Jill group, I did nothing but gape with my mouth open. I felt awe at the moment Dad, along with the entire Cabinet, raised his hand and took his oath of office, which was administered by the President. Dad's chest was sticking out and he was moving from leg to leg, as he did when he was nervous or excited. At the reception, we ate the delicious food and chatted with the President and First Lady and other Cabinet members and their families. It was wonderful to share with Dad this high point in his life.

After lunch, we all went home and Dad went off to his first day of work as secretary of commerce. That night, my parents called Mere to check on my great-grandmother's health. Mere told them that when she arrived at La Guardia Airport in New York, she waited for two hours in the terminal. Finally, she called cousin Roy and he came to pick her up. Apparently, instead of calling Roy himself, Morris had delegated the task to the driver who took Mere to the airport in Washington. And the driver never made the call. When my father heard this, he leaped out of bed and, wearing his Coke-bottle eyeglasses, called Morris, Morris, horrified, apologized repeatedly, but Dad kept on berating him. That was the beginning of Morris's education: Eventually, he became a trusted and responsible aide to Dad, and a close friend to our whole family, including Mere.

The day after Dad's swearing-in, we all went to the DNC's annual meeting and watched as Dad gave up the chairmanship so hard-won four years earlier. He ran the meeting, then turned the gavel over to the new chairman, David Wilhelm, handpicked by Clinton from his campaign staff. While Dad viewed Wilhelm as quite competent, he knew that the President would be the real head of the party for the next four years. At a luncheon afterward, Dad's mood was a bit sad because he was saying good-bye to his DNC family.

∼

Dad immediately plunged into being secretary of commerce, and as a new Cabinet member one of his first tasks was to undergo a briefing from Barbara Fredericks, assistant general counsel at the Commerce Department, on ethics and rules and regulations. Mom, Michael, and I also had to be briefed on what we could and could not do in keeping with the ethics rules governing members of the Cabinet and their families. We each received copies of the rules, which, it turned out, were stricter for us as part of the executive branch than they are for elected officials. For example, anyone in the executive branch is banned from accepting honoraria for speeches. No one may lobby the federal government for five years after one leaves the executive branch. The rules went on and on, supporting Mom's earlier misgivings about Dad's entering government service. The restrictions on all of us were great.

President Clinton had issued an edict that no one in the executive branch was to fly first class, even using his or her own money or frequent flier miles. The rule, which also covered employees' families, was enacted to prevent the image of government employees living it up on taxpayers' dollars. This caused Dad enormous grief the day he returned from a Congressional Black Caucus event in California. He was flying back to D.C. on Northwest Airlines, accompanied by Morris Reid. Unknown to either of them, when Morris had informed the airline that Dad would be on the flight, the airline upgraded both of them to first class. Remembered Morris, "When we got on the plane and were walked onto first class, he just lost it and grabbed me. He grabbed my shirt and suit as we stood in the aisle, so I said, 'What are you doing?' He blamed me for the upgrade to first class, so he put me in my place. We were on that plane, with the secretary sitting in the aisle and me at the window. Everybody walked by and he was humiliating me. He said, 'This is not going to be on you. This is about me. I'm going to be in the paper.' . . . Then, during the flight, he became real quiet and didn't say a single word to me, he was that furious."

While Dad was DNC chair, my parents often traveled together, with my mother interested and involved in Dad's work. All this would now change. Said Mom, "Barbara told us, 'The government is only responsible for Secretary Brown. You will not travel with the secretary, Mrs. Brown. You will not be able to do this. . . . You will not be able to do that.' "

Mom was devastated because the U.S. government treated spouses not as partners but as baggage: "I was fine in terms of the Clinton administration. But in terms of government, I was a nonentity—a devastating feeling for me because I had just come out of being very much a part of everything. The DNC felt I had a purpose, that I was contributing."

If Dad, as commerce secretary, was flying on a government plane and chose to take Mom with him on an overseas or even a domestic flight, he would have to pay for the equivalent of the cost of a first-class ticket on a commercial airline. As a result, she never traveled with him on any of his trade missions while he was secretary of commerce. The government also discouraged spouses from joining these trips, the rationale being that they'd be taking a seat away from a staff person. However, spouses were discouraged even when there were empty seats on the plane.

Dad, complying with the rules, did not encourage Mom to join him on his frequent overseas trips. But she did go along once or twice, including a trip to Paris during the summer of 1993. Mom and Dad flew together on a commercial flight, not first class, of course, and stayed at the American embassy in Paris, visiting with their friend and host Pamela Harriman, the U.S. ambassador to France. The government paid for my father's trip while my parents paid for Mom's room and board at the embassy. As the wife of a Cabinet member, Mom was welcome at dinners or luncheons (which my parents paid for), but, of course, meetings were strictly off-limits, which was difficult for her to live with after her participation in four years of DNC meetings.

Mom was told by general counsel Fredericks that she was

prohibited from fund-raising not only for the Democrats but for any organization, including charities. Barbara gave no leeway and was quite explicit in what she told Mom and Dad. Said Mom, "We both walked such a narrow line. Ronnie did everything right. He bent over backwards to comply. I had to do that as well because just about every industry comes through the Commerce Department. To avoid any kind of conflict of interest, to avoid even the appearance of conflict of interest, we did what we were supposed to do."

When Tipper Gore began a monthly luncheon gathering for spouses of Cabinet members, Mom and the others, both wives and husbands, took turns hosting the events. Tipper suggested that the group hire caterers, then seek reimbursement from the government, but Barbara Fredericks said that was not allowed. So Mom just paid for the luncheon when it was her turn to host it. The monthly gatherings allowed Cabinet wives, and husbands, to air their grievances. One of my mom's complaints was that Dad's car and driver could not pick her up to take her to an official event unless Dad left work and came home so he could accompany her in the car. Since the car was for his use only, she could not ride in it alone, even if she was meeting him to attend a government function. Said Mom, "We just about asked Barbara when we could use the men's room and the ladies' room. Everything we did, Barbara vetted."

My father loved his office at the Commerce Department, with its fireplace and aquarium, its wood-paneled walls and vaulted ceiling, its view of the Washington Monument and the Mall. Dad often had a fire going during the winter months when he was in the office. The room itself was so huge that his desk and chair took up only a tiny part; the space was filled with artwork and conversational groupings of couches, chairs, and tables. Over the fireplace Dad had placed a portrait of Averell Harriman, a former commerce secretary and Pamela Harriman's late husband. Students at Hunter Elementary School had made Dad a collage that he'd placed on an easel. Throughout the office were paintings, drawings, and sculptures of historical America and Africa as well as photos of all of us. His pride and joy was his enormous aquarium, filled with dozens of colorful and exotic specimens. And although he relished the hugeness of the office, he would often forget just how big it was and call out to Barbara Schmitz, his secretary. Of course, she couldn't hear him, since they were separated by a quarter of a football field.

From the very beginning of Dad's tenure as secretary of commerce, much of his time was taken up with answering various allegations against him. While the confirmation hearing may have quieted doubts Senate Republicans had about Dad, the press was not satisfied. There had not been a bloodletting and that may have led to scrutiny of my father's life, which began the day after the hearing. Any charges that anyone thought up, brought up, or made up, no matter how outrageous and untrue, were aired in the national press. Even after his death, Dad remains a favorite subject of news stories that tell and retell allegations against him that have long since been discredited. Today, the allegations are kept alive by Republicans, by some in the press, and by others who would like to blemish and dishonor his memory.

In a story on the front page of *The Washington Post* the day after the hearing, my father was said to have made mincemeat out of the committee despite its earlier threats to be tough on him. This may have led to a Republican effort to repair the party's hard-line reputation by going after my father, because go after him they did, without letup.

At the same time that Dad was becoming the focus of Republican critics, the Commerce Department required 100 percent of his attention, so he did what he had done all his life: He ignored negativity and moved forward. The first thing he had to do at Commerce was hire staff; after twelve years of Republican administrations, about two hundred political appointments were vacant because the Republicans who had held them had resigned after Clinton was elected. Dad wanted to hire people who would reflect his vision of an activist Department of Commerce. He was deluged with résumés, with people even putting them through our mail slot at home and at Mom's office: Everyone's mother, father, sister, brother, child, child's friends, and friends' friends wanted to work for Dad. Résumés were piled up in stacks both at the Commerce Department and at my parents' house. Dad received hundreds of calls from people who wanted jobs or from people who had friends who wanted jobs.

My father had brought some staff people with him to Commerce, including Barbara Schmitz; DNC finance director Melissa Moss, who became director of the Office of Business Liaison; and Rob Stein, who Dad hired as his chief of staff. It took many months to fill the vacant positions and Dad was still filling vacancies as late as 1996.

Although my father delegated considerable administrative responsibility to Rob and Melissa, he always had to be in control and had to feel certain that his team was tight, well organized, and loyal, so everything would go as smoothly as possible. To minimize his own stress, he needed an efficient organization around him. He also had a sense that when he traveled out of the United States, he could best project his authority and the power of the U.S. government with a well-run, effective organization. So while certain individuals may have criticized Dad's "too fancy, too this, too that" style, it was really his management style: He believed that in order best to govern, manage, and control the Commerce Department, he needed to project an image of authority and control.

Inside the vast Commerce Building, Dad worked to make sense of the department and tried to get a handle on running it. The first week or two, everyone was confused. Dalia Elalfi-Traynham, who came to Commerce from the DNC to be Dad's scheduler, recalled driving to work and hearing news about Commerce on the radio. "The announcer said, 'The Commerce Department says housing starts are up.' I walked into Ron's office and said, 'You know, I heard this on the radio and I thought, "Who authorized that, who does that?" ' And Ron said, 'Dalia, I heard it on the radio and I wondered the exact same thing.' "

African-Americans who had worked at Commerce before my father's tenure had been put in the background for a long time, so naturally they had high expectations of Dad. He did hire many more people of color into the Commerce Department while he was secretary and worked on changing general hiring policies. But in late 1993, during his first year in office, a group of Commerce employees filed a class-action suit against the department for not promoting and advancing African-Americans: Almost all the top career positions (as opposed to political appointments) were held by white men. Dad responded immediately, giving a major speech on diversity to Commerce employees and forming a Diversity Council composed of management and labor union representatives, along with representatives from minority groups. This resulted in a measurable improvement in the number of promotions of minorities and a drop in the number of complaints about the issue.

As he had at the DNC, Dad hired for Commerce the best and the brightest, young people whose potential he saw and nurtured. He surrounded himself with rising stars such as Naomi Warbasse, Kathryn Kellogg, and Gail Dobert. Sadly, all of them died with him in Croatia. And although he could not possibly know everyone at Commerce, he always acted as if he did, walking through the halls, saying hello to everyone he saw, giving many veteran employees of the department their first glimpse of a commerce secretary.

Remembered Wilma Greenfield, chief of protocol at Commerce, "He loved to do that. He'd go to the cafeteria and eat breakfast or just walk around. And people loved that."

As commerce secretary, my father was enmeshed in the protocol of international relations and learned the correct way to interact with foreign dignitaries. He enjoyed going into the reception area to personally greet representatives from around the world and would escort them back to his office, talking all the while. After a few minutes of Dad's joking and putting them at their ease, visitors would always relax.

Dad inspired loyalty, respect, and affection in his staff. His only real flaw as an administrator was his inability to fire people. Rob Stein recalled a meeting he and Dad had during Dad's first year as commerce secretary to talk over staff members who should be asked to resign. Dad couldn't do any of it and had other people do his firing for him. When he became angry at staff, he didn't yell or scream but still managed to show his displeasure. Explained Melissa Moss, "You could sense his disappointment and it was almost more painful to know that you had hurt him. He would never humiliate or berate anybody publicly. People loved working for him. He had so many people who were loyal to him. And so many of us stayed with him for so long, because he was loyal to us."

1993

Dad's first year at Commerce was both wonderful and awful. The first serious allegations against him appeared at that time, but he also became a grandfather in '93. Michael and Tami had identical twin sons, Morgan and Ryan, on July 15. The babies were born at Columbia Hospital for Women about five weeks early and so had to remain in the hospital for some time. Dad visited them almost every day. My sister-in-law, Tami, recalled how he'd walk into the hospital, put on his hospital scrubs, and then, in the neonatal intensive care unit, enjoy a nice long visit with his grandsons. "He used to come all the time. He was really proud. 'Look at these little smikes,' he'd say as he held one in each arm, a big grin on his face." "Smike" is slang for someone who thinks he's *so* together, and Dad used the word as a term of endearment for the boys. "Look at these smikes, just look at them!" he'd say to us as he held and rocked his grandsons. He was totally devoted to Morgan and Ryan and was always willing to change their diapers and feed them. He played with them, kissed, and hugged them all the time.

On the opposite side of Dad's world were the Vietnam allegations that first surfaced a month after the birth of Morgan and Ryan, in August. A newsletter, presenting itself as a POW-MIA publication but more accurately an outlet for racism because of its racist slurs, language, and tirades, accused Dad of accepting payment from the government of Vietnam in exchange for convincing the Clinton administration to normalize U.S.-Vietnamese relations.

To those who worked with Dad and understood the politics, the allegation had been fabricated by the same conservatives who had been dubious about Dad when he was nominated for commerce secretary. After the Vietnam allegation hit the newsstands, these individuals were able to say, "I told you so." At the Commerce Department, some employees who weren't close to Dad and didn't know him at all thought the sky was falling. A friend of Dad's, echoing the feelings of many other friends, said he'd been correct in his initial advice that Dad avoid government service: "I told him not to go over there; now they're trying to rip him apart."

Dad was enraged. He couldn't believe that journalists with whom he had amicable relations would write stories about a lie. They should know better, he told us.

Many news organizations ran the story, and even today it is still brought out and aired when Dad's name is mentioned in the media—despite the fact that the allegation was not true and was proven to be not true. It was heard by a grand jury in a federal court. The grand jury dismissed the charge for lack of evidence and the Justice Department publicly exonerated my father. In December 1993, the Justice Department sent him a formal letter stating that the entire issue was dead: The charges had been investigated and found to be false. Recalled Melissa Moss, "The Vietnam stuff was very tough, but he got up every day, he came to work, he was good to everybody, he never complained, and he never cried victim. It was horribly unpleasant for him, but he never complained publicly."

~

Two key issues my father worked on during '93 were NAFTA, the North American Free Trade Agreement, and GATT, the General Agreement on Tariffs and Trade. He traveled domestically for NAFTA and internationally for GATT to drum up support and also networked with business leaders to gain their support for NAFTA. He remained convinced that these trade agreements would benefit all Americans. On December 8, 1993, after NAFTA passed, Dad spoke in Mexico City at the American chamber of commerce.

Said Dad, "NAFTA's passage in the face of furious opposition was a defining moment for the Clinton administration and a triumph of our Global Commercial Strategy. Our commitment to free trade cannot now be questioned. Our understanding of the relationship between trade and growth has been confirmed. We have prepared the way for private exporters to vastly expand their Mexican operation and create tens of thousands of jobs." Trade agreements were high on President Clinton's agenda, and Dad worked hard for their passage, both because he was solidly behind the President and because he believed the agreements would benefit the U.S. worker.

∼

Despite the responsibility of his position—and its vulnerability as seen from the fabricated Vietnam allegation—Dad found time to have fun and to be with family and friends. On Memorial Day weekend of '93, one of my best friends, Lisa Handley, was having a crisis. She and her fiancé had called off their upcoming wedding. Lisa called me, crying, in extreme distress. Dad took the phone and said, "Lisa, just get on the next plane and hang with us for the weekend." She flew to D.C. the next day, Saturday. Recalled Lisa, "Your dad came home from a meeting at the White House with 'Bill and Hill,' as he called them, and as soon as he saw me, gave me the Mr. Brown bear hug, for which he was famous. I thanked him for inviting me down and he said, 'Lisa, you are like family.' He made me feel comfortable, not like I was infringing on a family holiday weekend. He said, 'Let's talk. What happened?' "

We all went to dinner and Dad pointed to the chair next to his and said, "This is Lisa's chair." He said, "Okay, since this is a family caucus, we'll go around and I want everybody to assess the situation and give their opinion." Said Lisa, "He was very Dr. Feelgood. Always made you feel good about yourself. Made you feel comfortable and supported. It was such a hard time for me, and he made me feel like it was my fiancé's loss, not mine." Dad was helping my friend as he had helped me and Michael so many times: He offered guidance so she could explore her situation and options and try to come to a conclusion. Lisa, who already loved Dad, loved him even more after he helped her out during that Memorial Day weekend crisis.

Dad never missed a chance to have fun. One day, Dad, Clyde Robinson, who now worked at Commerce, and two other staffers, were having lunch at Wilson's Soul Food Restaurant on Georgia Avenue, one of Dad's favorite restaurants. He had just delivered a speech to Howard University business students and was tackling his meal with relish when he noticed Robert Pack, a point guard for the Washington Bullets. At the time, Pack was on the bench due to a knee injury. Clyde Robinson recalled seeing Dad change from secretary of commerce into a basketball fan, as he and Pack chatted. After commiserating with the athlete over his injury, Dad turned to his companions, excited over having talked to a basketball great, and said, "This guy can play. He can shake and bake." A half hour later, he was back at the Commerce Department working on a complicated technology issue.

As the first post–Cold War secretary of commerce, Dad's goal was to turn Commerce into a powerhouse and to aid President Clinton in "growing the economy." Dad wanted to boost U.S. imports, create jobs, and gain primacy over foreign powers, such as Japan and Germany, whose economies had long been considered healthier than ours. Since my father thought that trade would eventually count almost as much as human rights or military alliances, he worked hard to help create within all relevant government departments, especially State, and within the U.S. foreign ambassadors, a sense of commitment to the commercial agenda.

Exploring the many different areas under control of the Commerce Department, Dad found NOAA (National Oceanographic and Atmospheric Administration) and the National Weather Service fascinating. He even asked the Weather Service to advise him when a major snowstorm or heavy rains were predicted. After he made that call, my parents' house was deluged with an endless stream of faxes containing daily, weekly, and long-range weather reports. The career employees at the Weather Service were so thrilled that a commerce secretary had taken an interest in their work that they even faxed Dad weather reports in the middle of the night.

One of my father's major goals was for the U.S. government to be an advocate for American business. He talked often of how heads of state of the great European powers, especially France, Germany, and Great Britain, aided their country's business community, whereas the U.S. government had never been an advocate. He intended to change that, and he did. Under my father, one of the Commerce Department's most important mandates was to assist U.S. companies in securing overseas contracts. And the companies he worked with later communicated to him and others in the administration how much they'd benefited from having the government on their side.

For the first time, American CEOs of both persuasions, Republican and Democratic, were enthusiastic about Commerce's role in helping them secure international deals. The CEOs clamored to get seats on trade missions, knowing these seats would mean large earnings and profits for their companies.

Since Dad's ability to schmooze was unequaled, he used his talents to weave new global relationships between the United States and foreign countries. In addition to bringing multinational big bucks into the country, he saw himself as the U.S. liaison between industry and foreign trade. He wanted Washington and business to team up to develop America's products and production, at the same time pressuring foreign governments for access to overseas markets.

Now that the Cold War was over, Dad succeeded in influencing the administration to change some Defense Department export limitations that had in the past hampered America's ability to market certain high-tech products overseas. Along with U.S. Trade Representative Mickey Kantor, Dad did some tough bargaining to force Japan, China, Ireland, Spain, and Russia to open their markets to our exports. And he did not focus much of his energy or time on regions or countries in Europe that already had healthy trade relations with the United States. He opened markets where previous administrations had never ventured: Malaysia, India, Israel, Qatar, Senegal, and Chile. This was often done over the objections of the State Department, which considered venturing into previously unexplored economic markets to be its province. Dad was the first secretary of commerce to use the department to expand markets for U.S. goods, and the State Department had difficulty with the aggressive nature of Dad's exploration of these markets and his developing relationships with foreign heads of state.

As commerce secretary my father worked harder than he had ever worked in his life. If he wanted to take time off, he had to tell someone on his staff to "hold" that day. Then, of course, he would forget all about what he had planned and say, "What's that hold for?" He did take time to play golf with Michael, or go away for weekends with Mom, and once he came to L.A. to see a jazz concert with me. He and Mom continued to see their good friends. Most of all, he made sure he had fun; Dad loved life and loved a good joke. Some time earlier, when my parents were visiting the home of Ted and Victoria Kennedy, my father got involved in looking at a fish tank that belonged to Vicky's son and daughter. Dad knew so much about tropical fish that he amazed the children by naming every fish in the tank. Except one.

"He really liked that fish and wanted to find out what it was," recalled Senator Kennedy, "Later, he invited the children to come down to the Commerce Department to see the tank he had there."

When the Kennedy family arrived at his office to see his tank, it contained that same mystery fish. Everyone made a fuss: How did he get it? What kind of fish was it? Dad made it into a big joke by refusing to tell, saying he was sworn to secrecy. Eager and willing to take time out to enjoy a funny moment with two young people, Dad "was great fun, charming, full of a spectacular love of life," Kennedy recalled.

On a day-to-day basis, when my father was not off on a trade mission or dealing with a crisis, work at Commerce was stimulating. There were briefings on trade figures in which he heard statistics compiled for the previous month. These would be followed by morning news conferences in which Dad would announce the trade figures to the press. Once, the press conference was to be held at the White House and Dad was briefed on the way over: Economic growth during the Clinton administration had been 3.2 percent as compared to zero during a comparable time during the Bush administration. Said Jim Desler, "He didn't appear to be paying attention. . . . I don't even think he looked at the statement. Then he stood up [at the press conference] and not only did he say it, but when he got to the zero growth, he held his hand up and made a zero. Cameras were flashing all around him.

In politics, alliances are formed, then unformed; enemies are made and unmade. I knew how fond my father and President Clinton were of each other; beyond the political connection, they saw in each other kindred spirits and they liked one another. But although they agreed on most issues, Dad did not approve of all the President's decisions. During the course of his three years and three months in the administration, Dad opposed some of Clinton's policies.

Dad and Mickey Kantor occasionally did not agree over an issue that was relevant to both Commerce and the office of U.S. Trade Representative. Sometimes, though, their disagreement was part of a "good cop, bad cop" negotiating tactic, with my father the conciliator and Mickey the hard-liner. Dad traveled with Mickey to Colombia in March 1996, shortly before the Bosnia trip, for a meeting with trade ministers from North and South America. Colombia presented difficulties for the U.S. government, which certifies countries as legitimate trading partners only if they have cooperated in drug-enforcement efforts. Colombia was not compliant and lost its certification. Dad disagreed with President Clinton about this because, as he had repeatedly said, he felt the United States must commercially engage a country in order to affect its human rights and other policies.

Although he ordinarily traveled without security, on this trip to Colombia, Mickey Kantor surrounded himself with Secret Service agents because he feared an assassination attempt; my father generally traveled with Department of Commerce security only. Kantor also refused to appear onstage alongside Colombian President Ernesto Samper Pisano because he viewed him as sympathetic to the traffickers. My father had a different attitude. Said Dad, "What am I going to do? Not shake the man's hand? That's absolutely ridiculous. Of course I'm gonna shake his hand." Pisano was grateful that my father had treated him like a human being, so his speech reflected this and didn't attack the United States.

Dad also opposed the Clinton administration's policy on ArmsCorp, a South African company that shipped arms to Iran under the de Klerk regime. This was a major violation of arms accords that continued under the regime of Nelson Mandela, the new South African president. When the United States levied a large fine against his country, Mandela was angry. He saw it as a sovereignty issue and said the United States had no business telling South Africa with whom they could trade. Dad, agreeing with Mandela, argued that since South Africa was no longer under apartheid, the United States could no longer stand on its high moral ground and judge that country's leadership and policies. The fine was not levied.

Despite minor differences between my father and policies of the Clinton administration, Dad remained one of the most interactive and collegial people in government. He always included representatives from the State Department, the National Security Council, and other agencies on the trade missions he led. He was named chairman of the Trade Promotion Coordinating Committee (TPCC), an interagency group that includes all federal departments and offices dealing with trade policy: State, Defense, Treasury, CIA, USTR, and OPEC. With Dad as chair, the committee became a force and at TPCC meetings, agency heads and Cabinet secretaries participated in steering commercial diplomacy strategy.

Because of his interaction with so many other agencies, the loss when he died was even greater. Individuals in other agencies, people all around the world, had lost someone whose warmth and ability to conciliate and bring diverse participants together could not be duplicated.

Trade Missions

Dad devoted considerable time as secretary of commerce to trade missions, and they received more publicity than anything else he did at the department. Using trade missions as his vehicle, Dad became the quintessential advocate for U.S. businesses as he traveled to emerging markets around the world with business leaders in tow. Dad brought in approximately forty billion dollars in new business to U.S. companies as a result of his advocacy and total commitment to trade negotiations between the United States and countries around the world.

A major aspect of his work as commerce secretary, his concept of commercial diplomacy, emerged from an early trade mission Dad made to Saudi Arabia and another he made to China in August 1994. Both countries had dismal reputations in the human rights arena. After the trip to China, Dad gave a speech about commercial diplomacy that received considerable press attention and in which he discussed affecting human rights policies and other political issues by improving economics. By engaging China in business relations, Dad believed, U.S. businesses could help influence that country to improve its human rights policies. Dad defined commercial diplomacy as engagement, rather than withdrawal, encouraging political stability and dealing with human rights and national security issues by improving international economic relations.

At some point during the China trip, my father and his team were debating sanctions with the Chinese when a reporter asked him about a little spat he'd had with Madame Wu Yi, the Chinese trade minister. Dad told the reporter, off the record, that Madame Wu, with whom he was very good friends—they walked around holding hands—had made a comment about him that he didn't like. She said that while he often acted nice, and one did not think he expected a lot, in the end, he always got what he wanted. Despite this minor tiff, Dad and Madame Wu always maintained smooth relations. On Dad's first trade mission to China, his advocacy led to the signing of agreements that would earn U.S. companies six billion dollars, including a billion-dollar contract for McDonnell Douglas.

Dad also learned from trade missions that he could bring the concepts of international economics to U.S. cities, universities, and communities. According to Jim Desler, Dad always included a range of American businesspeople, including women and people of color, on all trade missions. Said Desler, "His death was so untimely in so many ways. He was about to take off on a totally different level. He wanted to spend the [remaining months of his term] at Commerce . . . taking the lessons that he had learned globally, letting people understand it so they could really help our [minority] kids."

My father also used the trade missions to carry a message about African-Americans and other minorities to countries around the world. "When I get off the plane," he said, "it's a U.S. government plane, and I have the seal of the United States government behind me and they see a black man with a very mixed group of people—it changes their whole perspective of what our people can accomplish and can't accomplish and what we're capable of doing. People realize, 'Oh, they're not incompetent, stupid, lazy, shiftless, in jail, or on drugs.' "

In 1994, Dad started the U.S.-Russia Business Council, a government-to-government partnership, driven by the private sector. Dad and Viktor Chernomyrdin, currently Russian prime minister, negotiated for twenty-five U.S. companies and twenty-five Russian companies to build business partnerships that would benefit the two countries. In March 1994, for example, Dad led a trade mission to Russia that included corporate executives from Westinghouse, Duracell, Tenneco, Raytheon, and other companies; they did more than four hundred million dollars in business in Russia as a result.

In December 1994, Dad led a trade mission to Northern Ireland to encourage the peace process through commercial engagement. With him were ten CEOs, two members of Congress, and representatives from the White House and other federal agencies. Jim Desler recalled the rainy, pitch-black dawn when their group landed at Belfast airport. He and Dad drove an hour and a half to Derry, where Dad was to give the keynote speech at a black-tie dinner that evening. Jim remembers being concerned because my father had gotten almost no sleep in two days. Dad began his speech just as dessert was served. Five minutes into his talk, the members of the audience had put down their cutlery, stopped eating, and were listening intently.

My father spoke about a spirit of hope in Northern Ireland, about the civil rights movement in America, about his own experiences as an African-American, and about his favorite theme: unity and strength through diversity. He said his own life had led him to conclude that this was the only answer, and he believed it was also a lesson that Northern Ireland would begin to learn. Recalled Desler, "It was done in a cadence and manner that white Belfast had never heard or seen before, this African-American delivering an address that built to a crescendo. There was no applause during the speech, just complete attention and silence. At the end, there was a five-second delay, then slowly they started clapping and a standing ovation. It was the greatest speech I'd ever seen, a speech that to this day people I know in Ireland talk about."

A year later, in December 1995, Dad returned to Ireland,

where he spoke in Dublin, then met with representatives of a Dublin business. He was then scheduled to fly to South Africa after that but had about four hours before his flight. With several options to choose from, Dad and his staff members opted to spend a few hours in Kitty O'Shea's, a Dublin pub. Jim Desler remains amazed to this day that Dad, a black man raised in Harlem, was able to transform a bar filled with white people in the heart of Dublin into "his own world, with people coming up to him and talking and him responding and talking back."

Dad drank two Guinnesses, quite a bit for a lightweight drinker, and he and his staffers sat around eating lunch, talking, laughing, recalled Jim. Then Dad started in. "First he goes, 'Jim, how's your Irish coffee?' Then he asks, 'Do you mind if I have a little taste of it.' He had his own meal, so he just had a little taste, and then he orders a whole one for himself. . . . It was a wonderful, wonderful afternoon," remembered Desler.

Dad ate seafood while the others ate steak, but "he wanted to make it surf and turf so he ended up eating his own and having some of ours"—yet another example of Dad's legendary appetite and obnoxious habit of eating other people's food. (Years earlier when he was at the Urban League, Maudine Cooper and Lajuan Johnson were mandated to sit on either side of him at meals. With their plates flanking his, he was able to munch from their dinners after his was long gone. "There was never enough on his plate," Lajuan said.)

Dad led trade missions to more than thirty countries, including Japan, India, Brazil, Chile, Argentina, South Africa, Ghana, the Ivory Coast, and Mexico. He was the first commerce secretary to visit Qatar and the United Arab Emirates. In February 1995, Dad went with twelve American business executives on a Middle East trade mission to Israel, including Gaza and the West Bank, Egypt, Jordan, Kuwait, Qatar, and the United Arab Emirates. Dad was enthusiastic about the Middle East as a new market for U.S. businesses. Maria Cardona, deputy press secretary at Commerce, recalled how Dad, as was his usual practice, talked to every corporate executive on that plane trip to the Middle East, calling each into his "office," one at a time. Maria said that Gene Goodson, CEO from the Oshkosh Truck

Corporation, was euphoric after his conversation with Dad, say-ing, "He loves my trucks!"

Dad was the first Cabinet member to travel to Gaza. Jim Zogby, president of the Arab-American Institute, recalled that on Dad's first trip there, in January 1994, he traveled to Gaza by car even though the American embassy had urged him to travel by Israeli military helicopter because it was so much safer. But Dad chose to make the trip from Cairo to Gaza by car so that he would not insult the people there. He met with Yasir Arafat at Orient House, a Palestinian government building where no American had dared to go.

On Dad's second trip to Gaza, the embassy suggested he talk about terrorism. Recalled Zogby, "But I said, 'Mr. Secretary, they have been suffering economic blockade. They have 60 per-cent unemployment. They can't do business; they can't grow their economy. What hope do they give to their kids if they can't give them jobs? You have to talk about that.' " The rep-resentative from the U.S. consulate told Dad that was not the U.S. position. Said Zogby, "Ron went into Gaza. And the first words out of his mouth at the press conference were 'The clo-sure is wrong.' So the headlines all over Israel and the Arab world said: U.S. SECRETARY SAYS CLOSURE IS BAD FOR GAZA AND BAD FOR PEACE. He understood that what you say and how you say it, how you relate to people, is as important as your policy, that you have to be respectful. He stood there and said, 'No, I am going to do it this way. I am going to be respectful.' "

Skirmishes

Less happy than memories of successful trade missions were recollections of the battles Dad fought throughout his three years as commerce secretary. Just as Dad's first year was marred by the false Vietnam allegations, 1994 and 1995 were also marked by a campaign begun by Republicans who had just re-gained control of Congress to dismantle the Commerce De-partment. Outspoken GOP leaders suggested reorganizing critical components of Commerce, merging them into other agencies, and creating a new trade department. Since these suggestions would clearly cost taxpayers more money, not less, and create more bureaucracy, not less, Dad viewed the attempt to dismantle Commerce as a personal attack on him. And he believed it was racially motivated.

"They're coming after me because it's me and it's this department which has done such great work for the President," he said. "The Republicans just can't swallow that; they can't accept it. They think because I'm the first black secretary of commerce that I'm an easy target."

I recalled an article I had read a year earlier, in the December 1993 *GQ,* which both shocked and horrified me. It described how black elected and appointed officials have historically been destroyed by witch-hunts, either assassinated—Malcolm X, Martin Luther King—or discredited—Adam Clayton Powell, Mike Espy, and countless others. The article detailed the measures that the white Establishment will take whenever an African-American becomes too powerful. I read parts of the famed Church Committee Report of 1977, issued by a senate subcommittee headed by Senator Frank Church, which detailed the numerous incidences in which the U.S. government was involved in destroying black leadership. So much for Dad's occasionally voiced goal of becoming the first African-American president.

The attempt to massacre my father's image and reputation was fomented by Republicans on the prowl in an early defensive strategy for the '96 election. Whitewater was not bringing President Clinton down, so his attackers went after several close associates, including my father.

Of course, Dad handled all of this as he had handled everything in his life, with optimism that he could turn it around. He went to talk to Republican senator Pete Domenici from New Mexico to find out what the Republicans were up to. Said Dad to Domenici, "Sunday, there I am watching *Meet the Press.* Alma's at my side, and all of a sudden Pete is saying he's going to eliminate the department. And Alma goes, 'Well, honey, is that true? Pete wants to eliminate the department?' So I say to her, 'No, I'll go talk to him.' So, Pete, is it true? Alma wants to know." The senator told my father that since it was the House, not the Senate, that was pushing to dismantle the department, he had nothing to worry about.

Dad's last full year as secretary of commerce was perhaps his most challenging because many forces in the Republican party came to bear against him and hounded him with a series of untrue allegations. In December 1994, just after the Republicans won both the House and the Senate, Dad was questioned about entries he made on his annual financial disclosure form. A month earlier, as the election returns came in, Mom and Dad watched the Democrats dropping like flies and talked about what it would mean to the administration and the country, never dreaming that the change in power in Congress would have such an effect on the remaining fifteen months of Dad's life.

A Republican congressman from Pennsylvania, William Clinger, had been writing to Dad about his financial disclosure form for some time. Dad gave the letters to his staff, for them to handle. Since at the time, Clinger had no committee, no power, and was in the minority, no one at Commerce was in a rush to respond. But after the election, Clinger gained control of the Government Oversight Committee and immediately went after Dad. Angry at my father for having ignored him, Clinger issued a press statement on December 15, 1994, in which he announced that he would examine Secretary Brown's disclosure form to see if he had filled it out correctly.

Clinger added that he had been corresponding with Secretary Brown for months, asking questions, and had not received a response. His main concern was four hundred thousand dollars my father had received for sale of his partnership interest in a company co-owned by businesswoman Nolanda Hill. Clinger knew Dad had received this sum because Dad had clearly listed it on his disclosure form. But the congressman contended the money should have been listed in the *income* section of the form while Dad listed it in the *transactions* section. Clinger was suggesting that since Dad entered the item in a different place, he was trying to conceal it.

Mom and Dad were on their way to the Greenbrier resort in West Virginia, where Dad was to speak at the Gridiron Club, a journalists' organization. An article about Clinger's statement ran that day in *The Washington Post* and, at Greenbrier, Dad saw the article but was unconcerned. He and Mom had heard that Clinger was "just the nicest guy." They found out much later, according to Mom, that a member of Clinger's staff was pushing the agenda against Dad. In January 1995, when the Republicans formally took over the House and Senate, the press statements from Clinger's office increased in frequency and vehemence. Said Mom, "Every two minutes he called for an independent counsel."

Dad truly believed that everything would work out, that it was really a nonissue. He had listed the item on the form; how could that be considered concealment? Dad refused to allow the questions to get him down. When Mom began her new job, at Chevy Chase Bank, on January 9, 1995, Dad called her to see how her day was going. She described her office, mentioning the two huge steel file cabinets filled with someone else's files that were in her way. He told her he would come in with her on the weekend to move the file cabinets, hang pictures, and fix up the office. And he did; they had fun moving furniture around and decorating Mom's office just as the two of them had decorated each other's offices, over the years.

~

At the time, Attorney General Janet Reno, under fire for her perceived weakness during the government and FBI actions at Waco and Ruby Ridge, attempted to placate the Republican-controlled Congress by ordering independent counsels to investigate administration officials: the President and First Lady; Mike Espy, secretary of agriculture; and Henry Cisneros, secretary of housing and urban development.

And my father. On May 16, 1995, Reno ordered an independent counsel to investigate allegations that he had improperly filled out his financial disclosure form. Dad was furious. He showed President Clinton Reno's twelve-page motion to appoint an independent counsel.

"This is ridiculous," the President told Dad. "She had no need to do this. It's uncalled for." The President stood by my father, but a handful of White House staff "walked away too easily from Ron and his so-called problems," recalled Ginny

Dad with Thurgood Marshall and Dr. Dorothy Height during his Urban League days

President Jimmy Carter with his "Black Kitchen Cabinet," 1979. Dad is second from left at the top of the photograph.

Dad in his office at Harvard, 1980–1981

Dad goes to bat again with a leader of the Tiananmen Square uprising, Wuer Kaixi

"I won!" Dad with Paul Kirk, getting the gavel and the chairmanship, February 1989

Rosa Parks Tribute, February 1990. *From left*, Cicely Tyson, Rosa Parks, and Dad

April 19, 1990

LEE ATWATER

Dear Ron:

A bonafide case of strategic genius! Because
of the thoughtfulness and timeliness of your
act, I am forced to give little Sally this
donkey. I am sitting here looking at her
and my other two daughters, Ashley and Sara
Lee fondle the little devil ...

You have literally been killing me with
kindness since this whole ordeal started,
and I will _never_, _never_ forget.

With thanks,

Thanks again,
Buddy

LEE ATWATER

MAR 7

Ron —
Thanks for Calling
and Thanks for the
flowers — This is the
Kind of week in
which so many
of the big important
things we do in Politics

look awfully small.
You have been a
very formidable man
and I have come
to admire you very
much.
Thanks again,
for your concern.
Lee

20 March

Dear Ron — It's always so wonderful
to see you — you give me instant
comfort (isn't that wierd ?!?).
       I'm glad you were so
amused by the James connection.
So am I. Boy, they sure don't make
Republican men like you all !
       Take care — with affection —

Dad had Republican friends as well—personal notes from Lee
Atwater and Mary Matalin

Democratic candidate "summit" at the estate of Pamela Harriman

Mario Cuomo, Dad, and David
Dinkins at the 1992 Democratic
convention in New York

Dad with Alexis Herman at the
Democratic National Convention,
1992

Dad with Hilary Rodham Clinton, 1992

Dad with Jesse Jackson and Ted Kennedy

Dad, building bridges, with Fidel Castro, Yasir Arafat, and
Yitzhak Shamir

Dad and Michael, with
(*left*) Dad's law partner
Tommy Boggs

Nelson Mandela
with Mom and Dad
at a White House
state dinner, 1994

Dad conferring with
President Clinton

Dad shooting hoops with President Clinton

Dad with the troops at Tuzla air base, April 3, 1996

The only piece of the plane left intact, Croatia, 1996

Terzano, Dad's press secretary at the DNC, now press secretary for Vice President Gore.

These staff members saw Dad as a liability to a president with problems of his own and urged Clinton to seek Dad's resignation. Or at the least exclude him from policy decisions and keep him out of the loop. This effort against Dad failed because of Clinton's loyalty to my father and also because of the efforts of key people at the White House, including Alexis Herman, Ginny Terzano, and John Podesta, assistant to the President. There were rumors at this time that the President intended to ask my father to lead his reelection campaign, and, beginning in February 1995, Dad had been included in reelection strategy meetings. But after the independent counsel was let loose on my father, some White House staff members tried to freeze him out of these meetings.

Of course, it was most awkward for my father after this, as he would see Janet Reno at Cabinet meetings; he was never rude but had very little to say to her. If their departments were involved in some project together, he would have to sit next to her at a joint press conference. He told us that while he did what he had to do, he had little respect for her. Reno always said that she called for independent counsels on everyone who was accused of impropriety because she didn't want these issues to become political. The irony is *that* made the issues political; she was acting on the Republicans' allegations and so could not avoid being political. It seemed to me that she didn't want to be perceived as favoring the Democrats, her party; so, she made certain to favor the Republicans.

The false allegations against Dad continued. He was next accused of selling seats on trade missions to Democratic party donors. Of course, these charges were proven to be false by a paper trail detailing the process of how individuals gained seats on trade missions. Melissa Moss, who directed the Office of Business Liaison at the Department of Commerce, worked to ensure that neither politics nor donations were ever considered in awarding seats. In fact, the vast majority of companies didn't donate to any political party; and those who did gave substantially more to Republicans. Dad told us that his goal was to make certain that small and minority- and women-owned businesses were represented on trade missions. Explained Moss, "We wanted some diversity in the trip and some of those were very small companies. We chose people who had been winners of awards, who had shown that they were outstanding in their business field, and we chose them specifically because they had a product or service that we thought could advance their business in the country." All of those who went on trade missions went through a complex screening process and had to be approved by the general counsel at the Commerce Department. "There's a real paper trail to show how we chose people for the trade missions, which was based on merit. We'd start with whatever country we were going in, look at the emerging industries in the country and what industry sectors were expanding. . . . It was all straightforward."

1996: Three Months

My father led a normal life despite the stress and pressure of responding to lawyers, requests for documents, and news stories that repeated over and over the allegations against him. The only time I saw Dad truly disturbed was when Michael or I were dragged into the morass. Dad was livid when the independent counsel subpoenaed my law school tuition records, presumably in an effort to track Dad's expenditures, Michael's problem arose from a four-thousand-dollar campaign contribution he made in 1994 to Senator Edward Kennedy. When Michael told Dad, Dad, realizing he had contributed more than he was legally permitted, was furious at Michael's mistake and had Michael ask for the contribution to be returned immediately. Unfortunately, three years later, in the midst of campaign finance investigations, the Justice Department pounced on my brother's error, and in August 1997 he admitted a campaign contribution violation and paid a five-thousand-dollar fine.

"Ron was the subject of a series of investigations that threatened his public reputation and his professional future," remembered Mark Steitz, Dad's old DNC staffer. "They were unfair, darkly politically motivated, involving people who had lied to him, some of whom had been close to him. The rest of us would be fleeing to a cave, holed up with a shotgun, shooting at people we know. But he was basically convinced, and much of his life and accomplishments were evidence, that if he just were himself, and was true enough to himself, and positive enough, and outgoing enough, the world would fundamentally deal with him in basically decent fashion."

The allegations did not cast a shadow over Dad's last year despite the seriousness of the charges, despite the fact that no article about him was written without rehashing allegations that had already been proven to be untrue. He viewed the whole mess as an annoyance, an inconvenience, a bump in the road. As commerce secretary, he had thousands of employees to manage and a job to do. He would not allow himself to fail at this job and never for one moment doubted that he would eventually be exonerated on all the allegations. Dad's attorney Reid Weingarten agreed. He recalled, "There was never a moment in time when I thought Ron was going to get prosecuted, because A, he hadn't committed any crimes and B, I thought any ambitious prosecutor would realize, if he could bring together some sort of half-ass case, he would get killed in court. So I never thought Ron was at legal risk."

Ginny Terzano recalled the last time she saw Dad, the day after the blizzard of '96. He had come into work, dressed for the weather in jeans, boots, and the inevitable jacket and tie. Dad was intrepid: Only he would show up the day after a blizzard when no one else was at work. He entered the building happy, smiling, as if he didn't have a care in the world—or a single allegation against him.

"His basic nature was optimistic and hardworking," said Mom. "He had a goal, he knew the charges were unfair and untrue, he trusted Reid [Weingarten]. He saw how the President went to work every day with many charges hanging over him. So Ronnie moved on, he kept going, he never let it get him down."

Mom shared Dad's optimism. They never walked around with their heads hanging low, feeling sorry for themselves. They went to work, spent time with friends and family; they still had fun.

One of the last, best things my father did was to help save

affirmative action. To this day, I still use Dad's explanation of why we need this policy. "There's a gap right now between the achievements and successes of people of color and those of white people," he told me. "And the reason we need affirmative action is to close that gap."

When this federal program was in danger of being dumped, Dad told the President that minority contracting had to remain on the table. At a Cabinet meeting, he spoke out and made it personal so those in the room would get his strong message. Dad told Clinton and the Cabinet secretaries that when he ran for chair of the DNC, he encountered opposition. "It wasn't that I wasn't a good lawyer or a good fund-raiser or a good organizer," Dad said. "It was because I was black." And, too, there were objections when he was nominated to be secretary of commerce. "It wasn't because I wasn't competent. It was because I was black. . . . Race still matters in this society and people still do not have opportunities because of their color."

According to some who were present, the President reacted immediately and said, "Okay. We're defending it." At that moment, Clinton's policy of "Mend it; don't end it" was born. That night, Dad called President Clinton and said, "I saw your clips today." All the news had been about Clinton saving affirmative action. *The New York Times* had given Clinton his best editorial to date. Under the headline LEADERSHIP, the editorial stated that when the chips were down, the President had taken a position and stood firm. On the phone, Dad said, "Liked your press, didn't you?" And he and the President laughed.

As soon as I step out from the cover of the front porch, it starts raining, a light summer drizzle. The air smells sweet and reminds me of camp. I place the flowers I'm bringing to Dad on the backseat of my car. I wanted to wrap them in a silver necklace he had brought me years ago from a faraway place. The necklace has a silver heart on it and, inside that, a smaller heart made of turquoise. But the necklace is too long to wrap around the bouquet once and not long enough to wrap around twice, so I settle for a gold ribbon and tie the gladiolas and yellow roses and purple, pink, and violet blooms together.

At Arlington National Cemetery, the guard waves me through the entrance because everyone there knows me. I park in my regular spot and, when the rain stops, walk toward Dad's grave site, carrying the flowers and a wad of tissues. The tissues are for tears and to wipe off any debris from Dad's stone. I smile as I see his tall shining black headstone standing out from all the others. I made an excellent choice, I think. Then I perform my ritual: I kiss the three middle fingers of my right hand and place them on the "o" of "Brown," engraved near the top. "Hi, Daddy," I say. I scan the words and symbols. Then I walk around to the front of the stone and, still holding the bouquet, kiss my fingers again and touch Dad's middle name, Harmon, the name I plan to give my daughter someday. I arrange the flowers on the bench that serves as the headstone's base. "Daddy, I love you and I miss you so much," I say. Then, facing the stone, I read it word for word to myself.

The sun has broken through the clouds, so I take off my raincoat and lay it on the base, next to the flowers. I stare at my reflection in the shiny black granite. I wonder what Dad is doing right now. I stare at the ground and see tiny white flowers growing in the lush grass. I take off my shoes and walk barefoot on my father's grave. It feels wonderful, blades of moist grass between my toes, the sun on my feet. If the grass were dry, I'd lay down next to him and look at the beautiful sky. I see my reflection again and focus on "Harmon." My daughter will never know her grandfather, never feel the comfort and protection of his hand on hers. Never hear his silly laugh and watch as the corners of his eyes crinkle up. Never hear him clear his throat, as if he were parting the Red Sea. Never feel the warmth of his big hugs. My daughter will never understand how lucky I was to have my Dad.

I sit back down on the base and wait for the sign that never comes. I wish he would ruffle the grass. Or touch my hand. Or, better yet, walk right up to me as I sit here and chat with me for a while. Come on, Dad. Do something. Show me that you are watching. I don't want to wait until I die to be with you again.

It's time to go. I'm upset and lonely and my tissues are used up. I begin my farewell ritual. I stand up and kiss my fingers and trace the word "father" on the front of the stone. "Bye, Daddy. I love you." I pick up my raincoat and slide my shoes back on my feet. As I walk back to the car, I glance over my shoulder for one last look and see, high on the hill, Dad's big, beautiful, shining black monument.

Going Home

Friday, April 5, Unicorn Lane

MOM, Michael, and I had been waiting for Dad to come home since Wednesday, the day of the crash. Finally, we were told that he and the others who were on the plane would be brought to Dover Air Force Base the next day, Saturday. Mom did what she had to do: She chose a few people to go to Dover with us and the President and First Lady on Air Force One. And Michael did what he had to do: the casket and the calling.

"By Thursday, the day after the accident, Michael had talked to the families of everyone who was on the plane with Ronnie," said Mom. "He called every family immediately after the accident."

I was still unable to do anything other than weep and wail over what I had lost, what we had all lost.

We were told that the State Department and the military were overseeing Dad's homecoming and burial, a public affair that would last for several days. President Clinton had ordered flags to be flown at half-mast as a sign of national mourning, and bells were tolling at the Washington National Cathedral. The thirty-three caskets would be flown home from Croatia on a large C-17 military transport. Two of Dad's closest aides and friends, Morris Reid and Lauri Fitz-Pegado, were on the plane with him. Morris had been with my father in Croatia and Lauri, then an assistant secretary of commerce, had volunteered to fly over so she could also accompany Dad home.

Saturday, April 6, Dover

Mom was so right when she decided that Dover would be too difficult for Nan and Mere. Dover was too difficult for all of us. Dover was the worst day of my life.

My family and I left the house in the morning and were driven in a caravan of cars to Andrews Air Force Base, just outside of Washington. It was freezing cold. On the plane, Mom, Michael, Tami, and I sat with the President and First Lady; later, we talked and roamed around the plane during the forty-five-minute trip to Dover, Delaware. I got to know Christine Meissner, who is my age and who also lost her father in the crash; Charles Meissner had been assistant secretary of commerce for international economic policy. When we landed at midday, the President said, "Alma, you'll walk down the stairs with me, and your children will follow. Hillary will bring Doris [Meissner], and her children will follow them." We all walked down the stairs holding hands: first Mom with the President; then me and Michael; then the First Lady with Doris Meissner; finally, Chris and Andrew Meissner.

At Dover, we first went into a chapel, where I saw families huddled together in the chill, some praying, some just sitting quietly. Next we walked into a large holding room in a freezing-cold military building; there was coffee and people stood around and talked. Tami said she felt ill and wanted to lie down, so someone took her back to Air Force One. In the holding room, a White House staff person took Mom, the President, and the First Lady aside. After a few minutes, Mom walked over to me and Michael and said that the thirty-two families were in various holding rooms, that the President and Hillary were going to visit with them and then we would do the same. Mom believes those visits got us through Dover: By sharing pain, theirs and ours, we were able to control it.

Before we went in to see the first family, Mom said, "You know, we can't go pay our respects to the other families if we're going to fall apart. That's no help to them." So we went into each of those holding rooms strong and brave. And Mom was right because while I was giving comfort, I would forget that I needed comforting too. Holding hands, Mom, Michael, and I would knock on doors, then enter rooms filled with despairing mothers, fathers, husbands, wives, sons, and daughters—each with a teary, worn face. Each time we walked into a room, the family inside would break down and we'd hug and cry together. Some of them had pictures of the person they had lost. Some were people we knew.

A couple of incidents occurred that relieved the tension and almost made us laugh. First, we entered a room in which sat a divorced couple whose daughter had died. We all hugged, then the father asked Michael a question about a statement issued by the Air Force about the accident. When Michael answered him, the man said to his former wife, "I told you. You get everything wrong." Then they began arguing with each other, so we said, "We'll talk to you later. We're going on to the next family." I don't know if they even noticed us leaving, they were fighting so hard. Out in the hall, we held on to each other. All this tragedy and they were fussing about nothing. When we saw the parents at the ceremony later, they were holding each other for support, their squabble over.

As we went from room to room, I alternated between feelings of numbness and grief. Then, as we visited a family who'd lost their daughter, a woman ran over, grabbed me, and screamed, "Your daddy is dead! Your daddy is dead." I almost lost it then, but she was so hysterical that I calmed down and held her until she stopped sobbing.

After an hour or so, we finished the visits and went outside for the ceremony. We sat in stands on the airport tarmac. There were about a thousand of us: families, friends, colleagues, Cabinet members, foreign diplomats, and government officials. After an opening prayer, President Clinton spoke. He first paid tribute to all of the victims. Then he reminded everyone of Dad's enthusiasm for the mission to Croatia. He recalled that Dad was thrilled to be able to advance America's economic interests while contributing toward saving the peace in the Balkans.

Said President Clinton, "[He] was a noble secretary of commerce who never saw a mountain he couldn't climb or a river he couldn't build a bridge across. . . . The sun is going down on this day. The next time it rises it will be Easter morning, a day that marks the passage from loss and despair to hope and redemption, a day that more than any other reminds us that life is more than what we know. Life is more than what we can understand. Life is more, sometimes, than we can even bear."

Then he sat down next to Mom and we all watched in the freezing wind as, with ceremony and precision, eight teams of military pallbearers unloaded the caskets and placed each one in its own hearse. Thirty-three caskets into thirty-three hearses, one at a time. It took about twenty minutes although it seemed to take hours; in the background, a military band played "Stars and Stripes Forever." My thoughts were out of control: Dad was in the first casket. Dad was in the last one. Dad was not there at all. There was nothing to identify him or anyone else. Just thirty-three mahogany caskets draped with American flags.

That was the worst day, sitting and watching, not knowing where Dad was. Michael and I held hands the whole time and the President was crying as he held Mom's arm. There was a nineteen-gun salute, then the long line of hearses drove off. We got back on Air Force One and went home.

Sunday, April 7, Unicorn Lane

I had time on Easter Sunday, time to remember. I took no part in planning Monday's lying-in-state or Tuesday's memorial service or Wednesday's funeral. On Sunday, I lay on my parents' bed and looked at my rings that I never take off and relived the moment when each had been given to me. On my seventeenth birthday, Dad gave me a sapphire and diamond ring, and for high school graduation, a ring with rubies and diamonds in the same setting. When I turned eighteen, my gift was an emerald and diamond ring, also in the same setting. I wore all three on the ring finger of my left hand until Dad gave me a stainless-steel Rolex watch for law school graduation. He and I agreed that both the rings and the watch on the same hand would look gaudy, so I switched the rings to my right hand. I've gotten compliments on them for years and love telling people that they are from Dad.

Looking away from my rings, I saw a photo on the wall of my parents' bedroom, of all of us in the Dominican Republic. I thought about Dad's love of the beach and ocean. A year earlier, Mom and Dad had flown to L.A. and taken me on a mini family vacation. Chuck Manatt, a former DNC chair, and his wife had loaned us their house in Laguna Beach. Dad and I got up early each morning, went down to the beach, and ran or walked. Sometimes, we'd race along the shoreline. No matter where we went on our family vacations, Dad and I always took morning walks or runs on the beach. He especially loved to jog without shoes on, in the sand along the water's edge.

Then I relived Christmas. Every Christmas morning, from when I was as young as I can remember until Christmas 1990, the last one before Michael got married, he and I weren't allowed to go downstairs to open presents until Dad checked to make sure everything was in order, that Santa hadn't had a change of mind. My brother and I would hover impatiently as Dad did his morning ritual: Since he only wore his glasses in his bedroom, we had to wait while he washed his hands and put on his contacts. Then big, ole twenty-five-year-old Michael, six feet five, and I, twenty-three, sat on the stairs waiting for Dad to tell us that it was okay to come down.

He always took his sweet time and we'd call out, "Dad, come on, can we come down or what?" He'd say, "I don't know, things look a little out of place, hold on." Finally, he'd say it was okay and we'd go tearing down the steps to open our presents. When Dad would call us down, he'd never say, "Okay, Tracey and Michael" because he never called us by our real names. I was Boli, and my brother was Mick, Mickey, Sonny, or Sweetpea. Mom was Mumbelina. Everyone Dad was close to had a nickname. President Clinton was the Prez. Even coworkers were nicknamed: For example, Maudine Cooper, from the Urban League, was Mogee, and Lauri Fitz-Pegado was Fitzaroonie. Nicknames were Dad's way of expressing closeness. He was warm and fuzzy, and calling people by warm and fuzzy nicknames made them cuter and more lovable.

All these memories of Dad were racing through my mind on Sunday, as I tried to avoid reality. I thought about happy times, such as the day when I found out I had passed the California bar exam. I was so nervous that morning that I got up at dawn and went to the gym to relieve my anxiety. When I walked back in the door, the first message on my answering machine was Dad: "I was calling to find out if you called to find out. Please call me as soon as you know." Then, Mom: "Did you call? Did you call?" There were messages from a study partner and from a friend. But the last message, from another study partner, Jennifer Baltimore, was a shout of joy: "Congratulations! We both passed!" I felt thrilled but then doubted it was true, so I tried to call and hear the results for myself.

The number was busy for a while, so I called Dad and he called Mom and on three-way, I said, "Jennifer said that I passed, but I can't get through. It's busy, busy, busy." We decided that all three of us would keep trying; Dad and Mom both called on their other office lines. Then Dad came back on the phone and said, "I got through and they said your name is on the successful list!" But I still had to hear it myself, so then I dialed and got through and heard the same good news. But to be absolutely certain, I called again. I called a total of four times, with Mom and Dad listening in, to hear the magical words: "Tracey Brown is on the successful list." Mom, Dad and I were laughing and so excited. Dad said he was proud of me and always knew that I could do it. "Now," he said, "everything else is gravy."

～

Sometime during that long day, my grandmother, Mere, called me downstairs because I had a visitor. I had been spending most of my time upstairs, avoiding people. But this visitor was special. Katie Hamilton Gewirz, a close friend from high school, had lost her mother to cancer several years earlier. I was eager to see her; she would tell me how to make everything all right.

We hugged at the door and sat on the steps leading down to the family room. When Katie asked me how I was doing, I couldn't answer. It was hard to speak without crying. And crying made my aching body hurt even more. So I just listened.

"When my mom died all I did was cry," said Katie. "If I looked at pictures, or even just thought about her, I cried. Eventually—though it took a long time—I'd think of her and smile, or even laugh. I still cry and I still miss her, but now when I think of her, I smile much more than I cry.

"I know you can't imagine it, Tracey, and you don't believe it will happen to you, but it will. There will come a day when you think of your father, and smile or even laugh out loud at an incident you remember." I stared at her. She couldn't understand what I was feeling if she thought that I would smile or laugh or feel happy again. I thanked Katie politely for her visit, but as soon as I closed the door behind her, I cursed her audacity. I erased all memories of how close she'd been with her mother. I told myself that if they had felt about each other the way Dad and I did, she would grieve forever, which is what I intended to do.

Monday, April 8, Commerce Department Rotunda

Monday morning, we were escorted by Vice President Al Gore to the Commerce Department Building, where Dad was being brought to lie in state in the rotunda. Outside the building, we stood slick with rain despite the umbrellas held over our heads, as the hearse pulled up and the military ritual began again. Dad's casket was carried into the building and we followed him in—Mom, Michael and Tami, Nan, Mere, Chip, Dad's cousin Nick, and my boyfriend, Marcelino. We each had some time alone with Dad before the rotunda was opened up to the thousands of people waiting in line to pay their respects.

When it was my turn, I walked into the room and sat in the chair next to the casket. I wanted to open it and see if Dad was really in there. I didn't believe he was. But I didn't touch it, of course, afraid to find proof of what I didn't want to know. I cried and cried and tried to say something final but couldn't. There was no way I could say good-bye to him. I could not believe that I would never see him again. So why say good-bye? I walked out and other people went in, one at a time, to be with Dad. After family, some of Dad's closest staff people, like

Barbara Schmitz, went in. We walked back out into the rain and went home, leaving Dad lying in state.

Tuesday, April 9, Metropolitan Baptist Church

For days, dozens of people had been in and out of our house, organizing Tuesday night's memorial service, "Ron Brown: A Celebration of Life." Alexis Herman devised a structure; speakers would be grouped around the periods in Dad's life—his early years, early career, Washington, and Commerce. Mom, Michael, and I went over the list of speakers and discussed who we thought Dad would have wanted to talk about him.

Tuesday evening, we were driven to the church and spent a short time in the minister's office. When we finally walked into the hall of the Metropolitan Baptist Church, I could see that it was packed, but it wasn't until later that I realized nearly two thousand people were there. I sat in the front row with Mom, Michael and Tami, Nan, Mere, Chip, and Nick and smiled, laughed, and relished the joy of Dad as folks told funny stories about him. They talked about his gargantuan appetite. They imitated his physical gestures, such as the way he shook his leg or cleared his throat. They discussed his accent: Dad didn't pronounce his h's so "human" would sound like "uman." They recalled the way he said, "That's just turrible, turrible," rather than "terrible, terrible." The stories were funny, irreverent, and incredibly joyful, as speaker after speaker recalled my father's eccentricities and his warm, loving heart.

Kent Amos introduced the speakers. When I think back, a few people stand out. Charlyn Goins, Dad's childhood friend from White Plains, whose husband was Mom's childhood friend from Brooklyn, talked about my parents' friends, couples from New York and Sag Harbor who have stayed married and remained close for thirty-six years. Bryant Gumbel gave a moving speech. The Reverend Jesse Jackson's eulogy was strong and eloquent.

Five hours later, the memorial service ended. When we went outside, I saw friends from camp, from high school, friends who lived across the country. I got to hug everyone and spend some time with different people before we left. The memorial service was, for me, almost a diversion because it was so upbeat—the speeches, seeing all my friends. For a few hours Tuesday night, I was . . . almost happy.

Wednesday, April 10, Washington National Cathedral

In the morning, Michael and Chip left early so they could escort Dad's casket from the Department of Commerce, where he had been lying in state, to the Washington National Cathedral. Vice President Gore was there, also. Later in the morning, Mom and I and the rest of the family met Michael and the others at the cathedral for the funeral service. We went into a side room with the President, Hillary, and Chelsea and Al and Tipper Gore. We talked for a while; then, after the processional, we entered the enormous, flower-decked gothic cathedral, which, for Dad's funeral, held nearly five thousand people. This was the vast National Cathedral on Wisconsin Avenue; my high school, National Cathedral School, was just next door.

There is a photograph of us standing in a clump, looking confused, because inside the huge and crowded cathedral we couldn't see the rest of our family and didn't know where to sit. Not even the President knew where to sit. After a few minutes of whispering—Where do we go? Is there a special seating arrangement? Should we go to the right or the left?— we were finally led to our seats in the front row.

The service was short, about ninety minutes. There were readings. Alexis Herman—"Blessed are those who mourn, for they will be comforted." Bob Johnson, chairman of Black Entertainment Television—"Though much is taken, much abides." And George Fischer, CEO of Kodak—"Blessed is he who seeks out the wisdom of all the ancients and is concerned with prophecies." When Michael spoke, I was so impressed because I could not, at that moment, have even said my name. Michael's eulogy was strong and moving, and because, to me, he is still my obnoxious big brother, I was shocked to see him take command. The night before, at the memorial service, I so much wanted to speak and share some wonderful memories of Dad. I even thought about what I would say and had planned to introduce Jesse Jackson.

But when the time came, I was mute. If I stood up to speak, I would only have cried. So as I listened to Michael, I was so proud and knew that Dad would have been also. I could imagine Dad teasing me: Boli, can't you get up and talk to the folks? Are you going to let Michael do all the talking?

Said Michael, "My father kept us so close. . . . Some people thought our family was weird . . . [because we were so close, but] it's helped us deal with the loss." Looking at Mom, he said that she is "the person who made [my father] what he was and what he will always be. Mommy, you are now my role model. . . ." Michael concluded with these words: "Daddy, I love you and so do a lot of other people."

The President gave a beautiful eulogy, including some words Dad would have especially loved: "On a personal note, I want to say to my friend just one last time: Thank you. If it weren't for you, I wouldn't be here."

Dad would also have loved the music: "Amazing Grace," "The Battle Hymn of the Republic," and the singing of Santita Jackson, Jesse Jackson's daughter. At the end of the service, Wynton Marsalis played "Flee as the Bird to the Mountain," the sweet piercing sound of his trumpet reverberating mournfully in the vast cathedral.

I sat there and wanted it to be over. I couldn't wait for this last day of the public mourning process to end. The past week had been a blur, with only a few moments that stood out: When Alexis walked over after her reading to hug Mom, she broke down, so the two of them just stood there holding on to each other. The thousands of Commerce employees and other people standing in the rain to pay their respects to Dad. The phone calls and letters from people all over the world. And so many friends, broken up at losing Dad, whom we had to comfort.

After the President spoke, we followed the casket down the aisle and out the door. There, we stood as the military people carried Dad down the stairs toward the waiting hearse; his casket was on a caisson. Suddenly, one of the men tripped and a leg of the caisson began to collapse. The casket tipped and started to fall but they quickly brought everything upright. We got into cars behind the hearse and drove through the historic black Shaw neighborhood, around Fourteenth and U streets, where Dad was born. Hundreds lined the streets, many holding up signs: WE LOVE YOU, RON BROWN and GOODBYE, OLD FRIEND. There were banners on buildings and people waving and throwing flowers, or holding them. Michael rolled down the window and people leaned into the car to hug and kiss us and hand us flowers and cards. We sat there and held hands through the interminable ride.

Arlington National Cemetery

At Arlington, a military honor guard removed the casket from the hearse and placed it on a horse-drawn carriage, which proceeded slowly up a hill to the grave site. As the procession began, we saw rows and rows of military personnel marching in formation. First came the carriage carrying Dad, then our car, then a line of vehicles that included the presidential motorcade. When our car stopped, we got out near a fountain adjacent to the Tomb of the Unknown Soldier, which is where Dad's site is located. Linked arm in arm with Mom and the President, I walked to the site, where chairs had been set up. Dad's casket, still covered with the American flag, was sitting on the grave site. There were flowers all around.

The service was performed by the Reverend James Tate, from Harrisburg, Pennsylvania, whose wife, Dolly, was Dad's first cousin. Just as he began to speak, a gust of wind blew and little pellets of snow or hail showered down on us for a minute. The wind was light and airy, not heavy and wet, despite the weather, which had been freezing for the past week. This was followed by a soft, foggy mist that passed right over where we were sitting. Michael and I looked at each other: Dad was there.

Recalled Commerce staffer Larry Parks, "Then when it started snowing in the cemetery, I [thought] he is here. . . . Yes, oh, he's here. . . . He's fine. He's letting us know he's fine. I thought, 'You're making monkey business here in a cemetery.' He's up there with that twinkling eye going, 'Got them. I got them.' "

The Reverend read some Scripture and gave a sermon and I was doing all right until he said, "Ashes to ashes, dust to dust." I could not believe that Dad was going into the ground.

Soldiers representing the branches of the service stood beside the casket. The navy wore navy and white knickers tucked into white lace-up patent leather boots. Only moments after bottomless despair, Michael and I were hysterical at how funny those knickers and boots looked and how Dad would have cracked up at those outfits.

Off in the distance I heard a twenty-one-gun salute, which startled me but was also exciting, as were the fighter planes that flew over in formation. As a special mark of respect, the members of the firing squad handed us the shell casings and a white glove. The military guards next to the casket then folded up the flag that had covered the casket and handed it to the President, who gave it to Mom saying, "From a grateful nation." She broke down. I found myself walking toward the casket with a white lily in my hand. I put the lily on the ground, then kissed my hand and touched the casket. Michael and I walked back to the car with Mom between us, clutching the flag in one hand. Inside the car, we just sat for a few moments; then people came over and leaned in the car to hug us.

Back at Unicorn Lane, we had a receiving line and a reception at Kent and Carmen Amos's house next door. The receiving line was endless but it gave us a chance to see folks we hadn't seen during the preceding days' events. At Arlington, there were only twenty-five seats and standing room for a small number of people. Mom had to decide who would go to the cemetery, and although the decisions were difficult, she made them. Many, many people came although there were no seats for them and stood during the ceremony. We had something to eat at Kent and Carmen's and chatted with our friends. Mom stayed only a short time, then went home and got into bed. Michael and I remained but periodically went to check on Mom. I avoided going home and going to bed. I didn't want to lie there, thinking about the past—or the future.

The Next Day

I visited my father in the cemetery the day after the funeral. The site was marked by a green stake in the ground holding a plastic card bordered in white and green. It said, "Ronald Harmon Brown. Date of Death: April 3, 1996. Date of Interment: April 10, 1996. Branch of Service: Army. Rank: Captain." There was no sod yet and the dirt was still a mound, not flat or even. I wanted to dig in the dirt and make sure he was in there. Since the dirt was still fresh, I knew I had a chance. I even thought about how long it would take me, if I could do it before the police came to arrest me, how dirty I would get. I didn't want to go to jail. And I didn't think I could get to him using only my bare hands.

Finally, I convinced myself that I was ridiculous: Of course he was in there. So I began to talk out loud, telling him how much I missed him, how much I wanted him to come back. It was a sunny but cool morning. I put my coat down, next to and partly on the mound of dirt. Sitting on my coat was as close to Dad as I could get; I asked him how everyone was—Bill and Carol and Kathryn—and said they should look out for one another. Most of the time, I cried and said over and over, Please come back.

Two days later, I brought flowers when I went back to see Dad. Two men were laying the sod and we chatted for a while. One man said, in a soft southern voice, "Are you kin to him?"

"Yes, he was my Dad."

"Oh, my, we are so sorry. He was such a great man," he said. He told me that they wanted to lay the sod fast and right for Mr. Brown. In the middle of their work, they wandered off to give me private time. Then they came back and started to put down the sod and I left because I couldn't watch.

After that, I visited Dad almost every day. The first few times all I did was beg him to come back and tell him how much I loved and missed him. One time, a group of tourists were staring at Dad's little white and green plastic marker; his site had been added to the official Arlington tour. There was a family from Tennessee and we talked a little. The woman asked why we had chosen this site. "It's kind of crowded here," she said. I told her that was exactly why we picked this place. Dad loved being in the middle of the action and would not have wanted seclusion. We also chose a site high on a hill so Dad could have a view of the Washington Monument, the Commerce Department, and the Capitol, structures that had been important to him.

During the summer of 1996, I went to see Dad every couple of days. As it grew colder, I went every week or two. Shortly before his headstone went up, I went to see him on November 6, the day after Election Day. President Clinton had just been reelected and Rick Greenfield, Michael's best friend, had left something for Dad that he would have loved: that day's *Washington Post* headline about Clinton's victory, copied and cut to fit in an acrylic frame. And Rick had written: "The seeds you planted continued to grow. I miss you, Rick." I was so moved that I wanted to take the frame and its contents because I knew that, after a few days, the groundskeepers throw away flowers and memorabilia. But then I realized that Rick had left it for Dad, so it wasn't mine to take.

~

Mom put me in charge of selecting a headstone for Dad because she and Michael were working full-time and I had taken a leave of absence from the D.A.'s office. I researched the possibilities using guidelines from Arlington National Cemetery. And unspoken guidelines from Dad. He would want something shiny, big, noticeable, and grand, so the first thing I did was find out the largest size the headstone could be. We wanted Dad to stand out and wanted the stone to be visible from far away.

I liked Frank Bias from All Stones Memorial immediately because of the poster on his office wall: a photo of George Bush that said, "Help Wanted—I need a job." When Mr. Bias and I discussed dimensions, I came up with the idea of setting the stone on a large base that one could sit on, almost like a bench. Mom and Michael liked the idea. After rejecting all shades of white, gray, brown, tan, and copper, we chose a shiny black, like the Vietnam Veterans' Memorial. I chose letters cut into the granite, which is guaranteed to last forever.

Frank Bias suggested engraving on the stone "beloved husband and father." We wanted to include "grandfather" because of how much Dad loved Morgan and Ryan. And since "beloved" was not a word Dad ever used, we came up with a better word. My parents used to call each other "Wondy," short for wonderful. So we used "wonderful" on the stone.

The front is engraved: "Ronald Harmon Brown. August 1st, 1941, to April 3rd, 1996. United States Army Captain, Germany, Korea. Wonderful husband, father, and grandfather." On the back is the seal of the Department of Commerce and the words "United States Secretary of Commerce" and "Chairman Democratic National Committee."

~

After the headstone was installed, in November 1996, I had a place to sit that was close to Dad. I go to see him often. Sometimes I stop by for a quick visit, just to touch the stone and feel connected. Or I walk up to the Tomb of the Unknown Soldier and watch the changing of the guard. Most of the time, there are other people at Dad's site; the sod has been replaced three times because he gets so many visitors, which I'm certain he loves.

I talk to Dad about everything: this book, my boyfriend, Mom and Michael and Morgan and Ryan. When I discuss what to do with my life now that the book is finished, I can hear him laughing and see him shaking his head. "Boli, just make a decision. You'll be a star whatever you decide to do." If I tell him that he is still getting negative press, I hear him say, "They're not bothering your daddy, so don't let them bother you."

And, now, it turns out that my friend Katie was right. I laugh and smile far more than I cry when I think of Dad. The twenty-eight years that I was blessed to have him with me were full of love, nurturing, and support. There is nothing sad about those years. And I feel lucky to have so many wonderful memories of him. Even though my life will never be the same and I will miss him forever, I can fill the hole in my heart with memories of the great moments we shared as father and daughter, and as a family.

The cemetery has become the place where I can talk to Dad about my life and my problems. If I ask for advice, I listen, hoping to hear it. And, if I listen very hard, I can hear his voice and his laughter coming from somewhere inside my heart.

Why the Plane
Crashed

AFTER a brief investigation, the Air Force determined that three factors caused the crash—or "mishap," as the Air Force calls it: failure of command, pilot error, and an improperly designed airport approach. These factors, not the weather, caused the crash.

A. *Failure of command:* Air Force personnel disobeyed Air Force Instruction 11-206, which mandates commanders to review non–Department of Defense (DoD) airport approaches before a flight is undertaken. (Non-DoD airport approach means an airport does not follow stringent U.S. military approach procedures.) The commanding officers of the Eighty-sixth Airlift Wing—the division that oversaw my father's flight and the flights of other officials to and within the former Yugoslavia— requested a waiver to this regulation. Pilots of the Eighty-sixth, believing they could fly these prohibited approaches because of their superior skills, continued to fly the non–DoD-approved approaches even after the waiver was denied for safety reasons in January 1996. The approach flown by the crew of my Dad's plane was a non-DoD approach and had not been reviewed by command and should not have been flown.

The Eighty-sixth command did not adequately train pilots for landing in airfields using non-DoD approaches. Had the pilots of my father's plane been trained correctly, they would have known that their plane did not have appropriate equipment. It had only one Automatic Direction Finder (ADF) instead of two; that's the receiver on the plane that is tuned to beacons on the ground. One ADF was needed for final approach guidance and one for identifying the final approach point, which was missed.

B. *Pilot error:* (1) Mission Planning. Although the pilots knew for at least one day that they would be flying into Dubrovnik on April 3, they failed to recognize that they couldn't make the approach with only one ADF. Also, the flight plan of the route was improperly done, adding an unnecessary fifteen minutes to flight time.

(2) Rushed Approach. As a result of this planning error, the pilots arrived late in the Dubrovnik area. They rushed their approach and did not properly configure the aircraft; this means they did not set the dials, put the landing gear down, and line up the plane correctly for landing *before* beginning their approach. They crossed the final approach point without receiving clearance from the Dubrovnik tower. They were also eighty knots above the correct final approach airspeed. They were going too fast to configure the plane.

(3) Missed Approach Point. If they'd had a second ADF they would have realized that they had missed the final approach point. Since they had no visual contact with the airfield—they were nine degrees off course—a second ADF would have signaled to tell them they had missed the final approach point. Once they knew it was time to land, but couldn't see the runway, they should have turned right, over the water, to circle in a holding pattern. It appears that at the last minute they did realize they were off course, but instead of turning right, turned left into the mountain.

C. *Improperly designed airport approach:* The approach in Dubrovnik was not properly designed and did not have enough obstacle clearance in accordance with internationally agreed-upon criteria. The minimum descent altitude (MDA) should have been higher. MDA is the lowest altitude the aircraft is allowed to descend to in attempting to accomplish a safe landing with visual reference to the runway. A properly designed MDA would have placed the plane well above the point of impact, even though the pilots had flown nine degrees off course.

The Families

The Families of CT-43 is a support group created by people, like me, who lost loved ones in the crash. The group's purpose is to get answers to our questions about the crash, to achieve legislative reform in the area of air safety, and to provide emotional support for one another. We are frustrated with the lack of empathy exhibited by the Air Force.

Said Colonel William Colwell, legal adviser to the Air Force Accident Investigation Board, to me on July 12, 1996: "We're the Air Force. We did it. We're sorry." We families have many unanswered questions. Why was the investigation of the accident undertaken by the Air Force alone with no help from the National Transportation Safety Board and the Federal Aviation Administration? Why were no flight data recorders or cockpit recorders aboard the aircraft? How did the Air Force conduct and conclude its investigation in six weeks when other investigations, such as that involving TWA Flight 800, take at least a year? Why were only four of the sixteen officers responsible for the crash named publicly? Who are the other twelve officers and what was their punishment? Why was no one given a court-martial? Are Air Force planes still flying non-DoD approaches?

None of these questions have been completely answered.

None of us are satisfied with the punishment received by the Air Force personnel responsible for our losses. While the armed forces has jailed, discharged, and court-martialed officers and enlisted personnel for sexual misconduct, no similar punishment was given to the individuals who caused the death of the thirty-five people aboard the CT-43. Instead, of the sixteen high-ranking officers held responsible, most were given mild reprimands and counseling.

Reforms

Our efforts for reform have been led by Ken and Maureen Dobert, who lost their daughter, Gail, and Darrell and Karen Darling, who lost their son, Adam. The Dobert and Darling families have coordinated a campaign to educate and lobby Congress regarding the crash investigation and report, officer reprimands, the Uniform Code of Military Justice (UCMJ), the Family Advocacy Act, and the Gore Commission on Aviation Safety. Several families are suing the Times Mirror Company, which designed the airport approach map.

We want an open and impartial examination of the Air Force's investigation of the crash and its reprimands of those responsible. We want inclusion in the Aviation Disaster Family Assistance Act of 1996, which currently excludes civilians traveling on government aircraft. We want repeal of the Department of Defense regulation in the Military Claims Act that excludes government employees (but not civilian passengers) from filing claims and from being protected by FAA standards. We are seeking the right to sue the U.S. Air Force for wrongful death and the right of beneficiaries to collect on all life insurance policies. We want enhanced ground-proximity warning systems installed in all aircraft, including commercial and government.

Pending Legislation

Representative Eleanor Holmes Norton has introduced a bill, H.R. 1334, the Ron Brown Tort Equality Act. The bill amends the Federal Tort Claims Act to permit plaintiffs who are government employees to sue the federal government for gross negligence. It also permits non-federal employees who are injured overseas to sue the federal government for negligence. This legislation would allow the families of Commerce and State employees who were killed in the crash to sue the government for gross negligence. It would also permit the families of others on the plane, including the corporate executives and the *New*

York Times reporter, to sue the government; current law only permits them to sue for injuries incurred in the United States.

Representative Robert Menendez of New Jersey has introduced a bill, H.R. 1483, the Single Standard of Aviation Safety Act, that would apply FAA requirements to government aircraft so that these planes would have to meet the same standards as commercial aircraft.

～

Our group of grieving families is not seeking revenge against the Air Force or the federal government for our losses. We hope to bring about safer flying conditions. And we seek to help our healing process by finally having answered our multitude of questions.

New Questions

There are several conspiracy theories surrounding the plane crash that killed my father and his delegation. Some of the stories are on the Internet, some in the press, but mostly they come by word of mouth. Some I've heard say that the plane was shot down by friendly fire or by enemy fire; that an assassin shut down the airport beacon so that the pilots would fly off course, causing the plane to crash; and that my father was shot in the head before the crash. It's hard to believe any of the stories because they either contradict the evidence or are unsubstantiated. The only theory I'm interested in is one that I haven't heard: that Dad is still alive and being held prisoner in the Balkans. Then we could go rescue him and bring him home.

The latest speculation, that a wound on my father's head may have been caused by a gunshot, is the most disturbing to me. The finality of even contemplating a wound to Dad's head can't go unrecognized. Since the crash, I have lived every day with the hope, however small, that he wasn't really dead. Since I chose not to view Dad in the casket, I had something to hold on to. Maybe he wasn't in there. Although several people told us that they saw Dad, since I hadn't seen him, maybe there was hope. I remember grilling Morris Reid when he returned from Croatia: "Are you sure it was him? Are you sure he wasn't breathing? Could he have simply been unconscious?"

When the Air Force gave my family a briefing about the causes of the crash, they gave us several thick notebooks containing the full report of the accident investigation board. My mom asked that they remove any graphic or disturbing photos and reports concerning the condition of my father's body. We had decided that we wanted to remember him as he was, not as he died. As a result, we never saw any detailed report or photographs concerning cause of death. Just a one-page report stating that his death was caused by blunt-force trauma and head injuries due to an airplane crash. As a result, the fantasy that it was all a big mistake and Dad was alive had some room to fester. Eighteen months after the plane crash, I finally saw X rays and photographs of my father's body; the fantasy has been put to sleep. He is gone and he's not coming back.

Several events precipitated my need to see the X rays and photographs of my dad. A series of articles appeared in a publication owned by a far-right conservative that contained claims by Air Force personnel that a circular wound on the top of my father's head resembled a forty-five-caliber bullet hole. The pathologist who examined Dad's body inspected the wound closely and reviewed the full-body X rays before determining that the wound was not caused by a bullet. The examination of my father revealed no bullet lodged anywhere in his body—no exit wound, no metal fragments, and no trajectory path. In the opinion of the pathologist, the nature of the wound had been laid to rest: It was caused by the impact of one of many cylindrical objects found at the crash site.

The uncertainty remains among some because most pathologists agree that the most definitive way to determine if it was in fact a bullet wound would be to do a full autopsy of the body. No autopsy was done on my father. Once the Air Force determined that the wound wasn't caused by a bullet and therefore there was no foul play, the inquiry was treated as an accident investigation and no permission was sought from my family for an autopsy. The only autopsies performed were on the military personnel, per Air Force policy, and on one civilian, whose family had requested it. Had my family known about the suspicious wound at that time, we would have demanded an autopsy. Now there is only one way to know for sure: exhuming Dad's body and performing an autopsy.

After the articles appeared in the press, the "Ron Brown assassination" theory picked up steam. It created interesting bedfellows of the far-right and some African-Americans who suspected a murder and cover-up. They began demanding a new investigation of the crash. As a result, Mom, Michael, Tami, and I, armed with our own independent pathologist, our attorney, Vinnie Cohen, and scores of questions, met with some Air Force commanders and pathologists in December 1997. When it came time to get into a graphic description of Dad's body, Mom left the room. We went over the X rays in detail and I asked at least twenty questions. When the Air Force pathologist brought out graphic photos of Dad's injuries, he took Vinnie and our pathologist into a corner to look at them. It was then that I realized that if I didn't see a picture of my father's face, I would never truly accept his death. I explained my feelings to Michael and we slowly walked over to the corner of the room. I asked the Air Force pathologist if there was a relatively clean picture that showed Dad's face. He pulled one out, and although Vinnie suggested that I not look, I had to. I had to know. Michael and I stood firm, and with our arms around each other, we stared at the picture of our father's lifeless face. At some point I broke away and ran from the room in tears. The image hasn't stopped flashing in my head.

An odd thing happened to me that day. I stopped caring how my father died. It may seem strange, but whether his death was an accident or an assassination, he's not coming back. He and my mother won't be celebrating any more anniversaries; he and Michael won't play golf again; Morgan and Ryan won't get any more of his mustachioed wet kisses; and he won't ever hold my hand in his special way that told me everything was right with the world. He's gone forever.

My Father's Legacy

In June 1996, I stood offstage at the Indianapolis Super Dome waiting to accept an award that was being given posthumously to my father for his work on behalf of minority-owned businesses. I was planning to say a few words of thanks, accept the award, and exit.

As I walked onstage, however, the lights dimmed and Dad's face was projected onto a giant video screen while his voice was amplified by the sound system. I had been so unprepared to see and hear Dad this way, only two months after his death, that I felt as if I were about to pass out. I wiped away my tears and silently asked Dad to give me the strength to speak.

Finally, his voice and face faded. Feeling completely alone, I said, "I was not expecting that video, so please forgive me if I fall flat on the floor." Then I took a deep breath and made my remarks.

Thank you all very much for honoring my father in this way. It has been two months since his accident, and as you can imagine, it has been a very difficult time for me and my family. One of the things that helps tremendously is the enormous support we have received from so many of you. I constantly try to look for something positive that has come out of this tragedy, and this award today makes it clear. My father touched and helped so many people throughout his career. Whether it was his civil rights work with the National Urban League, his leadership in the Democratic party, or his policies of inclusion and the development of economic independence for people of color at the Commerce Department. It helps to realize the difference he made by providing opportunities for women-owned and minority-owned business. How appropriate that the Black Expo, an organization that seeks to advance minority business, should honor him.

The audience gave me a standing ovation. And as I stepped down from the stage, I was surrounded by dozens and dozens of people, some who wanted to talk to me, some who just wanted to give me a hug. I wasn't alone after all.

~

My family and I have discovered that many people besides us want to keep Dad's legacy alive. They have created numerous memorials, scholarships, and awards in Dad's honor. Immediately after my father's death, Mom received calls from corporate executives who were grateful to Dad for helping their companies compete abroad. They offered to endow programs and foundations within their corporations in memory of my father. Mom, Michael, and I decided that instead of this we would request that these individuals and others help us establish the nonprofit and nonpartisan Ronald H. Brown Foundation. We wanted the foundation to relate to four of Dad's main interests: young people, people of color, politics, and international business.

After applying for nonprofit status, we organized a board of directors that currently consists of the three of us, plus Tommy Boggs, Vernon Jordan, and Bob Johnson. There is also an advisory board and a steering committee, comprising scores of individuals who are leaders in their fields. Michael, with the help of friends including Lauri Fitz-Pegado, Mark Steitz, Courtland Cox, and Steve Selby, has worked nonstop for the last two years getting the Foundation off the ground.

The Foundation reflects both Dad's love of politics and the theme of his distinguished career, his work to create opportunities for people of every race, social class, and nation. Dad, who always told me and Michael that every single thing one does and every decision one makes is political, could never understand when people said, "I'm not into politics." My father believed that politics is involved in every aspect of life. The Foundation's goal is to transform my father's vision of a more just world into a practical legacy of tangible achievement.

The Foundation will draw its strength from the passions that marked my father's life: his activism; his passion to change and create and act, rather than argue; his faith in the potential of young people; his unshakable belief in the democratic process and in political participation; his groundbreaking work as commerce secretary; and his belief in inclusion. As Eleanor Holmes Norton recalled, "Somebody forgot to tell Ron Brown how a black man was supposed to act. He had an uncommon boundlessness. Many of us are brainwashed to believe that you can go but so far. He had no sense of limits."

The Foundation will carry on my father's missions and goals by administering several programs. The nonpartisan Ronald H. Brown Center for Politics and Commercial Diplomacy, located in Washington, D.C., will offer one semester of business and political development courses to college juniors and seniors and corporate executives. Seventy-five universities in the United States and around the world are currently participating.

The Foundation also includes The Ronald H. Brown Global Clearinghouse, reflecting Dad's interests in entrepreneurship, leadership, and the creation of opportunity. The Clearinghouse will provide information on emerging markets to small, women- and minority-owned companies interested in expansion overseas; will establish a mentoring program between large and small businesses; and will train small businesses in creating export and investment opportunities for American firms, particularly smaller businesses.

The Ronald H. Brown Business Roundtable, another aspect

of the Foundation, will be located in New York City and will conduct research on contemporary issues of domestic and global economic growth and political stability. It will also assist minority entrepreneurs in developing national and international policy agendas.

In February 1997, the Foundation held its first international trade seminar in the Bahamas, "A Day of Exchange: The U.S.-Caribbean Commercial Relationship International Trade Seminar." Future trade seminars are planned for South Africa and Korea. The Foundation also hosts Women's Leadership Teas, during which women discuss ways to increase their involvement in both the electoral process and the business community.

～

In addition to the Foundation, there are a range of other memorials, programs, and awards dedicated to Dad:

• The Ron Brown Scholar Program. Every year, ten African-American high school seniors will be selected as Ron Brown Scholars and will each receive a forty-thousand-dollar college scholarship based on academic excellence, leadership potential, community service, and financial need. During the program's first year, so many applicants were highly qualified that all twenty finalists received scholarships.
• The Ron Brown Award for Corporate Leadership will honor companies for outstanding achievements in improving employees' lives and the health of communities in which they operate. This concept was developed by President Clinton and business leaders as a way of recognizing companies who promote such programs as volunteerism, community development, protecting the environment, workforce diversity, family support, and employee training.
• The *Ronald H. Brown*, a 274-foot ship with meteorological and ocean data–collecting capabilities, was commissioned by the National Oceanic and Atmospheric Administration, part of the Commerce Department. Scientists aboard the vessel will study global climate change and other critical environmental issues.
• Summit 2000, an organization that assists the development

of minority-owned businesses, offers several awards in my father's name: The Ronald H. Brown Pioneer Award will honor a successful minority-owned business that has contributed to its community; The Ronald H. Brown Award for Leadership will be given to an individual for furthering the cause of economic self-sufficiency for African-Americans; The Ronald H. Brown Award for Vision will be awarded to a major corporation or business that has made significant contributions toward investment and ownership for African-Americans; and The Ronald H. Brown Award for Courage will be given to an organization or individual that best demonstrates the use of advocacy, diplomacy, intellect, and fortitude to accomplish access to opportunity.
• The A. Philip Randolph Institute's Community Service Award
• The National Black MBA Association—Ron Brown Scholarship and Ron Brown Legacy Award
• The National Child Labor Council Ronald H. Brown Award (1996 award presented to Oprah Winfrey)
• The African-American Institute Ronald H. Brown Award for African Business Development
• The Ronald H. Brown Man of the Year Award

Other honors to my father include renaming in his memory P.S. 155Q in New York City (now the Ronald H. Brown Community School); the Mt. Vernon Community School's Technology Center (now the Ronald H. Brown Technology Center); the Woodrow Wilson National Fellowship Foundation (now the U.S. Department of Commerce Ronald H. Brown Fellowship); Nansen Elementary School in Chicago (now Ronald H. Brown Elementary School); and the U.S. Information Agency Fellowship Program for Eastern European Studies (now the Ronald H. Brown Fellowship Program). In Mexico, the U.S. Trade Center has been dedicated to Dad. A bill, H.R. 29, passed the House of Representatives unanimously in September 1997, and is now before the Senate. The bill would rename the U.S. government building at 290 Broadway in New York City the Ronald H. Brown Federal Building.

~

My father lives on. The legacy he left me and Michael is one of family, community, and public service. He was our role model, so no matter how busy we are with our careers, we will always put our family and children first. He taught us to give back to the community, and that if we are more fortunate than others, we have an even greater responsibility to give back.

As devastating as Dad's death has been for me, I have been able to step back from my grief and appreciate what he did for the world. He lives on in the many, many lives he touched. No matter how high he climbed, he always left the ladder down for others. As Clyde Robinson said, "There will never be another Ron Brown. . . . The one thing that gives me some hope is that his presence here, presence as a public servant, has created a hundred thousand Ron Browns." He understood that if you want change, you have to stand up and work for that change. He was an example of leadership and courage to those who will continue his work and will eventually achieve what the last generation only dreamed possible.

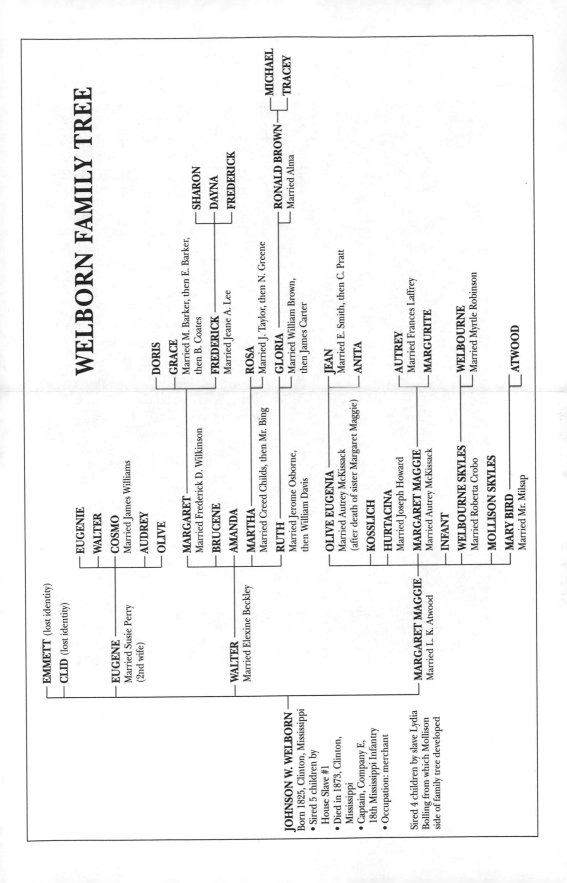

WELBORN FAMILY TREE

JOHNSON W. WELBORN — Born 1825, Clinton, Mississippi
- Sired 5 children by House Slave #1
- Died in 1873, Clinton, Mississippi
- Captain, Company E, 18th Mississippi Infantry
- Occupation: merchant

Sired 4 children by slave Lydia Bolling from which Mollison side of family tree developed

EMMETT (lost identity)

CLID (lost identity)

EUGENE — Married Susie Perry (2nd wife)
- **EUGENIE**
- **WALTER**
- **COSMO** — Married James Williams
- **AUDREY**
- **OLIVE**

WALTER — Married Elexine Beckley
- **MARGARET** — Married Frederick D. Wilkinson
- **BRUCENE**
- **AMANDA**
- **MARTHA** — Married Creed Childs, then Mr. Bing
  - **DORIS**
  - **GRACE** — Married M. Barker, then E. Barker, then B. Coates
    - **SHARON**
    - **DAYNA**
  - **FREDERICK** — Married Jeane A. Lee
    - **FREDERICK**
- **RUTH** — Married Jerome Osborne, then William Davis
  - **ROSA** — Married J. Taylor, then N. Greene
  - **GLORIA** — Married William Brown, then James Carter
    - **RONALD BROWN** — Married Alma
      - **MICHAEL**
      - **TRACEY**

MARGARET MAGGIE — Married L. K. Atwood
- **OLIVE EUGENIA** — Married Autrey McKissack (after death of sister Margaret Maggie)
  - **JEAN** — Married E. Smith, then C. Pratt
  - **ANITA**
- **KOSSLICH**
- **HURTACINA** — Married Joseph Howard
- **MARGARET MAGGIE** — Married Autrey McKissack
  - **AUTREY** — Married Frances Laffrey
  - **MARGURITE**
- **INFANT**
- **WELBOURNE SKYLES** — Married Roberta Crobo
  - **WELBOURNE** — Married Myrtle Robinson
- **MOLLISON SKYLES**
- **MARY BIRD** — Married Mr. Milsap
  - **ATWOOD**

ACTUAL FLIGHT PATH

BOSNIA-HERZEGOVINA

CROATIA

KOLOCEP

First Beacon

DUBROVNIK

119°

110°

Second Beacon

CV

DUBROVNIK AIRPORT

~ Index ~